THE INTERNATIONAL RELATIONS OF LOCAL AUTHORITIES

FROM INSTITUTIONAL TWINNING TO THE COMMITTEE OF THE REGIONS: FIFTY YEARS OF EUROPEAN INTEGRATION HISTORY

P.I.E. Peter Lang
Bruxelles · Bern · Berlin · Frankfurt am Main · New York · Oxford · Wien

EUROCLIO is a scientific and editorial project, a network of research institutions and researchers, and an ideas forum. EUROCLIO as an editorial project consists of two aspects: the first concerns studies and documents, the second concerns tools. Both are aimed at making the results of research more accessible, and also at opening up paths through the history of European construction/integration/unification.

The EUROCLIO series meets a dual objective:

- to provide reference tools for research,
- to provide a platform for this research in terms of the publication of results.

The series thus consists of two sub-series that satisfy these requirements: the STUDIES AND DOCUMENTS series and the REFERENCES series. These two series are aimed at general libraries and/or university history departments, teachers and researchers, and in certain cases, specific professional circles.

The STUDIES AND DOCUMENTS series consists of monographs, collections of articles, conference proceedings, and collections of texts with notes for teaching purposes.

The REFERENCES series consists of bibliographies, guides and other tools. It thus contributes to the creation of a database making up a "Permanent catalogue of sources and bibliographies on European construction".

THE INTERNATIONAL RELATIONS OF LOCAL AUTHORITIES

FROM INSTITUTIONAL TWINNING TO THE COMMITTEE OF THE REGIONS: FIFTY YEARS OF EUROPEAN INTEGRATION HISTORY

Fabio ZUCCA

Euroclio No. 72

This book is published with the financial support of CIRDS '900,
Fondazione Comunitaria della Provincia di Pavia - Onlus
and under the patronage of AICCRE - Federazione della Lombardia,
Università dell'Insubria - Cattedra Jean Monnet.

Centro Interdipartimentale
di Ricerca e Documentazione
sulla Storia del '900

Federazione della Lombardia
Associazione Italiana
per il Consiglio dei Comuni
e delle Regioni d'Europa

In particular, the author would like to thank
M. Milani, A. Baretta and R. Cinquanta.

Éditions scientifiques internationales
Brussels, 2012
1 avenue Maurice, B-1050 Brussels, Belgium
pie@peterlang.com ; www.peterlang.com

ISSN 0944-2294
ISBN 978-2-87574-002-1
D/2012/5678/94

Printed in Germany

CIP available from the British Library, UK and from the Library of Congress, USA.

"Die Deutsche National Bibliothek" lists this publication in the "Deutsche Nationalbibliografie"; detailed bibliographic data is available on the Internet at <http:// dnb.de>.

Mais le temps passe et l'Europe tarde sur le chemin où elle s'est profondément engagée... Nous ne pouvons nous arrêter quand autour de nous le monde entier est en mouvement.

(Jean Monnet, *Mémoires*)

Contents

Abbreviations

AEBR	Association of European Border Regions
AEG	Archives d'État de la République et Canton de Genève
AER	Assembly of European Regions
ACCE, Strasbourg	Archives centrales du Conseil de l'Europe, Strasbourg
ACCRE, Paris	Archives of the Conseil des Communes et Régions d'Europe, Paris
ACCRE, Roissy	Archives of the Conseil des Communes et Régions d'Europe, Roissy
AFCCE	Association Française du Conseil des Communes d'Europe
AFCCRE	Association Française du Conseil des Communes et Régions d'Europe
AFCCRE, Orléans	Archives Association Française du Conseil des Communes et Régions d'Europe, Orléans
AFE	Associazione federalisti europei
AICCE	Associazione italiana per il Consiglio dei comuni d'Europa
AICCRE	Associazione italiana per il Consiglio dei comuni e delle regioni d'Europa
AMFE, Torino	Archives of the Movimento Federalista Europeo, Torino
ANCI	Associazione Nazionale Comuni d'Italia
ASCFI	Archivio storico del Comune di Firenze
AST	Archivio storico della città di Torino
ASUPv	Archivio Storico dell'Università degli Studi di Pavia
AUSE	Associazione universitaria di studi europei
AVCL	Association villes et communes luxembourgeoises
CALRE	Conference of European Regional Legislative Assemblies
CECC	Communauté européenne de crédit communal

CEM	Council of European Municipalities
CEMR	Council of European Municipalities and Regions
CFFE	Comité français pour la fédération européenne
CIFE	Centre international de formation européenne
CIME	Consiglio Italiano del Movimento Europeo
CLRA	Congress of Local and Regional Authorities
CoR	Committee of Regions
CPRM	Conference of European Peripheral Maritime Regions
CRIE	Centro di ricerca sull'integrazione europea, University of Siena
CSF	Centro studi sul federalismo, Turin
DC	Christian Democratic Party
EAGGF	European Agricultural Guidance and Guarantee Fund
ECLA	European Congress of Local Authorities
ECLP	European Conference of Local Powers
ECM	European Common Market
ECSA	European Community Studies Association
ECSC	European Coal and Steel Community
EDC	European Defence Community
EEC	European Economic Community
EESC	European Economic and Social Committee
EGTC	European Group for Territorial Cooperation
EIB	European Investment Bank
EM	European Movement
EPC	European Political Community
EUF	European Union of Federalists
FAE, Geneva	Fondation Archives Européennes, Geneva
FRG	Federal Republic of Germany
IEHEI	Institut européen des hautes études internationales
IFHP	International Federation for Housing and Planning
IGM	Integrated Governance Model
IULA	International Union of Local Authorities
MFE	Movimento federalista europeo
MLG	Multi-level Governance

MEP	Member of European Parliament
MSEUE	Mouvement Socialiste pour les États-Unis d'Europe
NATO	North Atlantic Treaty Organisation
PRI	Italian Republican Party
REGLEG	Conference of European Regions with Legislative Power
SFIO	French Socialist Party
SYVICOL	Syndacat intercommunal à vocation multiple des Villes et Communes Luxembourgeoises pour la promotion et la sauvegarde d'intérêts communaux généraux et communs
UEF	Union of European Federalists
UIV	Union internationale des villes
USSR	Union of Soviet Socialist Republics

Preface

Mercedes BRESSO

President of the Committee of the Regions

The development of international relations between regions and local authorities has for years been a constant European policy objective. On this subject, it is sufficient to observe the importance of territorial cooperation in the 2014-2020 draft budget presented by the European Commission at the end of June 2011. From environmental protection to culture, from the mobility and security of citizens to cooperation for development, to research, the fundamental role played by local administrations in implementing the European Union's objectives and commitments on the international stage has become increasingly evident.

It is an extremely dynamic situation, which is at odds with the scepticism of so many players at all levels on the European political stage, and with the demagogic campaigns against the international status of local authorities. Visits to headquarters in Brussels, or participation in international fairs and events, have often been the object of controversy and political clashes, and it is certainly fair and useful to question the manner in which local initiatives and efforts integrate with national foreign policy. However, it is evident that, especially when it becomes weaker, the local authorities' capacity to establish relations at an international level is a vital element for the development of communities and can contribute to connecting them to opportunities and innovative processes beyond their national borders.

In this sense, structural funds have played a decisive role, not only because specific investments for territorial cooperation are established in operational programmes, but above all because they have encouraged regional and local administrations to acquire new organisational and relational skills needed to use the available resources, organising thousands of administrators into European and international networks dedicated to exchanging and sharing good practices in various sectors. In this way, over the past twenty years opportunities for opening local contexts to the European and extra-European scenario have multiplied, and regional and local governments have been able to benefit from new institutional relations, fuelled in part by shared experiences in fund management.

Nowadays, in order to have an idea of the vibrancy of the international relations established between local authorities, it is sufficient to pay attention to the agendas of European institutions. Subjects such as decentralised cooperation, macro-regions, and the aggregation of territories useful for local development are more frequently addressed, and consequently with ever-increasing interest.

This is not an easy path, but in some contexts it is increasingly evident that the approach used by national governments has not produced the hoped-for results. One should, for example, bear in mind the problems encountered by initiatives for the Mediterranean area, ranging from the promise to create a Free Exchange Area to the launching of the Union for the Mediterranean, which remained inactive for months and months just as North Africa moved towards momentous political and social change.

Nowadays, in order to measure the intensity of relations with this strategic area, in addition to the great questions concerning international politics and the development of economic and productive relations, one must certainly consider exchanges established between regions and cities in crucial sectors such as the protection of the environment, training, the recovery of artistic and landscape heritage, and culture.

Within the framework of European institutional law and current policies (in particular policies concerning cohesion and "Europe 2020"), the regions and the local communities increasingly seem to be a great resource and a great opportunity for the Union and for member states. This new form of European regionalism could open new ways for implementing policies addressed at the creation of public assets at a European level (the environment, sustainable development, human resources, etc.) in effective and legitimate forms. In this perspective of new macro-regional regionalism, a functional approach seems to represent an experimental path that should be followed. This basically means planning and experimenting forms of cooperation between European regions that go beyond the traditional logic of territorial proximity. We therefore find ourselves thinking about and establishing relations addressed at the development of territories, firmly convinced that territorial cohesion is at the basis of future growth for our old and beloved continent.

Following these reflections, Fabio Zucca's book is a fundamental contribution for the reconstruction of the international relations established by European local authorities, which, starting in the early 20th century, through the devastating experience of two world wars, regained possession of their political capabilities in supranational relations. The study on twinning, and the historical reconstruction of the origins of the Committee of Regions are precious not only for understanding history but also for creating the future of European citizens.

Presentation

Maurizio DEGL'INNOCENTI

Full Professor in Contemporary History, University of Siena

Fabio Zucca, the author of an excellent essay entitled *Autonomie locali e federazione sopranazionale. La battaglia del Conseil des Communes et Régions d'Europe per l'unità europea*, with a preface by Valéry Giscard d'Estaing, now presents a work on the international relations of local authorities that addresses European integration and includes a wide-ranging report on studies concerning the birth of the "movements" representing local autonomies in and for Europe, the "long march" towards a full legitimisation of local authorities within the European institutions, and the politics of twinning. Twinning, used as a parameter of real international policy implemented by municipalities, is the most original aspect of this book, which is based on archival sources. With only a few exceptions, it is not a subject matter often studied and one difficult to address, due in part to the dispersion of source material and because it is perhaps considered of secondary importance. It is no mistake to consider this delay in research, even in academic studies, as reflecting and supporting a way of considering European integration as achieved by states and government bureaucracies. Even leaving aside the somewhat significant information provided, the essay presented here deserves recognition simply for going against this trend.

It is possible to envisage five stages in this "long march". The first, that of its origins, is set at the beginning of the 20th century, when, faced with the emergence of a mass society, urbanisation and industrialisation, the national state became organised and strengthened. Conversely, the functions of territorial institutions and municipalities developed a more active role, presenting themselves as players in the economic, social and political-institutional field, thereby becoming interlocutors for the state. As central government grew, and with it the peripheral areas, there were those who saw municipalities as the main route for social progress. Political and social citizenry was shaped through local government, whose importance was soon perceived by the potentially mass political movements of socialist or Catholic origin. Associations of municipalities were formed, at times based on political affinity, and if the English experience is of any value, the associations represent a mutual journey of discovery and cooperation, a fruitful exchange of experiences and ideas; it would be difficult at a later date to find analogies that are as significant. One can thus confidently state that a European administrative conscience was being formed. The prospect of local government remained within the boundaries of the national states, but there was no lack of cosmopolitan initiatives, even those with pacifist characteristics. This was the era during which professional, political and trade-unionist international associations were formed.

The first international organisation of municipalities, formed in Gand in 1913, also dates back to that period. This event was inspired mainly by socialists who, ever since the 1900 Paris International Socialist Congress, have identified it as a decisive moment for political strategies in the management of territorial institutions. The organisation in question was the International Union of Local Authorities (IULA), or *Union internationale des villes* (UIV), of which Belgium's Emile Vinck was elected secretary. It is worth noting that participants included a number of names destined to play important roles in municipalist and Europeanist organisations, bearing witness to a long-term commitment that in some cases lasted over half a century. Of these politicians, Zucca emphasises the work of Edgar Milhaud and Alessandro Schiavi, both acute observers of international socialism. Milhaud became a professor of political economics in Geneva and was the founder and editor-in-chief of the *Annales de la Régie directe*, which in 1925 became the *Annales de l'Économie collective*, and after 1974 the *Annales de l'Économie publique sociale et coopérative*. Among his most important contributions one must at least mention *La marche au socialisme*, in which, against the "vieux État-pouvoir", he envisaged "l'État-industriel nouveau", founded "sur les organismes autonomes et souples, et harmonieusement représentatifs de tous les intérets sociaux en présence"; and, in answer to the critics of "étatisme", he opposed the new socialist formula of "confier la gestion de la propriété nationale aux intéressés eux-memes: producteurs et consommateurs associés". Schiavi was instead a public administrator and social-statistical scholar who worked for Milan's *Società Umanitaria* and was close to Filippo Turati, a man of acknowledged competence in the field of public housing. He was to become the AICCE's first president, and as such, in 1953, he supported the creation of an International Institute of Credit for European Municipalities by issuing bonds guaranteed by states and municipalities to ensure a home for everyone following the destruction caused by the war. The war and the consequent changes overshadowed the weak association to the extent that it was only in 1924 that a second congress was held in Amsterdam to set up its re-founding, which was finalised the following year in Paris. The *Fédération des conseillers communaux socialistes* was to suffer the same destiny.

During the 1930s, faced with the growing limitations of the League of Nations and the changes posed by totalitarianisms, in particular by Nazism, the European union seemed an indefeasible premise for a new international order seen as an alternative to the previous "anarchy" blamed as the primary cause of the war. As a priority, unity was perceived as a way of safeguarding peace. World War II and later the Cold War seemed to confirm this, but the idea merged with that of a convergence of "free people". At the end of the day, this was the crisis category, whether this refers to diplomatic equilibriums and those between the Great Powers, to a presumed and pre-existing continental "unity", or whether this is seen from the perspective of the destruction of human beings and assets or of values and civilisations. From a shared aspiration to the creation of a supranational institution, the federal hypothesis seemed to be the most coherent, lasting and stable solution, since it permitted the overcoming of the thorny issue of borders and minorities and the consequent transfer of people. According to socialists and progressive democrats, secular or Christian, this was also an opportunity to confer on Old Europe a more advanced social status. Thus two perspectives were outlined. The first one more liberal, oriented at re-launching on new bases the principle of a supranational organisation equipped with greater powers than the League of Nations, including its own military power and court of justice, projected at a global level from continental Europe and enveloping all the states, whatever their internal regimes. The other was more decidedly oriented at "revolutionising" social and political equilibriums, calling on the leading role of the people through elected institutions. The first relied on the part played by states that would voluntarily give up some of their sovereign power in exchange for the promise of greater reciprocal security, while the second option relied on the development of a political and social citizenry, thanks especially to the impulse provided by the working class. One must immediately specify that the first position consolidating or reorganising the national state while conceding little or nothing to a proactive stance by local institutions at an international level, decidedly prevailed over the second. However, it was precisely at a local level that the most interesting positions emerged in joining together external federalism and internal decentralisation. Zucca reconstructs the fundamental history of this process.

Compulsory references include the initiative of Count Richard Coudenhove-Kalergi, author of the book *Paneurope*, who, in October 1923, founded the Pan-European Union in Vienna and from 1924 to

1940 published the magazine *Paneurope* in French and in German. In the autumn of 1940 its headquarters were moved to Geneva and later to the United States. His proposal was addressed at all European countries, whatever their internal regimes, with the exception of Great Britain and the USSR: the first because of its imperial interests, the second because it was the homeland of Bolshevism. His idea was a union organised on an autarchic economic basis, with a Swiss-like constitution, a federal court of justice and dissuasive air power that would be more powerful than any other. In *Europe must unite*, the Count also attributed to European unionism the meaning of the safeguarding of the European race from the risk of domination imposed by a collectivity composed of the USSR, a pan-American Union, and even one of Mongol ethnicity led by Japan. In this perspective he ended up by also admitting the importance of British membership and, in order to achieve this, managed to set up a parliamentary committee directed by Duff Cooper, joined among others by Walter Layton. His association was joined by many authoritative French and German parliamentarians and cabinet members, obviously before 1933. It was therefore no surprise that, with the encouragement of foreign minister Aristide Briand, a project for a United States of Europe was presented to the League of Nations to oppose the revision of the Versailles Peace Treaties.

In the 1930's the idea of a court to resolve conflicts arising between states and of a military or police force capable of guaranteeing international order found significant consensus in the Anglo-Saxon world. The subject was extensively addressed by Lord David Davies in *The problem of the twentieth Century*, and then in *Une Europe fédérée*. Under his influence was the New Commonwealth movement that, between 1935 and 1942, published the magazine *The New Commonwealth Quarterly*, which from Great Britain quickly spread to almost all English-speaking countries. In 1940 the president of the British group was Winston Churchill, with Duff Cooper as vice-president. At the end of the summer of 1938, at the height of the Sudentenland crisis, thanks to the initiative shown by W. Beveridge and P. Ransome, the Federal Union was formed, based on the idea of a federation of free people under a shared elected government, the first step towards a global confederation. The Federal Union grew so fast and successfully that it became the most important federalist organisation in the world, joined by over 800 groups from all over the British Empire. They published thousands of brochures and posters, and in March 1940 created the Federal Union Research Institute, which requested committees of experts to study implementable programmes, made public in annual reports from 1939 to 1940-1941. These publications included essays by L. Robbins, *Les aspects économiques de la féderation*, and Beveridge's *Peace by federation.* The publications supported the creation of a United

States of Europe, with the participation of Great Britain and the exclusion of the Union of Soviet Socialist Republics (USSR), convinced that a federalism founded on a preventive union between France, Great Britain and Germany was the only possible way of guaranteeing international order and peace while preserving the characteristics and national culture of every country, including the smaller ones.

A distinguished conference was held at Oxford University on March 3, 1944, by Sir Walter Layton, formerly responsible for the economic and financial section of the League of Nations, editor-in-chief of the *Economist* from 1922 to 1938, and from 1930 chairman of *News Chronicle Ltd.*, and at the time of the conference director general of the planning offices at the Ministry of Supply. After the war Layton once again blamed global anarchy as the cause of war and emphasised the need for European union, guaranteed by the three Great Powers, with the creation of armed forces and a court of justice under the authority of a European council, in turn part of an organisation based on the model of the defunct League of Nations, of which all the states of the world would be members whatever their internal political regimes. In addition to the strong emphasis he placed on the impossibility of restoring full sovereignty to the 25 European states that existed before the war and above all on the insolubility of the German problem (borders, minorities and economic reconstruction) without unified policies throughout the Old Continent, Layton proposed a scenario in which everyone would have the right to both national and European citizenship.

The solution of the German issue within the framework of a new community of states, which would initially hinge on the alliance between Great Britain and France and then also be opened up to minor states, and which would be provided with a "superior" collective authority for economic and military control, was also a widespread belief in Labour circles. After a first document was approved in February 1940, it is worth mentioning *Labour's Peace Aims* by Attlee, who stated resolutely that Europe must "federate or perish". But after the Churchill Cabinet was formed, also including Attlee, the Labour Party no longer assumed a position on the matter, identifying with the government's foreign policy, which conflicted with previously expressed principles. A position against the reconstruction of Europe based on the full sovereignty of national states continued to be supported in minority circles following the ideas of Harold Laski and Aneurin Bevan, or in the Avant-Garde socialist group which, in April 1942, organised a congress, also attended by the Italian Paolo Treves. On this occasion, the emphasis was marked by political radicalism, as witnessed by an account published by *Socialist Commentary* in February 1944, which stated that while the future division of Europe into blocks or areas of influence seemed to be the catastrophic outcome of the current clashes, any remaining hope lay in the hypothesis of a federation of states, guaranteeing Europe's economic and political unity in peaceful cooperation with other powers, on condition, however, that a socialist economic and social programme would be adopted. A socialist Europe, in fact, would provide the best guarantee for the USSR, while an eventual Anglo-America hegemony would not, in their opinion, be in the best interests of Europe or of future peace.

Remaining in Anglo-Saxon circles, it is worth remembering the role played by Clarence K. Streit, the *New York Times* correspondent in Geneva, and the author in March 1939 of *Union Now*, which supported a "federal" link between the United States of America, the British Commonwealth and democratic European countries, also as a means of defence against totalitarian states and as the first step towards a federation of all the free peoples of the planet. This was a position widely shared by America's World Federal Union, a position totally autonomous from the British one, with the American constitution as its model. According to a survey commissioned in August 1942 by *Fortune* magazine, ten million Americans supported this idea.

Federalism as the path to the reconstruction of Europe in a stable security framework had supporters in the climate of resistance to Nazism and Fascism. On October 14th, 1939, in *Le Populaire*, Léon Blum committed to a federated and unarmed Europe. Similar opinions were expressed by the *Comité français pour la fédération européenne* (CFFE) in June 1944 and by European resistance movements the following months. In this context there was also the *Manifesto di Ventotene*, written in 1941 by Altiero Spinelli, Ernesto Rossi and Eugenio Colorni and published in secret by them in January 1944. This was a document created in a defeated country, and one in which it was firmly believed that the Fascist regime was unredeemable and that thus, for a free society, overthrowing an authoritarian or totalitarian state required a revolution. Colorni, a socialist also actively involved in armed resistance, so much so that he was killed a few days before Rome was liberated, was by education and persuasion a European intellectual who in some ways represented the ideal type of European federalist formed during World War II. Between 1946 and 1948 the various European socialist schools of thought converged in or remained close to the Socialist Movement for a United States of Europe, founded in London in 1947 by Pivert and Edwards, with *La Gauche européenne* as its newspaper. However, the creation of a supranational social democratic party aimed at removing Europe from excessively binding Atlantic agreements without, however, lessening controversy with the USSR, for which the most important representatives were the groups

Pensée Socialiste and *Iniziativa socialista*, remained a minority position within the Left. In the end this party merged with the re-founded Socialist International, which stated it belonged to the free peoples group, where the Europeanist ideals would always be held high.

Zucca correctly emphasises the importance of neutral Switzerland, a land of cosmopolitan and pacifist traditions (it is sufficient to bear in mind the Lugano *Coenobium*), and one very hospitable to exiles and neighbours: truly a vital centre for federalist plans. There was also no lack of hopes for a "Swiss Europe" based on the cantonal model. Switzerland's destiny was singular, changing from an inexhaustible crossroads of projects and initiatives with a strong Europeanist bent to a silent and absent spectator in the real European integration process. Among the many possible points in this regard, one should remember that after the third congress of the Pan-European Union held in Basel in 1932, it was the Swiss section that left Kalergi's Union, considering it too elitist, creating in 1934 the federalist movement Europa-Union together with the Basel section of the Union Jeune-Europe, subsequently adopting *Der Europaer* as its official newspaper in 1935. In Geneva in December 4th, 1944, the *Centre d'action pour la Fédération européenne* was created, presided over by René Jaccard, aimed at encouraging economic and political cooperation between European states and establishing an "alliance fédérative". By collecting in the *Europe de demain* federalist messages and documents, there was an admission that the project was still only "un acte de foi" against the prevailing language inspired by the "réalisme" that stamped the post-war period, with Europe divided into areas of influence, Germany broken up and, even worse, entire populations moved ("sans y prende garde, on nous brosse un tableau de la paix dont toutes les perspectives dressent de nouveau devant nos yeux l'image délirante de cette paix allemande qui a falli faire de tous les hommes libres des esclaves dans une Europe sans Européens"). Hence only the federalist solution remained to oppose this "Carthaginian" peace, within the framework of a renewed world organisation in which Europe needed Germany, which was only feasible in the context of a federal Europe (a United States of Europe) in which Great Britain acted as a counterweight. The Swiss experience was often quoted in the same series entitled *L'évolution du monde et des idées*, which aimed at expressing "aspirations and new ideas in view of the world's current situation" and contained publications addressing democracy "today and in the future", peace and federalism. Edmond Pivat published *Trois expérciences fédéralistes. États-Unis. Société des Nations. Conféderation suisse*, Raymond Silva *Au service de la paix. L'idée fédéraliste*, and Van Vassenhove *L'Europe Helvétique*. In other circles, fame was achieved by William Rappard's book, *Cinq siècles de sécurité collective, 1291-1798*.

On this subject, Zucca emphasises the decisive influence, above all at a theoretical level, exercised by the Swiss historian Adolf Gasser. Educated in Heidelberg and in Zurich, after studying with the historian Karl Meyer, while also a great admirer of de Tocqueville, he became a professor at Basel University. It was here that in 1939, in the midst of a fully committed struggle against National Socialism, he published *Geschichte der Volksfreiheit und der Demokratie* (which appeared in a clandestine edition in Milan in 1945 entitled *Storia della libertà popolare e della democrazia*). In this book he stated that, on the basis of its original organisation as a community formed of free and armed peoples' communities, the highest expression of which were the medieval cities of the 11th century, the West was a hotbed of communitarian state conscience, achieved not due to command but in the spirit of the trust and co-responsibility of individuals, since everyone voluntarily agreed to obey communitarian order. "In the organisation of state and society," he wrote, "every individual freedom always means freedom within the framework of the community, hence freedom that acknowledges naturally the interdependency between elements of a community and the traditions of the community itself (...). All people socially organised are a community of free people bound by bonds of trust based on self-education". In conditions of freedom, a healthy counterweight to the battle for power that was unheard of in Asia, he presented the foundations of European civilisation, so that for him the entire history of the West appeared to be characterised by the contrast between ideals of freedom and ideals of power (deriving from the ancient warrior spirit of nomadism). The message of 1939 against Nazism (as well as against Soviet Bolshevism) was a clear one: Western civilisation could only be saved if European elements, conscious of their responsibilities, would be prepared to sacrifice assets and blood to defend freedom of conscience. Everything depended on the "spiritual disposition" since, "at any time in the course of human evolution one might analyse, one always finds confirmation of the supreme truth; it is the spirit that moves everything". These ideas were again taken up in 1943 in the *Gemeindfreiheit als Rettung Europas*, still published in Basel. In the preface for the revised Italian edition, published in 1946 by La Fiaccola, Gasser wrote that the Italian title – *L'Autonomia comunale e la ricostruzione dell'Europa* – summarised the concept of "A basic broad municipal freedom as the indispensable premise for a lasting reconstruction of Europe", convinced that "two kinds of concepts are generally present in our times; a constitutional one and an economic one. Through constitutional guarantees there are attempts to ensure political freedom and democracy, while social freedom and social democracy are attempted to be achieved through economic reform". However, neither would last until merged with "administrative and therefore municipal freedom", the only

freedom leading to "a real acknowledgement and full comprehension of the state's ethical foundations", and the only one reconciling the opposite words, freedom and authority, with a decisive effect on the creation not so much of the state but of the state's administration, which directly affects the state's life (while a written constitution remains above all a theoretical element). To these two organisational principles of subordination and coordination Gasser links, respectively, both the top-down and bottom-up creation of the state, which depends on the authoritarian/
communitarian, bureaucratic/popular, dominion/federation, authoritarian state/communitarian or municipal state dichotomy. Convinced that, among the collective bonds inherent in the concept of public opinion, the most important are the ethical ones, it was only in the "federal spirit" that he saw a particularly active organisational element, even if only because of "the source of power closest to it: municipal freedom", on which he based that "sort of collective conscience" or "ethical collectivism (that) is always expressed in the existence of an extraordinarily compact public opinion". It is thus that every state animated by the spirit of municipal freedom is like a school of civility imposing on its students continuous self-education; like a school for the education of humankind from a peaceful and responsible perspective, always capable of mobilising "new regeneration forces". Conversely, he believed that "when a state is kept together by bureaucratic-mechanical bonds, then the spirit of command and subordination penetrates all aspects of collective life, and therefore every action involving economic exploitation bears the mark of domination and coercion". In centralised authoritarian states the social issue is a problem involving power. In quoting the Swiss pedagogue Enrico Pestalozzi, he expressed the hope that the West could return to the "original municipal principle" or, to express it better, to the underlying ethics of society, rediscovering fully the "art of being a man". Gasser was certainly induced by the Swiss experience to make an alleged original "municipal spirit" an absolute prerogative, in search of those ethical-cultural factors to which he entrusted the redemption/restoration of Europe. He was to be one of the sponsors of the *Conseil des communes d'Europe* and inspirer of the European Charter of Local Powers. In federalist circles, Gasser was celebrated as a precursor of the very idea of a federal European state, although he was accused of having neglected the otherwise essential problem, the only one considered capable of overcoming international anarchy. Others reproached him for an alleged Swiss "provincialism". One can also add that many of his interpretative passages, from prehistoric to modern times, do give rise to a degree of reservation. Few however have done better in describing the evocative element in

Europe's urban identity-making from a libertarian and progressive perspective.

Other opinions expressed the concept of communitarian freedom based on a morally responsible personality. An authoritative example is provided by Emmanuel Mounier, author of the *Manifeste au service du personnalisme* (1936). It is known that the terminology, chosen by Renouvier in 1903 to describe his philosophy, became popular in France during the 1930s, in particular with the *Esprit*, founded in 1932 to address Europe's political and spiritual crisis. According to Mounier, the absoluteness of the person does not isolate human beings, but on the contrary personalism opposes individualism, and it is a mistake to present personalism as an anti-collectivist reaction, just as it is to oppose the communitarian to the collective. This instead presupposes a hierarchy of communities, between the family, which is the social cell, or rather the "incorporated community," and the nation, which tends towards the universal, developing rational human beings and projecting them in a dimension better suited to expressing their potential. Based on these premises, Mounier was convinced that nations must renounce sovereignty in favour of a democratic community of peoples, so that the hoped-for union would be established not between governments but between their elected representatives. As an "orienting utopia" he considered federalism the "expression of personalism", and to this subject he devoted the November 1938 issue of the *Esprit* (*L'Europe contre les hégémonies*). Alexander Marc, Henri Brugmans, and Denis de Rougemont insisted on these aspects, and Mounier quoted them all as "personalists" committed to federalism. The magazine was to later turn its attention again to this issue with special editions published in November 1948 (*Les deux visages du fédéralisme européen*) with a more pacifist tone, and in February 1949 (*Révision des pacifismes*). The "personalists" mentioned by Mounier also included Marc, who, after reading Gasser (whom he accused, however, of "conservativism"), published *Du communalisme au fédéralisme integral* in 1948. Among those also inspired by reading Gasser was the French Catholic Jean Bareth, a primary school teacher and later a professor whose ideas matured in the Catholic corporativist movement *Justice sociale* and who, following France's defeat, became one of the leaders of the French federalist movement *La Fédération* and, together with Serafini, the heart and soul of the movement of European local institutions. In 1947 he wrote *Le fédéralisme: un principe, une action*, stating that the municipality is the basic political community to be placed as the foundation for more complex organisations.

It is important here to emphasise one point, and that is the distinction Mounier makes between the state and the nation, and how, to the notion of a "pluralist state" equipped with divided and opposing powers to protect one from abusing the other, he preferred the notion of a "state organised to serve a pluralist society". He considered Christianity to be experiencing a crisis, not only *per se* but more broadly as a sign of the decadence of religious values in contemporary ideas, and was persuaded that the philosophy of the Enlightenment led people to believe these ideas were artificial and would vanish. However, the experience of the 20th century should lead us to deduce that wherever the Christian aspects of those values disappeared, religious forms reappeared in different aspects, ranging from the deification of the body, the community or the species to an ascendancy to the aspect of a leader or a political party, so that "all the characteristic features attributed to the religious phenomenology could be found in new contexts, in a degraded and rather outdated manner compared to Christianity". He attributed the cause of this development specifically to the elimination of the "personal universe", making this elimination "one of the century's crucial issues." The point referred to here is needed to emphasise how the problem of the "spirit", of moral values, of civility, perceived to be in a critical phase, underlies the grand ideas for renovation in Europe on a federal basis with regard to the challenges posed by totalitarianisms and the world wars, parallel to and in support of diplomatic plans for a unionist reorganisation of a future Europe against the risks of new wars.

To restrict oneself just to one other example, one could quote the *Rencontres Internationales de Genève* – sponsored by a committee of Swiss citizens in September 1946 – which were later to become a real institution, which was the object of the discussion on the "European spirit". In 1947 a book was published entitled, appropriately enough, *L'Esprit européen*. It is interesting to consult the Italian edition published by Edizioni Comunità (1950) with an introduction by Umberto Campagnolo. Reflecting the MFE's position, Campagnolo considers it a mistake to refer to a "disease of the European spirit" rather than to that of the social community, thus rendering it a moral rather than a political problem. In an internal note, the editor reproached Campagnolo for presenting a European federation as a "pause" in a pre-war crisis in which the entire world had lived for four years, as a "niche" under the protection of which a social revolution could take place. Quoting as an example the *Comunità* experience, he countered that the federal solution should, if anything, be taken "from the level of the states and the large communities to a concrete level, a more daily one (and, nevertheless, a prior one) of the smaller cells of associated life, the communities, in which it would be possible to create a plurality of spheres of lively interest within which the wishes of the majority could be determined, with fewer possibilities of making mistakes and therefore with greater spontaneity". He reiterated the classical "person-community relationship" in order to aspire to that "civilisation of culture and justice towards which all today's humankind projects its hopes" as the lasting and profound foundations of a renewed European society.

After the war, albeit reflected in many European countries' cultural and political elites, the federalist ideas were not transformed into rigorous progress; that is, in the creation of a supranational power equipped with effective means of coordination and control on an elected basis. The logic of the weapons in the field as a consequence of the division between the winners and the losers; the division of Europe and the world into areas of influence and then into opposed blocks of states in view of, or at least at the risk of a return to arms, now with a nuclear threat; the reconstruction of identity-making codes and administrative apparatuses as well as the economic fabric of national states with input from the large mass territorial parties; all this gave the existing turmoil a very different outcome than the one originally hoped for. If, however, one looks carefully, these ideas were not totally neglected, and, like seeds thrown to the ground, they took root or were grafted onto other tree trunks. European union, in part and not only as a solution to the German problem (including partial rearmament), had now become a real objective, albeit following anything but a "revolutionary" path, just as, more in general, the re-foundation of an international organisation had become real following the unfortunate outcome experienced by the League of Nations. The need for a broadening of political and social citizenship, partly as an answer to totalitarianism but above all to achieve social cohesion, became an issue of the utmost importance, which in some cases was explicitly referred to in new constitutional charters. In European left-wing political parties centralising and even Jacobean demands prevailed, and the significant federalist elements remained a minority, while groups and movements remained active with an organisational continuity bearing witness to their ethics and ideals. One could say that federalism's political time had passed, but it did not thereby lose importance as a new political category or a force-idea, summarised in the coexistence of the values of freedom and democracy, or of a state serving its citizens. In the days of the Cold War federalism appeared as a noble aspiration of the "free" world, which, with its formula of a federal union of free peoples, "open" between democratic countries within the framework of a global confederation, overlapped that of a Federal European Union.

The immediate post-war period saw the beginning of a season of congresses that led to the founding of the European Union of Federalists (EUF), the European Movement (EM), and the Council of Europe (CoE), created in 1949 and which was perhaps the most advanced form of intergovernmental cooperation, although the British and the

Scandinavians negatively conditioned its potential. Finally, the Council of European Municipalities (CEM) was founded. Apart from the intergovernmental committee, these were mainly elitist pressure groups which shared a tendency to become institutionalised in order to become interlocutors of states. In this new phase, federalism and municipalism (the system of local authorities or administrative decentralisation), and the international and national context, developed along parallel paths, at times conflicting but more often intertwining. The centre of initiative progressively moved towards France. On June 16th, 1949, Jacques Chaban Delmas (mayor of Bordeaux), Pierre Mendès France, François Mitterrand, Maurice Schumann and Eugène Claudius-Petit voted a document on the defence of municipal and departmental freedoms and created a national committee. The *Centre d'études institutionnelles pour l'organisation de la société francaise* addressed the need for administrative reform characterised by decentralisation, and in March 1952, under the aegis of the *Université internationale*, "une session d'études municipale" was organised.

Zucca convincingly reconstructs its history, based mainly on contacts established at the end of 1950 between Gasser, de Jager, Bareth and Chaban-Delmas. This resulted in the idea of a movement of municipalities working in favour of both administrative decentralisation and European unity. With assistance from Milhaud, the exiled German trade-unionist Alida de Jager organised a first meeting in Switzerland in the autumn of 1950, followed by the assembly summoned in Geneva on January 28th-31st, 1951, which led to the creation of the *Conseil des communes d'Europe*, which excluded Eastern European countries. The French had the largest delegation, but the organisation's headquarters remained in Geneva until 1955, when they were moved to Paris; de Jager was appointed secretary, a position she held until 1953. In 1984 the movement changed its name to the *Conseil des communes et des régions d'Europe*. In 1952 the *Associazione italiana per il Consiglio dei comuni d'Europa* was also founded, adopting as its newspaper the monthly *Comuni d'Europa*. Umberto Serafini, who worked closely with Adriano Olivetti and was a militant in the *Movimento Comunità* within the framework of a project involving territorial community centres, was appointed secretary. By April 1952 this association had over two hundred members among local administrators and municipal councils. As Zucca reminds us, the Italian association remained more closely linked to the federal idea, while the decidedly more influential French one stood more in favour of administrative decentralisation, due in part to the previously mentioned national requirements.

In October 1953 in Versailles it approved the European Charter of Local Freedoms, drafted with Gasser's contribution. This brotherhood of municipalities, as a premise for a European federation guaranteeing Western Europe's security, was still supported by Bareth, who relied on the political experience of France's André Voisin (André Bourgeois) and Luxembourg's socialist mayor Hubert Clément, while Marc continued to support the indefeasible connection between European unity on a federal basis and the advancement of municipal and regional demands through the creation of the *Assemblée représentative des communes et collectivités locales*, in a freely elected European parliament. However, in the end the position that prevailed was the more pragmatic one assumed by Bordeaux's authoritative mayor Chaban-Delmas, aimed at gradually including the representation of local institutions in the ongoing European integration process, albeit in exclusively consultative forms and restricted to local and regional interests. To achieve this, on January 12th-14th, 1957, the first European Conference of Local Powers was convened in Strasbourg at the Council of Europe, where the decisive role played by Chaban-Delmas was once again confirmed.

The results appeared apparently modest compared to expectations. It is known that the 1951 Paris Treaty establishing the European Coal and Steel Community (ECSC), the 1957 Rome Treaty that led to the founding of the European Economic Community (EEC), and the treaty on atomic energy (Euratom) make only a marginal reference to local institutions. Yet new prospects appeared which, through the involvement of territorial institutions, could and did allow closer relations between the new European institutions and the communities, and hence the citizens. With a degree of delay, this was also understood by authorities in Brussels. The problem of overcoming the restrictions posed by the previous phase, in one sense elitist ones and in another bureaucratic-governmental ones, was all too real. This need was changed by the fact that in 1954 the MFE boasted 50,000 members, and in 1957 the federalist wing led by Spinelli proposed a congress of the European people with primary elections to express a constituent desire.

At the end of the 1950s, having created the European Common Market (ECM) and on a wave of economic expansion and the spreading of welfare policies, there was now also the problem of development and territorial and social imbalances, and of the forms of governance required to best address these issues. Intermediate institutions for achieving local development started to be considered with growing interest, in view of a territoriality which was considered to be their responsibility. It was to this that the principle of territorial planning and economic programming was also linked, an idea that fascinated both the democratic and socialist left as well as European Catholics. It was, as Zucca calls it, "a long march", and, using the CEMR archives preserved in the Historical Archives of the European Union in Florence, he provides a concise but exhaustive overview of communitarian institutions that were linked to the world of local autonomies, emphasising the role of administrators, in some cases destined to hold important positions at a national level. It would be useful to have biographical essays for them, as well as for other culturally and politically important personalities, in order to contribute to the reconstruction of the many paths followed to implement the Europeanist school of thought, thereby enlivening and colouring it as well as probably also contributing to overcoming a certain hagiographic tendency that one perceives on this subject from a strictly institutional perspective.

During the 1960s and 1970s another issue appeared with greater clarity, one all too perfunctorily assimilated to the system of local autonomies, and however, at the time and also later, always considered as an element for safeguarding the local autonomies from excessive state interference as well as valorising them. The issue was that of regional institutions. This intermediate level between the municipalities and the state was addressed in Belgium, Denmark, Great Britain, the Netherlands, Switzerland, Italy, France and Spain, in the form of a unification of the municipalities, an implementation of supra-municipal organisations, and the creation of regional institutions (in Italy in 1970). The problem of sub-governments was being addressed. Some have considered this one of the most important institutional changes in modern Western states after World War II and have now linked it at times to the reaction to unequal development and cultural homogenisation. At other times it was linked to a second urban revolution tending towards suburban areas, and sometimes to the growth of the welfare state with regional planning, as well as to a broadening of the territorial area in the daily lives of individuals and an ideological emphasis on decentralisation as a factor in democratic growth and efficiency. At this time the concept of "regionalisation" or "regional policies" also entered European communitarian circles. Following the December 1961 conference in Brussels, three groups of experts studied the problem, with their findings included in the "first statement by the EEC's commission on regional policy" presented by the Commission to the Council on May 11th, 1965. Real European regional policies were being drafted, entrusted to four financial instruments: the European Agricultural Guidance and Guarantee Fund (EAGGF); the European Social Fund; the European Investment Bank (EIB); and intervention established in Articles 54 and 56 of the ECSC Treaty, albeit applied solely to the coal and steel sector. In 1975 the European Fund for Regional Development was created.

Although still restricted to technocratic and bureaucratic issues rather than political and parliamentary ones, there was a stronger tendency to perceive the regional instrument as best suited for establishing and optimising policies to support peripheral and poorer areas. Although mainly created to address alienation phenomena, rather than a means for ordinary intervention based on efficiency and participation, "the regionalisation method, created and implemented as the coherent instrument for the organisation of a general and global economic development programme based on centres of decision-making and power," did, however, become more familiar. It finally became associated with the idea of development with qualified and decisive institutional participation. In a sense, some aspects of this are not extraneous to the expansion of the public administration, which characterised European history before the 1973-1974 energy crisis, due in part to greater socialist or social-democratic influence. Compared to the 1950s and to the impetuous but disorderly development of private consumption, there was later a determined revival of "policies" regarding the alleged free market mechanisms and the adoption of reform policies marked by programming and technocracy. The idea of a country-system was for the first time placed at the centre in terms of the prospects for modernisation. However, the addition of a regional circuit at a European level did not occur without conflict with the state. The controversy concerned above all the regions' roles in implementing EEC provisions concerning agriculture, which the government believed was its own exclusive competence, thereby opening another front, as happened in Italy, between new regional institutions and local ones concerning the functions of orientation and coordination or management and the transference of competences. A new phase was beginning in the governing of cities.

Zucca revisits the fundamental stages in these events. In October 1962 the EEC Commission published a Memorandum on the Community action programme during the second stage, which expressed some elements of long term territorial policy, making no reference, however, to local institutions. In 1963 the EEC managed to involve the Commission in the organisation in Brussels of the Congress for Territorial Planning and Regional Policy, which ended with the acknowledgment of the competences of local institutions in territorial planning. In 1964 the Commission formally invited the EEC to produce a first memorandum on the Common Market's regional policy, which, drafted early in 1965, was approved on May 8, 1966. One could perhaps join Zucca in clearly stating that local government at this point formally joined the European institutions. It was definitely the sign of a growing desire to emphasise the role of representatives, in particular that of parliament, also in the hoped-for perspective of direct elections that would be held on June 7th-10th, 1979.

Expectations for the involvement of regional and local authorities now increased. In December 1982 the EEC considered that the time had come for amending the preface to the treaties in order to institutionalise the consultative committee of local and regional institutions. On January 25th-27th, 1984, the European Community's Conference of Regions committed the European Parliament to encouraging the participation of regional and local authorities. The premise of the new Draft Treaty establishing the European Union, sponsored and drafted by Spinelli, voted by the European Parliament on September 14th, 1983, and approved on February 14th, 1984, at last indicated its acknowledgment "of the need to enable local and regional authorities to participate by appropriate methods in the unification of Europe; the need to allow the participation of local and regional institutions." On April 13th, 1984, the European parliament approved a resolution in this sense and later placed on its agenda the creation of a Committee of Regions. The first institutional appearance only took place in 1988, when, with decision no. 88/487/EEC dated June 1988, the committee created the Consultative Council of Regional and Local Authorities. Sworn in on December 20th, 1988, as a subsidiary institution, the Council remained active until 1993.

The last, and still ongoing phase, was inaugurated by the Maastricht Treaty dated February 17th, 1992, and by the formal implementation in 1994 of the Committee of Regions, which took office on March 9th and 10th, 1994, thereby becoming one of the Union's representative bodies in addition to the Council of Ministers and parliament, with the authority to express opinions on social, cultural and public health policies, trans-European transport networks, telecommunications and energy, and economic and social cohesion. The Treaty of Nice, signed on February 26th, 2001 (the Constitutional Treaty was signed in Rome on October 29th, 2004) established that the Committee of Regions, appointed as proposed by the central governments, was also one of the European parliament's consultative bodies, and therefore became a means for possible multi-level governance in a new Europe.

Taking into account previous considerations, one can better appreciate Zucca's choice to make the twinnings of European cities the object of his studies. These twinnings appeared to be minor events, partly because of the mistrust of those who saw them above all as a reason for sponsoring tourism, or, even worse, and not entirely unreasonably, as an intellectualist quirk. As a whole, this event was part of a far more important history in which turmoil, attitudes and commitments provide us with an image of a pluralistic Europe, with its cathedrals and state palaces, squares and markets, academies and universities, attempting to establish contact and mutual acknowledgment among its members.

Twinning began in the 1950s and was a French initiative, perceived as "the symbolic act with which two cities or villages belonging to different nations decide to establish and develop bonds of close brotherhood with cultural, economic and political objectives". There was initially an attempt to cooperate at a linguistic level with the Anglo-Saxon world, soon accompanied by a search for a dialogue with Germans, as shown by the founding in 1947 of the *Union internationale des Maires pour le rapprochement franco-allemand et la compréhension entre les peuples*. In some cases the initiative contributed to resolving shared problems, as with Metz and Luxembourg in 1952. In January 1952 a study-conference was organised in Paris, and the EEC finally saw the positive potential in promoting a Europeanist culture, leading to the first twinning between Troyes and Tournai. The phenomenon spread from the French-speaking regions while a ceremonial code was being drafted. Events were to move faster only in view of the first elections of the European parliament. In order to sensitise public opinion, the commission allocated funds for the EEC, which on September 28th and 29th, 1978, sponsored a conference in Mainz for one thousand twinned cities. From then on this custom became more important, and in 1983 there were twenty-thousand twinnings. It would take the Maastricht Treaty, and later the one signed in Amsterdam, before European citizenship was considered complementary to the national one. With provision 1904/2006/EC dated December 12th, 2006, the European parliament and Council adopted the programme entitled Europe for Citizens for the 2007-2013 period, in order to sponsor a series of initiatives to involve citizens in European integration, with twinning as one of its elements. The programme relies on structural funds, which envisage investments in territorial cooperation, also aimed at social cohesion, as stated in the programme "Europa 2020". It is too soon to address the possibility of Multi-level Governance (MLG) as an alternative at a European level for the Integrated Governance Model (IGM), which has characterised relations first within the Community and later the Union. Perhaps, however, the problem has been posed.

Zucca presents three significant cases of Italian cities active in twinning policies, Florence, Turin and Milan. Florence, which joined the AICCE in 1952, became twinned in 1954 with Reims, repeating the experience another eighteen times. Initially, apart from the role played by the Republican Menotti Riccioli, a member of the European federalist association since 1945, and the Christian Democrat Giancarlo Zoli, in line with De Gasperi's Europeanism, the central figure appeared to be that of the Christian Democrat Giorgio La Pira, president of the municipal council from June 1951 to May 1956, in 1956-1957, and in 1961-1966. Envisaging a new constitutional organisation, "of a personalist and pluralist kind", hence in his opinion "human and therefore Christian" rather than individualist and statist, La Pira refers to that part of the Catholic culture – from Ketteler to Toniolo, Maritain, Renard, La Tour du Pin, Blondel and, above all, Mounier – that supported the "creation of a city that is human in its organisation, which at most requires a reinstatement of the needs for brotherhood expressed in the Gospel". His starting point was humankind, to which he attributed the original autonomy (freedom), which he did not at all consider asocial, because the individual personality is expressed within a series of institutions, from the family to the territory, to work, to the cultural and political environment, each involving a person's subordination to the good of all. Assuming the creation of a republican Italy as a reference point, La Pira emphasised its importance in having made Article 6 the cornerstone of the entire charter ("guaranteeing the fundamental rights of individuals and social associations in which their personalities are expressed"), allowing the human being to be appreciated in the entirety of his/her status as a member not only of the state community (*status civitatis*) but also of the family community as *societas naturalis* (Art. 23 and others), as well as of the Catholic Church (Art. 7) (to which he acknowledges the nature of independent and sovereign law), the local community (106), even the class organisations (Art. 35), since these represent "an essential part of the social fabric", which clearly owes a debt to Toniolo's corporatism of Thomistic origin. In this framework he therefore considers the territorial community, like all others, as having its own charter or objective that must be respected and valorised by the state, the sovereignty of which, however, is in turn limited by the law of the people (*res pubblica christianorum*) (*Architettura di uno Stato democratico*, Rome, 1948). Hence it was not surprising when in 1955 La Pira organised a meeting of mayors from all over the world. Having attributed to Western Europe, as the expression of Christian Europe, the mission of uniting the continent's Christian family, though from a universal perspective, La Pira considered that the city could provide encouragement to defend life, "faced with the real danger of a death sentence" due to weapons of mass destruction. He thus attributed to the mayors a sort of basic diplomatic mission by creating a union of cities, to be culturally and spiritually enriched for new generations. In this role, La Pira took part in the second States General of European Municipalities held in Venice in 1954, where he supported the idea that through the "solid fabric of its cities" Europe presents "only one cultural, social, spiritual and historical reality". His basic objective remained to make Europe a bridge between the East and the West ("a bridge of friendship and goodness"), with conciliatory objectives in the Cold War era, though the accent placed on Christianity as Europe's connective and identity fabric sounds no less significant.

The second case studied concerns the international activities of the city of Turin sponsored by its Christian Democrat mayor, Amedeo Peyron (1951-1962), who organised the twinning with Chambéry (1957) and Liège. Once again support came from the Curia, but the scenario was different due to cooperation with the *Centro Comunità* in Turin. One can say that Peyron represented all the autonomist and federalist turmoil for which Piedmont and the nearby Val d'Aosta were a fertile breeding ground. It was thanks to the citizens of the Val d'Aosta and the Waldenses, who met with the Catholic E. Chanoux, that the so-called *Carta di Chivasso* was drafted on December 19th, 1943, and published in the *Unità europea* July-August issue in 1944, theorising a state of autonomies and regions to oppose a centralised and levelling state, within a perspective of internal and international federalism. Peyron always remained active in European institutions, and an acknowledgement of his influence came with the organisation in Turin in December 1953 of the 5th National Congress of the *Movimento Federalista Europeo,* which accepted the juridical-political charter of the *Associazione italiana per il Consiglio dei comuni d'Europa* for the purpose of linking local administrations to European federalism.

The third case studied is Milan, the one to which Zucca assigns a particular Europeanist vocation ("European city"). The opportunity was provided by the founding of the MFE on August 27th -28th, 1943, on the basis of the *Manifesto di Ventotene* and the federalist thesis, and by the intense relations cultivated with federalists operating in Switzerland. He was assisted even more by the fact that until 1948 the MFE was headquartered in Milan, where *L'Unità europea* was published until 1945, when it was suspended due to lack of funds. Zucca quite rightly emphasises how the local Christian Democrats were sensitive to federalist ideas, but above all he underlines the importance of Socialists, or rather Social Democrats, who for a long time governed and continue to govern the city. From Antonio Greppi, already a supporter of European federalism during his exile in Switzerland, to Gino Cassinis, promoter of the *Manifesto degli universitari italiani per la federazione delle nazioni d'Europa,* to Pietro Bucalossi and Virgilio Ferrari, as well as councillor Lamberto Jori and Renato Brugner, who worked with Serafini and promoted the European Institute of international Studies and Relation in Lugano, and including Ugo Alfassio Grimaldi, Ivan Matteo Lombardo and Aldo Aniasi: these were the representatives of Milanese and Lombard socialism's reformist culture, the one most oriented towards Europe in the Italian Left.

These are stories of cities that, within cultural pluralism, have a shared history and are Europe's greatest identity-making legacy. They are an asset if and when individually they manage to connect and, by recognising themselves in others, create a network. It is hard to say if and when, in this long march towards and within the European institutions, local government developed a renewed and shared administrative conscience on the basis of aspirations that had already emerged at the beginning of the 20th century, albeit in an embryonic manner; or if and when the communitarian institutions and state policies linked to them did benefit and whether their institutional performance has improved. There is a lack of in-depth and well-thought-out studies on this subject, and therefore Zucca's contribution provides a fundamental reference framework. There is, however, one thing that can be said; without the "esprit", the shared values and the acknowledged identities, without support from citizens, over the long term institutions are destined to implode, incapable of renewal.

Introduction

Fabio ZUCCA

Jean Monnet Chair, University of Insubria - Varese

The book reports the results of research lasting many years on the international prominence of local institutions within the European integration process, taking as examples significant cases involving the retrieval of a capacity for action by local communities that the advent of centralised and sovereign states in the 19th century seemed to have all but abolished.[1] The definition of the international role of municipalities and regions, leading institutional participants in multilevel governance within the European Union, are two aspects little explored by historical research, but which nowadays are clearly evident in both the context of current political as well as territorial and economic affairs.

The strengthening of the European Union, on the basis of a bottom up process, involves local institutions at all levels of representation, while the global crisis, which powerfully affects the very structure of European institutions with the single currency as well as the living standards of citizens, emphasizes the need to overcome the current incapacity of national governments to adequately react to change. In fact, the cities and intermediate institutions have increasingly become

---

1 The contents of the book are the result of new research on twinning undertaken by the cities of Florence and Milan or analyse in-depth subjects I have addressed in individual essays thanks to contributions discovered while studying papers in archives for which inventories have only recently be created (the Umberto Serafini archives deposited with *Archivio Storico dell'Università degli Studi di Pavia*) or are still being indexed and reorganised (the Aldo Aniasi Archives at the *Circolo De Amicis* in Milan). One exception is the previously published study on twinning for the city of Turin – Zucca, "I gemellaggi della città di Torino e l'azione di Amedeo Peyron" – which I thought would be useful to re-present. In fact, the city of Turin and Mayor Peyron, in his dual role of local administrator and president of the Italian section of the Council of European Municipalities, assumes particular importance within the context of the local authorities' recovery of autonomy to act within the framework of international relations, thereby establishing a useful means of comparison with action taken by other cities. The edited text has partly been rewritten also in view of more recent research.

the playing fields on which the challenges of European policies are unfolding. Hence, the impact of local authorities on the creation of Europe must become increasingly powerful in order to encourage effective cooperation between the various levels, from a European to a local one, involved in implementing policies and interventions promoting a sustainable approach at an economic, environmental and social level. In this sense, debates about the future of the European Union's cohesion policies will enter a new phase after 2013, with the Committee of Regions (CoR) committed to supporting the causes of the mayors and presidents of regions. In February 2011, about eight hundred politicians and representatives of institutions attended the forum on cohesion organised by the European Commission. The President of the CoR, Mercedes Bresso, emphasised "Our message is clear. We want to be sure that after 2013 cohesion policies will have the resources needed to continue to pursue the reduction of economic, social and territorial disparities between European regions. Cohesion policies remain a fundamental instrument since they involve the European Union's regions, cities and social partners".[2] One should also bear in mind how the distribution of the European budget for the 2007-2013 period has allocated 36.5% of the total amount[3] to cohesion policies for growth and employment and is mainly destined to territorial authorities. In summary, the intervention of mayors and regional presidents has provided the Fifth Report on Cohesion with local feedback that includes specific indications based on the experience acquired thanks to the direct administration of citizens. The result has been a strengthening of the Cohesion Fund as a means for measures for territorial development, not only until 2013, but also for the years to come. On June 16, 2011, the leaders of European local and regional institutions therefore urged José Manuel Barroso, President of the European Commission, to equip the European Union with an "ambitious" budget. This budget would take into account their role in the Europe 2020 strategy, since stimulating the economy requires the regions and municipalities have an active role in planning and budgetary matters in order to achieve the objectives of European cohesion policies.[4]

In this perspective, which stimulates historical research, it is at times useful to propose a number of reflections collected over the past twenty

---

[2] Press release dated January 31st, 2011, from the Committee of Regions at http://www.cor.europa.eu/pages/PressTemplate.aspx?view=detail&id=545cd53a-9dc3-427f-876b-0706e7bbefe3.

[3] See *Régions et communes d'Europe*, 72 (April-May 2011), p. 5.

[4] Press release dated June 16th, 2011, from the Committee of Regions at http://www.cor.europa.eu/pages/PressTemplate.aspx?view=detail&id=5cd9a64f-8ce0-411a-a29a-8f130c3f6c85.

years of studies, which are part of a process that, over the years, has resulted in the publication of books and essays.

A group of researchers at the universities of Genoa, Pavia, Siena and Turin, as well as from a number of research centres and foundations,[5] started and consolidated a vast *corpus* of studies on the history of federalism and European integration, with particular reference to the field of political ideas and philosophies, the work of movements, of their leaders, as well as the unification process itself. The adoption of such a perspective has resulted in a broadening of the field of research, both from a chronological point of view, since it is known that the precursors of modern Europeanism and federalism are to be found between the end of the 18th and the beginning of the 19th centuries,[6] and from a consideration of the political parties, movements, territorial institutions, and economic and social forces, so as to assess and understand the creation of the *acquis communautaire*.

The first specific contributions followed the work began with exceptional results by Walter Lipgens[7], which was continued after his premature death by Wilfried Loth.[8] Lipgens's work was presented in its totality during the first international conference entitled *I Movimenti per l'unità europea negli anni 1945-1954* which, held in Pavia on October 19th-21st 1989, inaugurated a long and fruitful season of studies on federalist subjects, acting also as a stimulus for some younger scholars to follow the path of historical research on European integration,

5 In particular I would like to mention the pioneering work done by the Luigi Einaudi Foundation in Turin, which already in October 1974 had allowed the organisation of a study seminar and the publication of the book edited by Pistone and entitled, *L'idea dell'unificazione europea dalla prima alla seconda guerra mondiale*, and by the Luciano Bolis European Foundation, which, at the end of the 1980s sponsored and organised the first conference of studies on European federalist movements. On the role played by the Bolis Foundation, see Rognoni Vercelli, "Gli archivi dei movimenti per l'unità europea e il ruolo della Fondazione Bolis"; *idem*, "Gli archivi federalisti ed europeisti e il ruolo della Fondazione Bolis". To the work of these two foundations one must today add the study and research work done by the *Centro di studi storici sul federalismo e l'unificazione europea "Mario Albertini"*, and that of the *Centro di ricerca sull'integrazione europea* (CRIE) at the University of Siena, the *Centro studi sul federalismo* in Turin (CSF), and the Pavia University's *Centro interdipartimentale di ricerca e documentazione sulla storia del Novecento*.

6 Albertini, *Il federalismo. Antologia e definizione*.

7 The following books are of the utmost importance Lipgens, *Europa-Föderationspläne der Widerstandsbewegungen 1940-1945*; *idem*, *Die Anfänge der europäischen Einigungspolitik*, translated into English with the title *A History of European Integration*; posthumous books published by Lipgens and Loth (eds.), *Documents on the History of European Integration.*; Lipgens's collection, *Sources for the History of european Integration.*

8 Pistone, "Introduzione".

considered also from the movements' point of view, at that time, just like today, not very customary for the academic world. Attended by scholars from all over Europe, the first conference was followed by two others on Europeanist movements, in Genoa in November 1992 and in Siena in October 1997. Those conferences also attended by leading players who presented their papers among others, Umberto Serafini,[9] the founder of the *Associazione italiana per il Consiglio dei comuni e delle regioni d'Europa* (AICCRE), at the time of its founding the *Associazione italiana per il Consiglio dei comuni d'Europa* (AICCE). With his customary passion, he spoke at length in Genoa about the history of the Council of European Municipalities and Regions (CEMR) (at the time of its founding called the Council of European Municipalities (CEM)), which could rightly be considered his movement; about the mayors, local administrators and politicians linked to the world of autonomies and Europeanism, such as the socialist Alessandro Schiavi, first president of the AICCE; about heads of state and government; and about the men and women from the Old Continent who had fought alongside him for the United States of Europe and for the autonomy of territorial institutions. For the minutes of the next meeting in Siena he also drafted an important account.[10] The minutes of

9 Umberto Serafini (1916-2005) was born in Rome and attended the Normale University in Pisa, but World War II and his deployment to the Libyan front prevented him from graduating. He took part in campaigns in North Africa until December 1941, when he was captured. Having returned to Italy at the end of the war, he graduated in Philosophy from Rome University. He then began his political militancy in the *Movimento Comunità* becoming one of Adriano Olivetti's closest advisors. He also joined the *Movimento federalista europeo*, thus taking part in the battles for creating a federal Europe. In 1951 he started to work on the creation of an association of local authorities at a European level. In 1952 he founded the *Associazione italiana per il Consiglio dei comuni d'Europa*, of which he was elected Secretary General. He founded and directed the monthly magazine published by the movement *Comuni d'Europa*. Serafini's biography from then on mainly coincides with the history of the movement he contributed to founding, developing and leading until his death. On Serafini, see his autobiographies *I libri e il prossimo* and *La mia guerra contro la guerra*. Equally indispensible for setting his political work in a broader contexts are his books *Adriano Olivetti e il Movimento Comunità*; *Breve storia del Consiglio dei comuni e delle regioni d'Europa*; my books *Autonomie locali e federazione sovranazionale* and "Umberto Serafini e Altiero Spinelli fra federalismo infranazionale e sovranazionale"; and the monograph issue of *Comuni d'Europa*, n.s., 10 (December 2005), which is entirely devoted to him. The author is writing his biography as well as editing the collection of his editorials published in *Comuni d'Europa*.

10 In addition to the report written by Serafini, the minutes for the Siena conference also contain those by Jean-Pierre Gouzy, Gian Piero Orsello, and Carlo Ernesto Meriano, who spoke about Giuseppe Petrilli. One must also emphasise how some of the essays published in the various minutes mentioned were written by those who personally took part in the battle for the European federation.

the conferences were published in 1996 and in 2000, respectively.[11] The next conference on Carlo Cattaneo's legacy, sponsored by Pavia University's *Centro interdipartimentale di ricerca e documentazione sulla storia del Novecento*, in close cooperation with other universities and research centres, and held in Pavia from November 28th to November 30th 2001, not only focused the attention of scholars on a figure, that of Cattaneo, who was ahead of his times as far as 20th-century European federalism was concerned, but also proposed modern reflections on the European Union's institutional structure and the various players in the unification process. The two books of minutes bear witness to the attention now paid by a vast audience of European historians to the issues addressed.[12]

Among other things, these studies emphasised how, in Italian events, there were important and singular aspects concerning the history of Europeanism, federalism and European integration set within a regional context, which in a dynamic manner constantly interacted at a national and international level. On the basis of study experiences on international Europeanist movements, a series of research programmes were started that, following the example set by the pioneering Convention in Turin on November 28-29, 1991, on the origins of Europeanism in Piedmont,[13] resulted in systematic research with clear interrelations between contemporary history and that of the political ideas, philosophy and work done by federalists in Piedmont, Liguria, Tuscany and Lombardy.

The period analysed was different depending on the territory analysed, but the attempt to seize the European perspective in the ideas and the events between the 19th and 20th centuries was pursued with wide-ranging and precise historical reconstructions. Subsequently there were conferences addressing the subjects of *Europeismo e federalismo in Piemonte tra le due guerre mondiali. La Resistenza e i Trattati di Roma (1957)*, Turin, October 9th-10th, 1997; *L'europeismo in Liguria. Dal Risorgimento alla nascita dell'Europa comunitaria*, Genoa, October 18th-19th, 2001; and *Europeismo e federalismo in Toscana 1945-2001*, Siena, November 15th-16th, 2002.[14] Furthermore, a book was published with all the minutes of the last study conference held in Milan-Pavia-

---

11 The first edited by Pistone, *I movimenti per l'unità europea 1954-1969*, the second by Landuyt and Preda, *I movimenti per l'unità europea 1970-1986*.

12 Preda and Rognoni Vercelli, *Storia e percorsi del federalismo*.

13 Malandrino (ed.), *Alle origini dell'europeismo in Piemonte.*

14 The minutes for the first two conferences were published; Pistone and Malandrino (eds.), *Europeismo e federalismo in Piemonte tra le due guerre mondiali. La Resistenza e i Trattati di Roma (1957)*; Preda and Levi (eds.), *L'europeismo in Liguria*; the minutes of the third conference have not yet been published.

Brescia on May 28th-30th, 2003, dedicated to federalism in Lombardy.[15] This last conference was sponsored by the *"Mario Albertini" Centro di studi storici sul federalismo e l'unificazione europea* and by Pavia University's *Centro interdipartimentale di ricerca e documentazione sulla storia del Novecento.*[16] Interest surrounding this event was shown by the numerous prestigious sponsorships received[17] and the wealth of papers presented in a multidisciplinary context. Introducing this conference, Luigi Vittorio Majocchi[18] emphasised the importance of

---

15 Zucca (ed.), *Europeismo e federalismo in Lombardia dal Risorgimento all'Unione europea.*

16 The *Centro interdipartimentale di ricerca e documentazione sulla storia del Novecento* was created in 1998, thanks to the initiative of professors and researchers at Pavia University's Departments of Political Economics and Quantitative Methods, History and Geography, Political and Social Sciences, and the Institute of Statistics. Its charter was first amended in March 2002 and then again in 2005, both to allow the addition of the Department of Juridical Studies and Roman Law, and to conform the charter to new regulations passed by Pavia University's ruling bodies. In order to achieve its objectives, the centre collects and makes available to professors, researchers and scholars archival, bibliographical and documentary material of all kinds concerning the sector studied, with particular reference to the history of Pavia University, to local political history, the history of the Resistance, and the political-social aspects of the European integration process. To better achieve its objectives, the centre has participated in conventions with the Provincial Administration of Pavia, the Municipality of Pavia, the *Istituto pavese per la storia della Resistenza e dell'età contemporanea* and with the *Centro di studi storici sul federalismo e l'unificazione europea "Mario Albertini"*. Together with *Centro per la storia dell'Università degli Studi di Pavia*, it has promoted the creation of the university's historical archives which, thanks to fundamental contributions from the Cariplo foundation, has recovered and made available documentary material of extraordinary importance not only for the university's history, but also for scientific and political history as well as local, national and international economic history. See Negruzzo and Zucca (eds.), *Gli archivi storici delle Università italiane e il caso pavese*. This centre is now directed by the author and presided over by Giulio Guderzo.

17 Among these it is worth mentioning that of the Lombardy Region – The Directorship of the culture, identity and autonomies of Lombardy, of the Province of Pavia, of the Municipalities of Milan, Brescia and Pavia. Their creation was in particular helped by the *Associazione universitaria di studi europei* (AUSE), the *Centro di ricerca sull'integrazione europea* (CRIE), the *Fondazione Europea Luciano Bolis*, the *Istituto pavese per la storia della Resistenza e dell'età contemporanea*, Pavia University's "Carlo M. Cipolla" *Dipartimento di Scienze storiche e geografiche*, Milan University's *Dipartimento di Scienze della storia e della documentazione storica*, and the Province of Pavia's Agency for the Promotion of Cultural Activities.

18 Luigi Vittorio Majocchi, was born in Vigevano in 1937. After graduating in Law from Pavia University he specialised at Harvard University. A professor of history and philosophy in Lyceums, he taught at Portland State University; he also held the first Jean Monnet chair of History of European Integration from 1989-1990 to 1998. He is currently a professor at Pavia University where he teaches Western European History. At the beginning of the 1960s he came into contact with the Pavia federalist school, represented by Mario Albertini, who initiated him to aspects of the federalist

Lombardy's contribution to the history of federalism and European integration, referring in particular to the figure of Mario Albertini,[19] (to whom the Pavia day of the conference was devoted), who in his opinion stands as one of international federalism's greatest theorists. The capability of the federalist leader from Pavia, however, was also demonstrated in the creation not only of a federalist school but also of a generation of militants who, inspired by him, transformed the federalist idea into political actions and practices aimed at creating the European federation. Lombardy was thus the homeland for generations of Europeanists who, in various sectors of politics and society, supported the commitment for the creation of a United States of Europe. In Lombardy, more than in other Italian and European regions, federalism found a receptive environment in the political, economic, social and cultural fabric. In particular, Milan and its mayors, with Aldo Aniasi standing out among

---

culture, and with Altiero Spinelli, who encouraged him to become committed to the battle for Europe's federal unity. A militant federalist, he became the secretary of the *Movimento federalista europeo* from 1980 to 1987 and director of the International European Movement from 1984 to 1987. During this period he supported Altiero Spinelli's battle for the Treaty on the establishment of the European Union and subsequently continued his work for the conferral of a constituent mandate to the European parliament to be elected in 1989. In his dual role of scholar and militant federalist, in 1971 he founded and then directed until 1987 the *Centro studi sul federalismo, il regionalismo e l'unità europea* (CESFER); he published the study series entitled *I problemi della lotta politica per il federalismo*, which he also directed. In 1999 he sponsored the foundation of the *Centro di studi storici sul federalismo e l'unificazione europea "Mario Albertini"*, of which he is currently the president. However, above all Majocchi maintained a school of historical studies that has provided interpretative means to more than a generation of scholars of the history of European integration. Among his many publications, see Majocchi and Rossolillo, *Il Parlamento europeo*; Majocchi and Vitale (eds.), *Europa 1992. Dall'Atto Unico al governo europeo*; Majocchi (ed.), *Messina quarant'anni dopo*; Majocchi, *La difficile costruzione dell'unità europea.*

19 Mario Albertini can be considered one of federalism's greatest contemporary theoreticians. He was capable of merging ideas and action in a pure Mazzini-like spirit, also "bringing up" groups of young federalist militants. Born in Pavia in 1919, in 1945, persuaded of the historical need for Europe to achieve federal unity, he joined the *Movimento federalista europeo.* After graduating in philosophy in 1951, he embarked upon an academic career at Pavia University, but his commitment to the battle for a European federation soon became a priority, and in 1953 he became one of Altiero Spinelli's closest advisors, subsequently succeeding him in 1966 as the leader of the European federalist movement. Between 1975 and 1984 he was the president of the Union of European Federalists. The author of many books and essays, in 1959 he founded the multilingual magazine "Il Federalista", which is still published today. His strong personality and capacity for political synthesis allowed him to influence the policies of the Italian federalist movement until his death in 1997. See in particular the seminal work entitled Albertini, *Tutti gli scritti*, and also the chapters about him in Zucca (ed.), *Europeismo e federalismo in Lombardia*, pp. 377-529.

them with his work in favour of European twinning, as discussed in this essay, were leading players in the battle for a European federation. Many of the aforementioned studies have been published in the University of Siena *Centro di ricerca sull'integrazione europea* series entitled *Fonti e studi sul federalismo e sull'integrazione europea*, initially a series published by Pavia University's "Carlo M. Cipolla" Department of Historical and Geographical Sciences, and now published by Il Mulino and edited by Giulio Guderzo and Ariane Landuyt. This series has sponsored studies and research that emphasise the complexity of the factors that contributed to the Europeanist process and includes many essays devoted to the history of Europeanist and federalist movements and to the work done by political parties and individual leading players in the battle for a united Europe. These initiatives have established further important synergies with scholars in various countries, resulting in additional reflections, such as those arising from the debate on the "method" adopted during the Messina Intergovernmental Conference, planned by Luigi Vittorio Majocchi,[20] or the conference on the contribution of the Christian tradition to the creation of Europe,[21] organised by the Paul VI Ambrosian Foundation and presided over by Luigi Zanzi.

New stimulus for research came from the increasingly important activities of the *Associazione universitaria di studi europei* (AUSE) and from the European Community Studies Association (ECSA), for which AUSE is the Italian section, which have developed European study programmes and set up in Italy and in countries inside and outside units, chairs and multi-disciplinary research groups named after Jean Monnet within the framework of activities sponsored by the Lifelong Learning Programme of the Directorate-General for Education and Culture – European Commission. On this subject it is sufficient to mention how in 2011 AUSE, brilliantly directed by its president, Daniela Preda, organised in Turin its 15th Summer School, which, accompanied by an important international conference dedicated to *L'Italia e l'unità europea dal Risorgimento a oggi. Idee e protagonisti*, confirmed its traditional role of bringing together young scholars and the most important international leaders in the field of multi-disciplinary research on European subjects.[22]

---

20 The minutes were published in Majocchi (ed.), *Messina quarant'anni dopo*.

21 See minutes in Citterio and Vaccaro (eds.), *Quale federalismo per quale Europa*.

22 The minutes of the conference are being published. Confirming the vitality of studies sponsored by the AUSE, the minutes of the 13th Summer School held in Catania in October 2009 and the minutes of the international conference held in Certosa di Pontignano (Siena) on May 23rd and 34th, 2008, were published in 2010: Preda and Pasquinucci (eds.), *The Road Europe Travelled Along*.

One must emphasise how the centenaries of the birth of the two fathers of current European federalism, Altiero Spinelli and Eugenio Colorni, resulted in the creation of two national celebration committees, the first one led by the then Rector of Rome's "La Sapienza" University, Renato Guarini and Francesco Gui, the second presided over by Maurizio Degl'Innocenti, now president of the "Filippo Turati" Historical Studies Foundation. In different periods, these committees did commendable work in promoting research, seminars and publications that have enriched the world with studies on federalism, on the Europeanist movements, and on the history of European integration.[23]

Within this framework, particularly stimulating for research at a continental level, there is still a significant lack of studies on the effect territorial institutions have had on the European integration process. Although historiography has to a certain extent recorded the presence and work of decentralised institutions in the European unification process, there are still few papers that thoroughly addressing this aspect. This situation is mainly due to the presence of a large amount of documentation, which, however, is hard to consult, not only because it is spread all over the continent and mostly not in order, but also because it is not comprehensible and understandable on the basis of a significant reference bibliography that is just beginning to be created.

The need to emphasise the impact of local institutions on the European unification process is confirmed by written and spoken testimony provided by the leading players and by the objective fact that territorial institutions have now really become part of European institutions. From all this there emerges a cultural and political hinterland deeply rooted in attempts to propose political and ethical alternatives to the triumph of National Socialism and Fascism. Thanks to the work of territorial institutions, politicians and movements have emerged whose work was often the result of ancient schools of thought, resulting in the creation of the European Conference of Local Powers (ECLP), which then became the Congress of Local and Regional Authorities (CLRA) –

---

[23] While the work of the Spinelli committee was certainly significant for the number of initiatives undertaken – see www.altierospinelli.it and Preda (ed.), *Altiero Spinelli e i movimenti per l'unità europea* –, during the three years of its activity and with seriously few resources, the Colorni committee created a solid intellectual path, albeit a very varied one as far as the subjects addressed in these research papers are concerned. The results of this work have been published in three books: Degl'Innocenti (ed.), *Eugenio Colorni dall'antifascismo all'europeismo socialista e federalista*; Cerchiai and Rota (eds.), *Eugenio Colorni e la cultura italiana fra le due guerre*; Zucca (ed.), *Eugenio Colorni federalista*. The committee's work also ensured the republication, edited by Geri Cerchiai, of Colorni's book *La malattia della metafisica*, while only a current lack of funds is preventing the republication of federalist papers.

set up at the Council of Europe – the Committee of Regions (CoR), the Conference of European Peripheral Maritime Regions (CPRM), the Conference of European Regions with Legislative Power (REGLEG), the Association of European Border Regions (AEBR), the Conference of European Regional Legislative Assemblies (CALRE), the Assembly of European Regions (AER), the European Group for Territorial Cooperation (EGTC), and the United Cities and Local Governments.

A first scientific debate on relations between local communities and the creation of European unity occurred during a conference held in Turin and in Stresa on May 14th and 18th, 1961, for the centenary of the Unification of Italy. The event's official sponsors were the Institute for the Science of Public Administration and the president of the Exhibition of Italian Regions, Adrio Casati, but its real inspirers were the politicians, historians, jurists and economists linked to the world of local autonomies, men such as Jean Bareth, Amedeo Peyron, Umberto Serafini and Gianfranco Miglio, to mention but a few. The subject was debated from various perspectives: historical, juridical, administrative, economic, cultural and political. The extensive minutes, published in 1963, are a milestone in the historical-political studies on the subject of local authorities and Europe. A number of the leading speakers at that event later exerted political as well as intellectual influence, such as Gianfranco Miglio in the context of the internal reorganisation of European states, and Umberto Serafini, Jean Bareth and Amedeo Peyron in the battle for infra- and supranational federalism, and Mario Albertini for European federalism.

Later on, political and scientific magazines, *Comuni d'Europa* in Italy and *L'Europe en formation* in France, kept alive the debate and at the time welcomed the opinions of young promising figures such as Dario Velo and Alberto Majocchi, or teachers such as Alexandre Marc and Umberto Serafini.

So as to also provide answers to these issues, for about 15 years Giulio Guderzo and Luigi Vittorio Majocchi have promoted a basic research programme that has allowed the identification of the main players as well as the recovery of a number of archives on local authorities and the leading figures of this history that would otherwise have been forever lost. Within this framework, a study was carried out on the contribution provided to the European integration process by the CEMR and its national sections. In the 1990s, a new research group addressing local institutions, and in particular metropolitan cities, was created in France, which today refers to the Lyon 2 University and the *Institut d'Études politiques* in Lyon. In 2000, thanks to an initiative by Paris 1 University's *Institut Pierre Renouvin*, a series of research studies were addressed at the "espaces européens et temps de l'Europe", with the primary objective of studying territorial authorities, and in particular the regions, in the European integration process.[24]

In order to undertake these studies, finding and recovering the archives linked to the international work done by territorial authorities was of the utmost importance. In this sense the role played by the CEMR, the largest organisation of European territorial institutions, initially was the most important. The CEMR's international sector was initially headquartered in Geneva between 1951 and 1955, and since then has been situated in Paris. It was precisely in the Paris area, and more specifically in a *garde meuble* at the Roissy Charles de Gaulle Airport, that the CEMR's international historical archives were found, effectively forgotten there by the organisation itself, not preserved in the best of conditions, and with a number of important files missing, such as the one on the movement's foundation which has still not been found. Thanks to the interest shown by Pavia University's researchers and professors, the CEMR's archives where then placed with the Historical Archives of the European Union in Florence, where they were indexed and made available to scholars.

Furthermore, photocopies of the CEMR documents concerning the political activity undertake by this association in favour of the European integration process, and found in the archives, were deposited in Pavia. These files are the result of the initial recovery work done at the *garde meuble* and form the central nucleus of the archives on the subject of the relationship between local authorities and the European integration process. The archives contain the minutes of international meetings, the reports from the States General – the CEMR's great international assembly – correspondence between the sections and the international secretariat, between the latter and the movement's presidents, between institutional organisations and the various foreign ministries, government ministers, politicians, trade-unionists, federalist and Europeanist movements and various European personalities. Documents from the Paris headquarters of CEMR, not yet deposited in Florence, are available at Pavia University for consultation as photocopies, and for some subjects in the original. The original order has been respected for every file, and therefore individual documents can easily be retraced to their place in the original archives.

International research has also identified archival sources in the various national headquarters of the Association of European Territorial Institutions, which have been consulted for historical purposes for the first time. Of particular importance for the strategic role played at least

---

24 One of the first results of this work was the book: Bitsch (ed.), *Le fait régional et la construction européenne*.

since the early 1980s are the documents from the *Association française du Conseil des Communes et Régions d'Europe* (AFCCRE), preserved in Orléans, and those of the *Association villes et communes luxembourgeoises* (AVCL) – now the *Syndicat intercommunal à vocation multiple des Villes et Communes luxembourgeoises pour la promotion et la sauvegarde d'intérêts communaux généraux et communs* (SYVICOL) – preserved in the city of Luxembourg. Neither of these archives is open to the public, but they can be consulted after obtaining authorisation from the governing bodies of these associations. One must also acknowledge the importance of the discovery and recovery of a significant number of personal archives of mayors and politicians such as Giorgio La Pira, Mayor of Florence, Aldo Aniasi, Mayor of Milan, Amedeo Peyron, Mayor of Turin, Celeste Bastianetto, senator and Mayor of San Donà di Piave, or infra and supranational federalists such as Alexandre Marc, co-founder of the Movement of Local European Autonomies, Alida de Jager, founder of the CEM, Umberto Serafini, Adriano Olivetti, and the Florentine federalist Gastone Bonzagni, to mention only a few.

Research activities have also led to the recovery of personal papers that, either photocopied or in the original, have been placed with Pavia's University's historical archives. Important figures whose papers have been used for this book include Umberto Rossi, Mayor of Ivrea, one of Adriano Olivetti's main advisers in the Community Movement and co-founder of both the CEMR and the AICCRE; Giacomo Centazzo, Mayor of Udine and an active federalist; Renato Brügner co-founder of the AICCRE, founder and director of the European Institute of Inter-municipal Studies and Relations with headquarters in Geneva; Magda Da Passano, a federalist and an activist in Adriano Olivetti's *Movimento Comunità*; the aforementioned Celeste Bastianetto, Mayor of San Donà di Piave as well as a Christian Democrat senator and one of Luigi Sturzo's oldest advisors. There are photocopies concerning the federalist and municipalist work done by Edgard Milhaud, promoter and founder of the CEMR as well as one of the main representatives of reformist socialism between the two wars, a candidate for the Nobel Peace Prize, founder of the Faculty of Economics at Geneva University, a member of various French cabinets, as well as the founder and editor-in-chief of the *Annales de l'économie collective*, at the time the most important economic reference publication for European reformists.

A temporary section has been set up at the *Archivio Storico dell'Università degli Studi di Pavia* to host part of the archives of Alberto Cabella, a founding member of the European Union of Federalists (EUF) and the *Movimento Comunità*, assistant national secretary of the *Movimento federalista europeo* (MFE), secretary general of the Congress of the European People's acting committee, and later director of the *Istituto italiano di cultura* in Paris. A written account about the founding of the CEMR provided by Alexandre Marc is preserved in a file with his name on it in this same archive.

In addition to paper documents, also entrusted to Pavia University, there are a number of recordings of interviews with federalist personalities such as Umberto Serafini; Jacques Jira, an prominent member of the French federalist movement *La Fédération* and a witness of federalist policies from the 1940s until today, as well as interviews with the aforementioned Alberto Cabella, Magda Da Passano and Umberto Rossi.

These archives were recently enriched by the addition of Umberto Serafini's personal archive and additional documentation that contains part of Adriano Olivetti's papers. Both have been indexed and recently made available to scholars.

It is with regret that I must report that the Italian section of the CEMR (AICCRE), the most active on the subject of federalism and European unity, has never created an archive. Documentation concerning its activities is therefore for the moment untraceable and probably lost, just like that of *La Fédération*, the most important French federalist movement at least until the end of the 1970s. Such news should lead historians, archivists and, in general, all those responsible for preserving the documentary heritage both at an Italian and a European level, to reflect on the rising need for valid subsidies for the selection of documentation, but mainly on the care required when discarding papers, which is of course necessary, since it is impossible to preserve immense quantities of material, but which at times can delete important clues for a correct reconstruction and interpretation of events.[25]

It is necessary to once again emphasise how the current political-institutional status of local institutions is the result of a complex historical evolution and provides ideas for research moving in different directions. Hence the archives at the Council of Europe, those of the European Union and those of individual territorial institutions are important.

The research presented was completed in 2001 with the publication of the book *Autonomie locali e federazione sovranazionale. La battaglia*

[25] Among the many books available on this subject, see Carucci, "Lo scarto come elemento qualificante delle fonti per la storiografia"; Zanni Rosiello, "Spurghi e distruzioni di carte d'archivio"; Guercio, "La selezione dei documenti archivistici nel recente dibattito internazionale".

del Conseil des Communes et Régions d'Europe per l'unità europea[26] as well as with later essays and monographs.

Other historical studies were later added to these papers, bearing witness to the rising interest in these subjects as well as the greater accessibility of documents, made possible in part thanks to the aforementioned recoveries. The excellent book by Laura Grazi, *L'Europa e le città. La questione urbana nel processo di integrazione europea (1957-1999)*[27] and Giulia Devani's essay, *Altiero Spinelli e il Conseil des Communes (et des Régions) d'Europe*,[28] which greatly depended on the CEMR archives entrusted to the Historical Archives of the European Union in Florence, are emblematic. The research and objectives of Patrizia Dogliani and Oscar Gaspari to a certain extent followed a different path. Nevertheless, they do provide an important contribution to the subject of the international relations of the municipalities with their book *L'Europa dei comuni dalla fine dell'Ottocento al secondo dopoguerra*,[29] just as the quoted minutes edited by Marie-Thérèse Bitsch on the relationship between the regions and European formation represent a summary of studies by various historians on this subject.[30]

Research on the role played by local institutions in international relations, and in particular in the European integration process, does not end with the publication of this book, which is addressed at providing elements of reflection for new scientific research that will help to clarify how the multiform action taken by municipalities and regions, in a context of federalism and multilevel governance, has played, and can increasingly play, a positive role in the creation of a United States of Europe.

---

26 Zucca, *Autonomie locali e federazione sovranazionale*.

27 Grazi, *La questione urbana nel processo di integrazione europea*.

28 Devani, "Altiero Spinelli e il Conseil des Communes (et des Régions) d'Europe".

29 Dogliani and Gasperi (eds.), *L'Europa dei comuni*.

30 *Le fait régional et la construction européenne*.

Part I

Bring Municipalities Together
to Bring Europe Together

CHAPTER 1

The Birth of the European Local Autonomies Movement

Western civilisation has its roots in the Greek *polis* and the continuation of this urban tradition in Rome and the system of Italic cities, which involved autochthonous experiences. When the Urbe started to dominate large territories, in Italy and then in the rest of the continental and Mediterranean world, it sent magistrates as administrators with the authority to impose the law of Rome in those more or less distant places. These were vast regions, at times coinciding with current national states or macro-regions, falling under the Roman *imperium* which was enforced through the presence of the legions. Administrative units were called provinces, and there were 87 under Domitian, spread over the known world. All traces of them vanished with the dissolution of the imperial system, and subsequent territorial reorganisation once again emphasised all over western Europe the central role played by cities.

The reorganisation of Europe during the Middle Ages began in urban communities, which provided the energy to progress following the impulse provided by political, economic and cultural life. Through a profound regionalisation process that started around the year 1000 and then was resumed with greater vigour in the 12th century, the Europe of cities was born or regenerated from below with autonomous growth that was to become the driving force of European civilisation. Cities were places of cohesive communities and centres of commerce and manufacturing, art and architecture, the seats of intellectual cenacles and schools, hubs for juridical and political experimentation led by republican regimes or noble families, and they represented the mainstay around which all European history revolved. For centuries Europe experienced the separation and divergence of more or less distant feudal territories, subject to the domination of lords, dukes, marquises, counts and barons, and represented a conservative world linked mainly to income provided by land and by wars.[1] Its cities were the seats of corporations and institutions of social and political representation, animated by enterprising bourgeoisies bearing an idea of mobile wealth

1 On this subject the immense bibliography includes the enlightening book by Settia, *Rapine, assedi, battaglie*.

not bound to land ownership. The city, to use an expression borrowed from Carlo Cattaneo,[2] marked the beginning of all history in Italy and, one could add, also in Europe.

That civilisation was characterised by regionalisation, founded on a multi-centrality of cities, which some now identify as the possible element in a new infra-national and supranational federal organisation of Europe.[3] Every city developed relations through exchanges with the surrounding countryside and also with nearby cities in a relationship that over the short or medium term developed as dominating or dominated. Over greater distances, cities developed relations through land or maritime connections that, from Europe, first developed towards the smaller and larger Mediterranean[4] and then expanded immensely across the routes of the Atlantic.[5]

Over the centuries European cities then built up institutional relations that one could describe as international. These relations developed through trade and fairs, but also through universities and religious institutions. Alliances were signed, as were commercial treaties, and wars were fought to control territory and trade. The evolution of the

---

2 To set his work and ideas within the framework of supranational federalism and European integration, see (also for the quoted bibliography) among the many papers written on Carlo Cattaneo the now published minutes of the conference on Carlo Cattaneo held in Pavia in November 2001: Preda and Rognoni Vercelli (eds.), *Storia e percorsi del federalismo*. The conference sponsored by Pavia University's *Centro interdipartimentale di ricerca e documentazione sulla storia del Novecento*, in close cooperation with other universities and research centres, emphasised how ahead of his time Cattaneo was in understanding and clarifying both the profound meaning of the need for European unity, dissociating himself from the exaltation of the national myth, and in his ability to point out possible ways of creating a federal state as the means for asserting democratic values and internal and external peace over vast political areas and for organising the broadest possible capacity for internal self-government. On infra-national and supranational federalism see also Momigliano, *Carlo Cattaneo e gli Stati Uniti d'Europa*; Cattaneo, *Stati Uniti d'Italia*; Levi, *Federalismo e integrazione europea*; Cofrancesco, *Europeismo e cultura*. On Mazzini's Europeanism see Salvatorelli, "Mazzini e gli Stati Uniti d'Europa"; Tramarollo, *L'Europa di Mazzini*; Chiti-Batelli, "Mazzini, précurseur de l'idée de la fédération européenne?". In general, on the idea of European unity during the Risorgimento see Visconti, *La concezione unitaria dell'Europa nel Risorgimento italiano e nei suoi precedenti storici*; Albertini, *Il Risorgimento e l'Unità europea*; Pistone, *L'Italia e l'unità europea*.

3 On this subject the thoughts of Luigi Zanzi contained in his book *Le Alpi nella storia d'Europa* are of the utmost importance.

4 For a historical-geographical definition of the concept of small and large Mediterranean see Braudel, *Civiltà e imperi del Mediterraneo nell'età di Filippo II*.

5 On European expansion following the Atlantic routes and the role played by cities, see the unmatched work of Chaunu, *L'espansione europea dal XIII al XV secolo*; *idem*, *La conquista e l'esplorazione dei nuovi mondi (XVI secolo)*.

economy and the consequent political-territorial organisation, stimulated by those same fruitful relations, determined the ruin of the independence of cities starting back in the 16th century. The advent of centralised national states, answering a need to economically and socially organise the development achieved in large and cohesive territorial areas, abolished relations between territorial institutions and, over time, declared them illegal. The modern state assumed for itself exclusive external representation and was therefore the only subject legitimised to hold international relations, regulating them, and at times totally preventing them, until the crisis of the European system of centralised sovereign national states became totally evident with World War II.[6]

Between the end of the 19th and the beginning of the 20th century, direct relations between local administrations were resumed with difficulty, encouraged by socialist and Catholic internationalism, as well as the desire of individual administrators and officials to compare their various management experiences at a national and European level. This resulted in the creation of a network that first became a movement for the administrative debate and then for the political one.[7] Contacts developed in an embryonic institutional form with the foundation, in Gand in 1913, of the first International Union of Local Authorities (IULA), at the time better known by its French name, *Union internationale des villes* (UIV).[8] The association came to life mainly on

---

6 For an overall review of the historiography that has the crisis experienced by sovereign national states at the centre of its ideas, see Kerr, "The Prevention of War"; *idem*, *Pacifism is not enough, nor patriotism either*; Robbins, *Economic Planning and International Order*; Luigi Einaudi, *La guerra e l'unità europea*; Dehio, *Gleichgewicht oder Hegemonie*; *idem*, *Deutschland und die Weltpolitik im XX Jahrhundert*; Spinelli and Rossi, *Problemi della federazione europea*; Albertini, *Lo Stato nazionale*; Pistone (ed.), *Politica di potenza e imperialismo*; Pistone, *Ragion di Stato, relazioni internazionali, imperialismo*; Levi, *Il federalismo*; Pistone, *Un'Italia federale in un'Europa federale*. Reflections on the thoughts of Ludwig Dehio contained in the essays by Pistone, *Ludwig Dehio* are also particularly interesting, as are Majocchi, "Ludwig Dehio"; Pistone, "Ludwig Dehio e l'interpretazione federalista dell'epoca delle guerre mondiali e del fascismo". For a comparison between the theory of international relations based on the concept of the primacy of foreign policy and the concept of the primacy of internal policy see Waltz, *Teoria della politica internazionale*.

7 One of the first to define as a movement the renewed dialogue between European administrators and territorial institutions was Giovanni Montemartini in his book *Municipalizzazione dei pubblici servigi*. On Giovanni Montemartini and his brother Luigi, a socialist member of parliament, see *La cultura delle riforme in Italia fra Otto e Novecento* and Magnani, *Luigi Montemartini nella storia del riformismo italiano*.

8 On the events that led to the creation of the UIV within the context of the reformist movement, see Gaspari, "Alle origini del movimento comunale europeo"; Payre and Saunier, "L'Union internationale des villes o l'Internazionale municipale (1913-1940)"; the introduction by Dogliani and Gaspari entitled, *Origini e sviluppo del*

the basis of the reformist experience, but other elements were not extraneous to the movement, among them municipal technical authorities anxious to hold a debate to find solutions to the problems already experienced by the municipalities.[9] In this context an important role was played by the scholar and socialist militant Edgard Milhaud[10]

---

movimento comunale europeo nel Novecento for the book edited by Dogliani and Gaspari *L'Europa dei comuni*. For an overall review see Rugge, *I regimi delle città*. After World War II, the UIV extended its network of members to the whole world. The organisation is divided into seven regional sections with headquarters in Quito, Djakarta, Washington, Guatemala City, Harare, Istanbul and Paris. After years of at times very bitter debates, the CEMR at the end of the 1980s became the UIV's European section, leaving global representation of local autonomies to the UIV. The complex relations between the UIV and the CEMR have yet to be reconstructed. For the years preceding the integration between the two associations, one indispensable source is the series of documents concerning the *CCRE-International Union of local Authorities (1982-1990)* preserved at the European Union's Historical Archives in Florence.

9 The needs of municipal officers, wishing for an international debate on the various administrative methods, were answered by the UIV, as were the aspirations of the internationalist and utopian world, not to mention the Freemasons (Dogliani, "La sinistra europea alle origini del movimento comunale internazionale".

10 Edgard Milhaud (1873-1965) was very young when he joined the French Socialist Party. His sensitivity for economic and social problems and his studies at the *Sorbonne* led him to address in depth those issues concerning the implementation of socialist principles within the context of a capitalist economy. He completed a study on workers and socialist movements in Germany, and the results of this work were published in his first essay, published in 1903, entitled *La démocratie socialiste allemande*. His papers particularly impressed Jean Jaurés, with whom he cooperated in an attempt to merge the various socialist movements into a single party. He then joined the new French socialist party, holding important internal positions and later also government appointments, supporting the creation of trade unions linked to the socialist movement. In 1902 Geneva University asked him to chair the first course on Political Economics. Milhaud therefore experienced all levels of an academic career at this Swiss university. In 1905 he founded the *Bulletin économique*, which paved the way for the foundation in 1908 of the international magazine *Annales de la Régie directe* – published in French, English, Spanish and German – which in 1925 was called *Annales de l'économie collective* and then in 1974 became the *Annales de l'économie publique, sociale et coopérative*. His intentions for this magazine were to provide the necessary theoretical support to encourage the development of cooperatives at a local and national level, as well as to demonstrate the need for and the financial advantages arising from important nationalisations such as that of the railways. The magazine soon became the most important economic reference point for European reformist socialism, consequently broadening the issues debated. To develop studies on cooperation, especially at the municipal level, he created, together with the international cooperative trade-unionist movement, the *Centre international de recherches et d'information sur l'économie collective*. Milhaud also fought to achieve lasting international peace by cooperating with the League of Nations. For his work in this context, at the beginning of the 1950s he was short-listed for the Nobel Peace Prize. In 1951 he was one of the promoters and founders of the CEM, providing the organisation of European municipalities with the support of his

who, in addition to having held important positions in the French Socialist Party (SFIO), had also cooperated with various government cabinets both as an expert and as an economic advisor. Milhaud founded and directed the magazine *Annales de la Régie directe*, later called *Annales de l'Économie collective*, published in various European languages. Together with his many colleagues from a variety of countries, he used the magazine to develop the concept of inter-municipality, on the basis of which municipalities were to cooperate in spreading the knowledge acquired and the experiences in technical and social progress gained in local administrations. The magazine also served to create representation of their shared interests, study issues linked to the construction of public works and the organisation of municipal life, and create and manage institutions and collective services.[11] The UIV's constituent assembly was not only attended by Milhaud but also, among others, by Alessandro Schiavi,[12] a socialist and fervent municipalist. Mihaud was to play an essential role in the creation of the European movement of local autonomies after World War II, while Schiavi did the same for the movement's Italian section, of which he became the first president.[13] Furthermore, Schiavi was one of the

---

magazine and his own intellectual contribution. In the Milhaud archives, preserved at the Archives d'État de la République et Canton de Genève, there is also biographical information used for his candidatures for the Nobel Prize. Also see: Milhaud, "Au seuil de la 50e Année des 'Annales'"; Babel, "A la mémoire du professeur Edgard Milhaud".

11 *Premier Congrès international et exposition comparée des Villes*, p. 343.

12 Dogliani, "La sinistra europea alle origini del movimento comunale internazionale", p. 182.

13 Alessandro Schiavi (1872-1965), a socialist from Romagna, had already come into contact with international and national socialism in 1896 when he attended the Congress of the Second International in London and the IV National Congress of the Italian Socialist Party in Florence. These two events, his appointment as secretary of the regional socialist organisation and as editor-in-chief of *Il Risveglio*, marked his progressive departure from local political life. In December that same year he joined the first editorial bureau for the *Avanti*, of which the editor-in-chief was Bissolati, and he remained there for a decade. During this period he strengthened his political relations and friendship with Filippo Turati, a bond that after World War II saw Schiavi become the first biographer and attentive curator of the publication of the works and files of the Italian socialist leader. In 1905 Schiavi was dismissed from the socialist newspapers staff but appointed secretary and then director of Umanitaria's council house sector. His work was always centred on the study of social phenomena linked to farming struggles and municipal socialism. These interests led him to cooperate with Edgard Milhaud, whom he met only after the founding of the CCE, and the magazines for which he was the editor-in-chief. He was a strong supporter of socialist liberalism, to which he devoted important studies published by *Critica sociale, Avanti, La Riforma sociale* and *I Problemi del lavoro*. From 1912 to 1919 he was a member of the board of directors of the Socialist Party's Milanese section. A convinced neutralist, he attended the Inter-Allied Socialist Conference in London in

links between Italian municipalist socialists and the European municipalist movement, of which Milhaud was one of the most important representatives. His studies on social and municipal problems resulted in cooperation with the magazine published by Milhaud, and he actively addressed political positions that often originated in Maximalism in Milan's municipal administration, from which he was dismissed with the advent of Fascism.[14]

The Gand congress elected as the UIV's general secretary the reformist and freemason Émile Vinck[15], who that same year, 1913, backed the foundation of the *Union des villes et communes belges.* Vinck remained president of the UIV from 1913 to 1948, one of the most difficult periods in the organisation's long history. The fact that Vinck was a member of the Masonic lodge *Les Amis Philanthropes*

February 1918 and, in 1919, sponsored the first project for hosting Austrian children in Italy. At the 19th National Italian Socialist Congress held in 1922, Schiavi presented a topic in which he emphasised the need to come to an agreement with the middle-classes, with the sole objective of protecting fundamental freedoms. In 1926 he returned to Forlì where, under police supervision, he devoted himself to economic-political studies while maintaining political links at an international level as well. In the winter of 1942-1943 he established contact with a number of republicans in Romagna and embarked on anti-Fascist activities which, after July 25th, led him to become one of the city's most important politicians. Schiavi was the elected Provincial Councillor for Forlì, a senator representing the Social Democrats, and later appointed a member of ECSC's assembly. He came into contact with the CEM's promotion committee thanks to mediation by Renato Brügner, a member of the same party and close to Umberto Serafini in founding the AICCE. In spite of his age, after being appointed president of the AICCE he embarked on an intense national and international campaign to promote the ideas and the organisation of this new movement he perceived as so close to his earlier theories. He was one of the strongest supporters of the project for the creation of a European Community of Municipal Credit, also assuming the presidency of this institution, which remained elusive, not having ever found the funds needed to operate. Among the many works on municipal issues see Schiavi, *Il comune ieri, oggi, domani*; *idem*, *Le piaghe d'Italia.* Su Schiavi see [Serafini], "La morte di Alessandro Schiavi"; Ridolfi (ed.), *Alessandro Schiavi. Indagine sociale, culture politiche e tradizione socialista nel primo '900*; Bianciardi, *Alessandro Schiavi. La casa e la città*, Dogliani (ed.), *Europeismo e municipalismo. Alessandro Schiavi nel secondo dopoguerra*; Schiavi, *Carteggi*. I. *1892-1926*; *idem*, *Carteggi*. II. *1927-1965*; Monti and De Maria (eds.), *Inventari delle carte e bibliografia degli scritti di Alessandro Schiavi negli archivi forlivesi*; Schiavi, *Diari e note sparse (1894-1964)*; Ragusa, *Il manifesto elettorale*; Schiavi, *Nel socialismo italiano ed europeo*. On events concerning the European Community of Municipal Credit see Zucca, "Amedeo Peyron. Un sindaco federalista".

14 Schiavi, *Nel socialismo italiano ed europeo*, pp. 32-34.

15 Émile Vinck (1870-1950), a socialist who worked as a lawyer and was a solicitor at the Belgian Appeal Court, was elected municipal councillor in Ixelles from 1904 to 1941 and then senator from 1912 to 1946 (Dogliani and Gasperi (eds.), *L'Europa dei comuni*, p. 15).

resulted in the hypothesis that he was influenced and supported by Freemasons, as well as the socialist movement and later the Catholic movement, in the creation of the first embryonic network of international relations between local European institutions.[16]

In 1913 the International Garden Cities and Town Planning Association was founded – later renamed the International Federation for Housing and Planning (IFHP) – which, although wishing to organise and in some way provide leadership for European territorial institutions, did not equip itself with political objectives but instead with a role involving technical-professional refresher courses and in-depth analysis.

The existence of the UIV led to the creation of corresponding national organisations between local bodies that, in turn, contributed to strengthening an awareness of possible infra- and supranational relations between territorial institutions. Following the example set by the great political mass movements appearing on the political stage, the International of Municipalities[17] appeared at the beginning of the 20th century.

In spite of the positive premises, the UIV's work was unable to develop due to the war that devastated the European continent. After World War I a number of French, German, English, Belgian and Luxembourg municipalities, encouraged by the same managerial class that had led the UIV at the beginning of the century, resumed direct relations, both in order to overcome together the trauma of a devastating war and because they shared the memories of the same tragic events.[18] However, it was only in 1924 that the UIV's second congress was held in Amsterdam, in a country that had been neutral, marking the resumption of institutional relations between the municipalities achieved through the movement's re-forming in Paris in 1925.[19] From then until the end of the 1930s, the association of municipalities devoted itself to an in-depth study of issues such as the financial organisation of local institutions, municipal companies, expropriations, town planning, and the study of local, national and international economic phenomena using statistics. According to research currently available, it does not seem that during this period initiatives linked to twinning, either in shape or substance, were undertaken, or initiatives that indicated any intention to

16 Gaspari, *L'Italia dei municipi*.

17 Payre and Saunier, *L'Union internationale des villes*.

18 Association française du Conseil des Communes et Régions d'Europe, *L'art du jumelage*, p. 3.

19 On the subjects debated at these two Congresses see *IIe Congrès international des villes, Amsterdam 30 juin et 1 juillet 1924*; *IIIe Congrès international des villes, Paris 28 septembre-4 octobre 1925*.

create European institutions going beyond the usual international meetings or conferences. After the advent of Fascism in various European countries,[20] the UIV progressively lost contributions first from local Italian administrators, then from the German and Spanish ones. Its activities therefore dwindled until the eve of the new European "civil war".

During this period, the idea of the role played by local authorities in European history was not abandoned however. The most enlightening example, which after the war provided a real contribution to the rebirth of the movement of local autonomies at a European level and the idea of a twinning of municipalities, came from the Swiss historian and political activist Adolf Gasser.[21] He attended Heidelberg and Zurich universities, where he graduated with a thesis on the study of the creation of ancient local freedoms in Switzerland.[22] His dissertation was published in 1927 and became the basis on which the Swiss historian developed his ideas and his work.

In 1932 the third congress of the International Pan-Europa Union, led by Count Richard Coudenhove-Kalergi,[23] was held in Basel, and the

---

20 Historiography concerning the advent of Fascism in Europe is extremely vast and the following are a few examples of such work. For Italy see De Felice, *Mussolini il fascista.* I. *La conquista del potere 1921-1925*; Santarelli, *Storia del movimento e del regime fascista*; Tasca, *Nascita e avvento del fascismo*; Quazza (ed.), *Fascismo e società italiana*; Lyttelton, *La conquista del potere*; Veneruso, *L'Italia fascista (1922-1945)*; Linz - Farneti - Lepsius, *La caduta dei regimi democratici*; Cofrancesco, *Per una analisi critica della destra rivoluzionaria*; Pombeni, *Demagogia e tirannide*; Roveri, *Le cause del fascismo*; Gentile, *Storia del partito fascista*; Vivarelli, *Le origini del fascismo*; Tranfaglia, "La prima guerra mondiale e il fascismo". On Germany see Collotti, *Nazismo e società tedesca 1933-1945*; Schulze, *La repubblica di Weimar*; Thamer, *Il Terzo Reich*. On Spain see Tamames, *La República*; Plana, *La Spagna franchista*; Morlino, *Dalla democrazia all'autoritarismo*. For a broader overview see Renouvin, *Histoire des relations internationales*. VII. *Les crises du XXe siècles. De 1914 à 1929* and *idem*, *Histoire des relations internationales*. VIII. *Les crises du XXe siècles. De 1929 à 1945*; Di Nolfo - Rainero - Vigezzi (eds.), *L'Italia e la politica di potenza in Europa (1938-40)*; Di Nolfo, *Storia delle relazioni internazionali 1918-1992*; Duroselle, *Storia diplomatica dal 1919 ai nostri giorni*.

21 Gasser's bibliography (1903-1985) has yet to be studied in depth, and such a study is made even more difficult due to the loss of his personal archives. See Esterbauer *et al.* (eds.), *Von der freien Gemeinde zum föderalistischen Europa*, pp. 9-42; Gasser, *Ausgewählte historische Schriften, 1933-1983*; Zucca, "Émile Chanoux e Adolf Gasser".

22 Staatsarchiv Basel, *Sammlung biographischer Zeitungsausschnitte*, *Adolf Gasser (1903-1985)*, p. 1.

23 In 1923 Richard Coudenhove-Kalergi (1894-1972) published the book entitled *Pan-Europa*, in which he hoped for the creation of a "confederation" of continental Europe based on the American model and on French-German reconciliation. The book was greatly appreciated by European public opinion, allowing the author to

following year, inspired by this important international event, the Basel section of the International Pan-Europa Union was founded.[24] One of its promoters was the engineer Hans Stettler, a member of the *Jungliberale Partei*,[25] who also involved Adolf Gasser in the organising committee. Between 1933 and 1934 Gasser became aware of the need for civic commitment addressed at analysing in greater depth the issues of democracy in Europe[26] to provide answers to the spread of Fascism, which, imposing political dictatorships and economic autarchies, risked bringing ruin to the entire continent, especially in multi-ethnic and free market states such as Switzerland.[27] He therefore abandoned his mainly juridical-constitutional studies to devote himself to an historical analysis of the origins of democracy in Europe. This intellectual effort was accompanied by an increasingly militant commitment to the ideal of European unity.[28]

His personal work coincided with the Swiss section of the International Pan-Europa Union, which had separated from the rest of the organisation led by Coudenhove-Kalergi, considered unsuited for

found the Pan-European Europe movement. This organisation soon had sections in all European countries. It was basically joined by politicians and cabinet members, among them, in Germany, the social democrat Paul Löbe, president of the *Reichstag*, and Finance Minister Joseph Koeth, and in France, Léon Blum and Aristide Briand, at the time Foreign Minister. Coudenhove-Kalergi's work was at the origin of the project on the creation of a European Federation that Aristide Briand presented on September 5, 1929, to the Assembly of the League of Nations. British and Italian opposition stopped this initiative, but Pan Europa continued its propaganda work until Hitler's rise to power; the annexation of Austria and the war destroyed the movement's network. After the war Coudenhove-Kalergi recreated Pan-Europa and through a series of conferences contributed to sensitising the European political world about the subject of the continent's unity. On the Pan Europa movement see the papers of its founder: Coudenhove-Kalergi, *Crusade for Pan-Europe*; *idem*, *Pan-Europe*; see also Curcio, *Europa. Storia di un'idea*, pp. 829-833; Duroselle, *L'idea d'Europa nella storia*, pp. 378-402; Brugmans, *L'idée européenne 1920-1970*, pp. 57-73; Agnelli, "Da Coudenhove-Kalergi al piano Briand"; Fondation archives européennes, *Le Plan Briand d'union fédérale européenne*; Saint-Gilles, *La Paneurope*.

24 Lipgens, "Swiss plans for the Post-war Order in Europe", p. 746; Jílek, "L'idée d'Europe devant la guerre", pp. 23-24.

25 Jílek, *L'esprit européen en Suisse de 1860 à 1940*, p. 56.

26 Gasser, "Three kinds of new Europe", p. 768. Gasser's paper was published in Der Europäer. Organ der Schweizer Europa-Union für die Einigung Europas, in number 11 dated February 1942.

27 On Switzerland's international position during the period in question, see Bianchi, *Neutralismo elvetico (1814-1944)*; Bourgeois, *Le troisième Reich et la Suisse*; Ruffieux, *La Suisse de l'entre-deux-guerres*; Rings, *La Svizzera in guerra 1933-1945*; Jost, "Minaccia e ripiegamento (1914-1945)"; Codiroli, *L'ombra del Duce*; Fleury, "La Suisse et la préparation à l'après guerre".

28 Staatsarchiv Basel, *Sammlung biographischer*, p. 1.

taking effective propaganda actions due to its elitist characteristics. The Swiss also blamed the exclusion of Great Britain and the Soviet Union from Coudenhove-Kalergi's plans for a confederation as well as the Count's criticism of the League of Nations.

In June 1934, those who had left the International Pan-Europa Union formed, together with members of the Basel section of the *Union Jeune-Europe*, the federalist movement *Europa-Union: Schweizerische Bewegung für die Einigung Europas.*[29] The new organisation's objective was to mobilise public opinion in favour of a European federation, in which each state, or rather each community, could maintain its own cultural and political characteristics. Within the framework of this new organisation, Gasser was a member of the Central Committee[30] as well as the movement's theoretician, which was far more important. In fact, he provided the *Europa-Union* with awareness of a historical perspective that viewed the experience of Swiss cantons, and therefore municipal and individual freedoms, as the basis for the creation of a democratic Europe.[31] Gasser developed this idea during lessons he began to hold at Basel University in 1936, as a *Privat-dozent* of Swiss history.[32]

This intense intellectual work led to a number of events. Gasser started to cooperate on a permanent basis with the monthly magazine *Der Europäer*, which in 1935 became the official newspaper for the *Europa-Union*,[33] as well as with the *National Zeitung* in Basel.[34] In

---

29 Lipgens, *A History of European Integration*, p. 117; Jílek *L'esprit européen en Suisse*, pp. 57-59. In the beginning the movement was able to rely on twenty sections mostly in the German part of Switzerland; See Jílek, "L'Union européenne a Bâle entre 1938 et 1946", p. 278. In spite of splitting from the International Pan-Europa Union in 1943-44, *Europa-Union* was perceived by Italian federalist activists, who had taken refuge in the Confederation, as the Swiss section of Coudenhove-Kalergi's movement (Archivio Storico dell'Università degli Studi di Pavia – from here on ASUPv – Fondi aggregati, Fondo Guglielmo Usellini, c. X, f. 1, report entitled "Gli attuali movimenti federalisti"). This indicates that, in spite of the propaganda provided by *Europa-Union*, the movement had not succeeded in comprehensively spreading its image and ideas beyond German Switzerland's cultural and political circles.

30 Pozzoli, *Il federalismo europeo organizzato in Svizzera*, p. 22.

31 Analysing the articles that appeared in *Der Europäer*, Walter Lipgens also warned that Gasser was the main leader-writer for *Europa-Union*. See Lipgens and Loth (eds.), *Documents on the History*, vol. I, p. 768.

32 *Ibidem*.

33 The paper began publication in May 1935 and was sent to the movement's members and supporters. In Germany *Der Europäer* was considered a subversive newspaper and its sale was immediately forbidden. So as to ensure the monthly's greater visibility, after January 1946 articles in French were published more frequently and the paper's name was changed to *Europa. Organ der Europa-Union. Organe de*

August 1940 the newspaper asked Gasser to write weekly editorials.[35] Throughout the war, the historian from Basel could therefore address not only his compatriots but also readers who were able to receive this newspaper in Germany, providing them with thoughts based on the issues presented by contemporary history, in particular the concepts of democracy, federalism and municipal freedom.

In the winter term of 1938-1939, Gasser held 16 lessons[36] at Basel University, in which he very thoroughly, albeit not yet completely, presented his own ethical-political idea of history. In 1939 these lessons were presented in a book published with the meaningful title *Geschichte der Volksfreiheit und der Demokratie.*[37] These considerations were useful to Gasser when, probably also in 1939, he wrote the preamble for *Unsere Leitsätze für das neue Europa*, adopted on February 4, 1940, by the *Europa-Union.*[38] In this brief paper he summarised a number of aspects of his ideas, identifying in the voluntary union of free municipalities, based on the values of individual freedom and Christian love, the path for the reconstruction of Europe.[39]

---

l'Union Européenne. See Lipgens and Loth (eds.), *Documents on the History*., vol. I, p. 747; Bauer *Les 50 ans de l'Union européenne de Suisse*, p. 10.

34 The *National Zeitung*, Basel's second most important newspaper, also had on its staff Hans Bauer, president of *Europa-Union* from 1934 to 1965. See Jílek, *L'esprit européen en Suisse*, p. 69-70.

35 Gasser, *L'autonomie communale et la reconstruction de l'Europe*, p. 5.

36 *Idem*, *Storia della libertà popolare e della democrazia*, p. 5; *idem*, *L'autonomie communale*, p. 5; "Storia della democrazia".

37 *Idem*, *Geschichte der Volksfreiheit und der Demokratie*. Considered a dangerous instrument for subversive propaganda, the book was banned in Germany in 1940 (see Staatsarchiv Basel, *Sammlung biographischer*, p. 1).

38 See Lipgens and Loth (eds.), *Documents on the History*, vol. I, pp. 753-758. The *Leitsätze* or *Principi fondamentali* were published in German in the January and November 1940 issues of *Der Europäer*. The French version was published in July that same year in the movement's magazine. After the League of Nations Federal Council requested a return to "total neutrality", the movement felt the need to specify its political charter in the *Leitsätze*. The federal petition, motivated by fear that sanctions would have to be applied to Germany following the *Anschluss*, clearly caused problems to a movement with European solidarity as one of its founding principles. *Europa-Union*, although fundamentally in line with the principle involving spiritual defence expressed by the Federal Council, which studied the concept in depth, proposed that the Swiss constitutional system should become the model for a future European federation. See Jílek, *L'Union européenne à Bâle*, pp. 280-285; *idem*, "Un choix d'Europe en 1938".

39 See Lipgens and Loth (eds.), *Documents on the History*, vol. I, pp. 753-754. The preamble is not signed but its contents are certainly attributable to Gasser. See also Jílek, "L'idée d'Europe devant la guerre", p. 27. The rest of the *Leitsätze* is attributed to a Working Committee presided over by Hans Bauer. See Lipgens and Loth (eds.), *Documents on the History*, vol. I, p. 753.

The intellectual path followed by the Basel historian achieved its full development following these reflections and was fully outlined in the book *Gemeindefreiheit als Rettung Europas. Grundlinien einer ethischen Geschichtauffassung*, published in Basel in 1943.[40] The ideas expressed in this book had Swiss federalism[41] and the work of Alexis de Tocqueville[42] as their main basis for reflection. Gasser stated that in history there are two fundamental forms of state organisation, one based on the principle of a commanded administration, and the other on autonomous administration. In the first case the state-building process is from the top down, through subordinated action, while in the second it is bottom up through a free union of communities. Basically, Gasser believed that all forms of centralised states, considered almost as a synonym for an authoritarian state, clashed with the decentralised state and at times overlapped in the history of the West.[43]

On the basis of these principles, the Swiss historian welcomed the critique of the absolutist and centralised state expressed by de Tocqueville in his *Démocratie en Amérique* and expanded in particular

---

40 Gasser, *Gemeindefreiheit als Rettung Europas*, which I consulted in the Italian version translated by Adelaide Koller and entitled *L'autonomia comunale e la ricostruzione dell'Europa*.

41 According to Gasser, the prototype of a free municipality was the Swiss medieval one, founded on the right of free, armed citizens to resist the power of the lords. He considered feudal power on the same level of that of the centralised state and the right to resistance to be equal to individual freedom, accompanied by a shared spirit of solidarity. This was the "pact" between free communities that, according to the Swiss historian, should have been at the basis of a Federal State. (Gasser, *Storia della libertà*, pp. 46-47, pp. 108-110 and pp. 156-157; *idem*, *L'autonomia comunale*, pp. 64-71). In his work there are obviously many references to Swiss historians that also reveal a similar perception of historical reality (Gasser, *Storia della libertà*, p. 48; *idem*, *L'autonomia comunale*, pp. 66-69).

42 Gasser continuously addresses the ideas expressed by De Tocqueville, finding inspiration and confirmation. He initially expressed his agreement with the concept of a "tyranny of the majority" (Gasser, *L'autonomia comunale*, pp. 15-16; De Tocqueville, *Scritti politici*. II. *La democrazia in America*, pp. 292-319), emphasising later how the French author had understood the fundamental role played by the free municipality of New England in the formation of the American democratic conscience and thus in the organisation of the North American state (Gasser, *L'autonomia comunale*, pp. 53-58 and p. 76; De Tocqueville, *Scritti politici*. II. *La democrazia in America*, pp. 78-121). Referring to *L'ancien régime et la révolution* Gasser said that, where the absolute centralising state implemented the destruction of the collective spirit of reciprocal trust, it had suppressed *in nuce* the possibility of achieving a vital and deeply-rooted democracy (Gasser, *L'autonomia comunale*, pp. 81-82; De Tocqueville, "L'antico regime e la rivoluzione", pp. 668-671 and pp. 681-703). In summary, Gasser, like De Tocqueville, identified in the centralised bureaucratic state the obstacle to be overcome in achieving that federation of free municipalities that, according to both authors, must be at the basis of a social system.

43 Gasser, *L'autonomia comunale*, pp. 9-18.

in *L'Ancien régime et la revolution*, analysing, however, the structure of European states in greater depth.[44] According to Gasser the process that in different periods saw the establishment of the national monarchic state in France, Spain, Italy and Germany, destroyed any possible basis for the birth of authentic liberalism, since it destroyed the ancient freedoms of the community pact already in force in medieval municipalities.[45]

Local communities were considered the only context in which personal freedoms, merged with the spirit of Christianity, could be totally and freely expressed. The concept of municipality was not, however, identified with a specific administrative unit, but expressed instead in every cell of social organisation in which a spirit of decentralised solidarity had developed.

In those countries in which the creation of the state was implemented through a centralising process, the municipalities were "subjugated to the state bureaucratic apparatus, to its wide-reaching power of command, its rigid control, and exposed to its arbitrary interference", and local administrations only obtained the responsibilities that the various central governments decided to entrust to them. Because of this, individual citizens became accustomed to expecting "all redemption always and only from the state authority instead of from the goodwill of citizens", thereby losing the capability to govern themselves and becoming used to trusting a "capable authoritarian government".[46] This created the conditions for the advent of the dictatorships that ruled Europe at the time Gasser was writing.

For Gasser, the issue involving the centralisation of power was not just a problem to be addressed at a territorial level, and thus an issue that could be summarised in the conflict between small and naturally democratic organisations and the large and inevitably authoritarian ones. He quoted the Italian and German principalities as examples of territorially restricted states, in which, however, local freedoms had been totally suppressed in favour of the prince's strongly centralised authority. In his

---

44 Compared to De Tocqueville's historical-political analysis, Gasser differed in his judgment of the history of the Swiss Confederation. His perception of the historical reality was in fact influenced by his basically positive opinion that, unlike De Tocqueville, prevented him from underlining existing contradictions that had also existed within this social and constitutional system at least until the 19th-century reforms (Gasser, *L'autonomia comunale*, pp. 64-65; "Relazione sull'opera di Antoine Élisée Cherbuliez intitolata 'La democrazia in Svizzera'", pp. 251-268).

45 Gasser, *L'autonomia comunale*, pp. 77-113. Émile Chanoux presented the same historical analysis as Gasser: See Chanoux, *Écrits*, pp. 281-282, p. 291, pp. 296-297, pp. 395-397, pp. 497-498.

46 Gasser, *L'autonomia comunale*, pp. 80-81.

opinion, the real watershed was in the administrative organisation of states. He therefore defined as democratic those states in which administration was autonomous, and as authoritarian those in which it was commanded.[47]

In the particular historical period during which he wrote, he saw the possibility that war could create the conditions for a sufficiently widespread disaggregation of central power to favour a reorganisation of European states on a municipal basis.[48] He was therefore aware of the need for his work to provide the keys for historical understanding, which he considered indispensable for ensuring that the re-organisation of European states would take place in the hoped-for manner.

Gasser hoped for a reform of the centralised bureaucratic system of continental states[49] preferred by Anglo-Saxon countries which would have imposed their administrative and social models. Europe would have become a "world of general decentralisation, hence equipped with wide-ranging municipal freedoms", and individual states would therefore have ceased "to be an element disturbing the peace"[50] while municipalities would have reacquired a central role in the organisation of Europe.

In this manner, however, his ideas differed from the interpretation of European history provided by federalist and Europeanist movements, in particular the *Movimento federalista europeo* (MFE),[51] which arose from

---

47 Ivi, pp. 78-84, pp. 95-98, pp. 125-126, pp. 141-142. In particular, Gasser acknowledged, as a characteristic of states with a centralised organisation, the faculty of the government to appoint at its pleasure its representatives, which generally were not chosen among local managers, but were intentionally extraneous to the territory and removable simply by issuing an administrative order. They thus created a bureaucracy separated from the local community. Conversely, wherever the principle of self-government was applied, magistrates, officials and representatives of the people were locals and were generally elected. Hence, while in the latter case trusting communities of free men were formed, in the former there was a lack of participation and trust between citizens and the institutions, be they monarchic, republican or socialist.

48 Ivi, p. 132.

49 To ensure these reforms would be applied, the historian from Basel reached the point of hoping for the advent of a "semi-authoritarian regime, exercised by men with rigidly democratic ideas" who would acknowledge "the crucial meaning of municipal freedom" so as to implement a radical programme addressed at suppressing the hierarchic administrative system (ivi, pp. 148-153).

50 Ivi, p. 188.

51 The *Movimento federalista europeo* was created in Milan during a secret conference held on August 27th and 28th, 1943. On that occasion, the six political ideas that guided the work of constitutionalist federalists until modern times were approved ("Tesi politiche federaliste"). On the movement's constituent meeting see Levi and Pistone (eds.), *Trent'anni di vita del Movimento federalista europeo*, pp. 66-71;

the Resistance. These movements described the politics of power as the sub-product of international anarchy, a fundamental characteristic of that system of states within which the strongest was inexorably led along the path to hegemony regardless of the form of government or internal organisation. The solution proposed by federalist movements therefore tended to remove the very causes of war through the creation of a European federation.[52]

In *Gemeindefreiheit als Rettung Europas* and in later additions to the book, Gasser seemed instead to momentarily forget the need to create a European federal state.[53] This attitude led him to work between 1944 and 1949 in favour of the spreading of his "municipalist" ideas in Europe, in the sense of an internal administrative reform of the states that emerged from the World War which placed municipalities at the centre of national and international activities.

Rognoni Vercelli, *Mario Alberto Rollier*, pp. 85-112. For an in-depth analysis of the *Movimento federalista europeo*'s role see the following essays: Albertini - Chiti-Batelli - Petrilli, *Storia del federalismo europeo*; Levi and Pistone (eds.), *Trent'anni di vita del Movimento federalista europeo*; Levi, *L'unificazione europea*; D'Agata, *Le origini del Movimento federalista europeo*; Pistone, "La lotta del Movimento Federalista Europeo dalla Resistenza alla caduta della Comunità Europea di Difesa nel 1954"; Preda, "Declino e rilancio del MFE tra fine della guerra e Piano Marshall", pp. 489-525; Majocchi, *La difficile costruzione dell'unità europea*; Pistone, "I movimenti per l'unità europea in Italia", in *I movimenti per l'unità europea 1954-1969*; Morelli, "L'Unione europea dei federalisti e il Movimento federalista europeo sovranazionale"; Neri Gualdesi, "La battaglia dei federalisti italiani per costruire l'alternativa europea federale"; Pistone, "I movimenti per l'Unità europea in Italia", in *I movimenti per l'unità europea 1970-1986*; Morelli, "Il Movimento federalista europeo sovranazionale e l'Unione europea dei federalisti".

52 Among the various federalist movements created during the European war of resistance to National Socialism and Fascism – see Lipgens (ed.) *Documents on the History of European Integration*, vol. II; Lipgens, *A History of European Integration*; Dumoulin (ed.), *Plans des temps de guerre* – the MFE from the very beginning unequivocally stated, through the writings of its founders Altiero Spinelli, Ernesto Rossi and Eugenio Colorni, that the main objective of democratic political parties in the immediate post-war period should be "the creation of a solid international state" on a federal basis as the only reasonable solution to avoid a return to a system of sovereign states that would involve the danger of new and terrible wars.

53 In 1946 the French and Italian versions of the book were published: Gasser, *L'autonomia comunale*, was extended in paragraphs 13, 19, 20, 29, 32, 33; Paragraph 17 was added to Gasser's, *L'autonomie communale*. In the three editions of his most important work, Gasser did not return to the subject of the need for a possible European federation, so clearly set out in the introduction to the *Leitsätze*. He was convinced that internal reform of European states, in a municipalist sense, would have naturally led them to develop a spirit of reciprocal cooperation which would not prejudicially have required a supranational organisation (*idem*, *L'autonomia comunale*, pp. 143-153 and pp. 181-193; *idem*, *L'autonomie communale*, pp. 178-191 and pp. 222-237).

In this operation, Gasser was helped by the extraordinary success of his book on municipal autonomy. Published in German in 1943, the book was also published in French and Italian in 1946 and was widely distributed across the continent.

The turning point in inter-municipal relations occurred very clearly after World War II thanks to an acquired awareness by a number of integral federalist militants[54] who, also influenced by Adolf Gasser's ideas, perceived how, in order to achieve peace, it would be necessary to create a Europe of citizens with its organisational basis in the municipalities.

The main players in this course of action included the French federalist movement *La Fédération. Centre d'études institutionnelles pour l'organisation de la société française*, founded in July 1944 by a group of federalists linked to personalist Catholic movements, which included among its main objectives that of providing the political-theoretical means for the reorganisation not only of the state but also of French society.[55] Very soon its members realised that to achieve its objectives of infra-national federalism, or at least of reform in the sense of a decentralisation of the French state, they could not ignore the international situation, in particular the new European status. The federation therefore had to be formed "du quartier ou du village" to

---

54 For a quick overview of the birth and development of integral federalism and its relations with the idea of European unification, see Marc, *Du communalisme au fédéralisme intégral*; Loubet Del Bayle, *I non conformisti degli anni Trenta* (French edition *Les non-conformistes des années 30*); Greilsammer, *Les mouvements fédéralistes en France de 1945 à 1974*; Voyenne, *Histoire de l'idée fédéraliste*; Gouzy, "Alexandre Marc soixante-quinze ans de combat fédéraliste"; *idem*, "Alexandre Marc"; De Rougemont, *Œuvres complètes de Denis de Rougemont*. III. *Écrits sur l'Europe*; Marc, *Europa e federalismo globale*. There is also a variation of infra-national federalism, which, within the framework of possible European unity, envisages the implementation of the broadest possible autonomy for cultural, ethnic and linguistic minorities. This perspective holds out the hope for a reorganisation of current national European states on a regional, ethnic or linguistic basis. For an introduction to this subject, see: De Rougemont, "Vers une fédération des Régions"; Héraud, *Peuples et Langues d'Europe*; Salvi, *Le nazioni proibite*; Héraud, *L'Europe des ethnies*; Esterbauer - Héraud - Pernthalter (eds.), *Föderalismus als Mittel permanenter Konfliktregelung*; Chiti-Batelli, *La dimensione europea delle autonomie e l'Italia*; *idem*, *Regionalismo, federalismo, razzismo*; Salvi, *L'Italia non esiste*; Citterio and Vaccaro (eds.), *Quale federalismo per quale Europa*; Chiti-Batelli, *Oltre il sistema rappresentativo?*

55 To set the history of *La Fédération* within the overall context of the history of movements for European unity see Greilsammer, *Les mouvements fédéralistes*; Voyenne, *Histoire de l'idée fédéraliste*; Gouzy, "I movimenti per l'unità europea in Francia". On the birth and early development of *La Fédération* see Zucca, *Autonomie locali e federazione sovranazionale*, pp. 68-75 and pp. 114-128.

Europe, as written by Jean Bareth,[56] one of the founders of *La Fédération*, and in this sense directly influenced by Adolf Gasser's ideas.[57]

Between January 28th and 30th, 1951, the CEM was founded in Geneva; only after 1984 did this movement assume the name of *Conseil des communes et des régions d'Europe*, thereby officially involving the regions in the struggle for the United States of Europe. The constituent assembly was attended by fifty-nine people, mainly mayors and local administrators from nine countries in Western Europe linked to federalist and municipalist movements and to Socialist and Catholic internationalism. Analysing the composition of the various delegations that attended the founding meeting, it is clear that the largest delegation was the French one, but it was also the delegation that from a political point of view had the most important personalities present. Participants included Pierre Trémentin, president of the *Association des maires de France*, Joseph Lassalarié, president of the *Association des présidents des Conseils généraux*, André Voisin, secretary of *La Fédération - Centre d'études institutionnelles pour l'organisation de la societé française*, as well as the Mayor of Bordeaux Jacques Chaban-Delmas.[58]

Although able to rely on extremely important political personalities, the other delegations could not guarantee, through the support of the organisations of local authorities already widely established at a national level, the immediate massive adhesion of local communities to this project. Such support did occur in France, where just a few months after the creation of this association about eleven thousand people became members, out of a total of twenty-two thousand for the whole of Europe.

Such important representation by France can be understood only by revisiting the events that led to the Geneva meeting; otherwise it is not possible to understand why other countries, such as Italy, did not send

56 Jean Bareth (1912-1969) was, together with Umberto Serafini, the soul of the movements of European local communities, addressing both the movement's organisational and political aspects. For the moment no one has written his biography. To study his political ideas see Bareth, "Le fédéralisme c'est d'abord la commune"; *idem*, *Le fédéralisme par la commune*. Also see Defferre, "Depuis Genève, le C.C.E. fut son œuvre"; Poher, "L'Europe, cette commune patrie à laquelle Jean Bareth a tant rêvé"; Sergent, "Nous poursuivrons sa tâche"; Serafini, "Jean Bareth".

57 These ideas were presented by Jean Bareth in a number of leaflets between 1946 and 1947. See Bareth, "Le fédéralisme c'est d'abord la commune"; *idem*, *Le fédéralisme par la commune*; *idem*, *Le fédéralisme: un principe, une action*. A brief history of the evolution of the Europeanist and municipalist ideas within *La Fédération* in Martin, "Bilan de dix ans d'efforts 1944-1954".

58 On the role played by Chaban-Delmas within the movement of European local autonomies, see Zucca, "L'Europe des communes et des régions à travers l'action de deux de ses acteurs principaux: Jacques Chaban-Delmas et Umberto Serafini".

delegations having that same mobilising power over local institutions in their respective countries.

The starting point for this reflection was the underlying crisis that characterised French society and its administrative organisation the very day after the foundation of the Fourth Republic. Within this context it was to defend the local autonomies, the basis of all freedoms, that *La Fédération* gave itself the objective of reforming the French state's organisation in a federalist sense or, secondarily, to support a strong policy for administrative decentralisation. The organisation created a *Comité national d'études pour la réforme de la constitution* joined by senators, members of parliament, and the representatives of economic and social organisations.[59] The programme of *La Fédération* found a solid following among local administrators, to whom this programme was presented only in the form of a greater decentralisation of state power, in order to eliminate the problems experienced by mayors in their relations with the Paris bureaucracy, and later as an effective manifesto to oppose the centralism of the communist ideology and also organisations such as the UIV which accepted as members local institutions governed by communists. The federalist organisation therefore was able to join the ongoing political debate concerning the form of the French state.[60] While these activities did not immediately have a

59 Archives of the Association française du Conseil des communes et régions d'Europe in Orléans (from here on AFCCRE Archives, Orléans), c. *Divers a trier VIII*, f. *reforme constitutionnelle*. This file contains the documents concerning the campaign "pour la réforme de la constitution" of the French Republic from the end of the 1940s to 1953. They clearly indicate that it was *La Fédération* that set out and directed the work of the *Comité*. It also organised a survey to understand the opinions of local administrators on the subjects proposed. In 1953 it launched a new campaign for constitutional reform also involving the *Association française du Conseil des communes et régions d'Europe*.

60 The bibliography on the reform of the French state and the crisis experienced by the Fourth Republic is vast. For a quick overview see Werth, *France 1940-1955*; Fauvet, *La Quatrième République*; Elgey, *Histoire de la Quatrième République*; Bouvier *et al.*, *Histoire économique et sociale de la France*. IV. *L'ère industrielle et la société d'aujourd'hui, siècle 1880-1980*; Rioux, *La France de la Quatrième République*; Nicolet, *L'idée républicaine en France 1789-1924*; Bonin, *Histoire économique de la Quatrième République*; Berstein and Rudelle (eds.), *Le modèle républicain*; Becker, *Histoire politique de la France depuis 1945*; Bechelloni (ed.), *Metamorfosi di un modello repubblicano*. Among the many memoires written by the leading players and witnesses of the genesis of the Fourth Republic, see those written by Duverger, *La repubblica tradita*; Blum, *L'œuvre de Léon Blum*. IX. *1947-1950*; Auriol, *Journal du septennat (1947-1954)*; *Témoignages, Guy Mollet, 1905-1975*; Faure, *Mémoires*; Debré, *Trois républiques pour une France*; De Gaulle, *L'esprit de la Ve République*. The Fourth Republic is also considered as the great moment of the birth of European organisations. Therefore, many French historians have concentrated their research on the relationship between the creation of Europe and the Fourth Republic. See the extremely important books by Bossuat, *La France, l'aide américaine et la*

significant effect, they did allow the organisation to attract the attention of the municipal political world to its objectives.

On June 16th 1949, the movement organised a meeting between local administrators, national politicians and those responsible for organisations representing mayors and councillors. The meeting was attended, among others, by Jacques Chaban-Delmas, Pierre Mendès France, François Mitterrand, Eugène Claudius-Petit and Maurice Schumann. During this meeting a list of demands was drafted and decisions were taken to form a *Comité national pour la défense des libertés communales et départementales.* This document, signed by all those present, stated the need to proceed with administrative decentralisation, accompanied by a concession of financial autonomy to local authorities and the abolition of administrative power exercised by prefects over mayors. During the meeting, the connection between the problems involving the necessary reform of the French state and that of a possible creation of a European state also emerged.[61]

In order to publicise the document-programme, between 1949 and 1950 the movement organised the *Journées des maires de France* attended by thousands of mayors of small rural municipalities as well as

construction européenne 1944-1954; Grosser, *Affaires extérieurs. La politique de la France, 1944-1984* and Duroselle, "Les "invariants" de la politique étrangère de la France". For a broader overview of this subject see also Bloch-Lainé and Bouvier, *La France restaureé 1944-1954*; Bjøl, *La France devant l'Europe, la politique européenne de la IVe République*; Moreau-Defarges, "La France et l'Europe: le rêve ambigu ou la mesure du rang"; Girault, "The French Decision-makers and their Perception of French Power in 1948"; Guillen, "La France et la construction européenne dans les années cinquante"; Bossuat, "La France et les constructions européennes 1943-1957"; *idem*, *D'Alger à Rome (1943-1957). Choix de documents*; Girault and Frank (eds.), *La puissance française en question 1945-1949*; Girault, "La France entre l'Europe et l'Afrique"; Gerbert, *Le relèvement 1944-1949*; Grange, "La politique européenne de Pierre Mendès France vue par les diplomates italiens"; Guillen, "L'Europe remède à l'impuissance française?".

61 AFCCRE Archives, Orléans, c. *Courrier nat. 1972*, f. *documents historiques CCRE*, document dated 1950 entitled *Campagne pour la défense des libertés communales et départementales*. In addition to national politicians, the meeting was attended by the presidents of the *Association des maires de France*, Pierre Trémintin, and of the *Association des prèsidents de Conseils généraux*, Joseph Lassalarié, who were among the founders of the CEM. Furthermore, a list of members of the *Comité* indicates that it consisted of one hundred and nineteen members. Of these, thirty-six were senators and thirty-four were members of parliament. They included, Jacques Chaban-Delmas, Pierre Méndes-France, Maurice Schumann, but not Mitterrand. The number of parliamentarians attending should not be considered surprising, since in the French political tradition, mayors of important cities very often are also elected to the National Assembly or the Senate, and therefore the presidents of the Republic also come from the ranks of local administrators.

a number personalities of national prominence.[62] Among the various meetings of particular importance was the *journée* organised in Bordeaux by the president of the *Association des maires de la Gironde*, Jacques Chaban-Delmas. The Mayor of Bordeaux, in close cooperation with André Voisin, managed to involve in this initiative not only the mayors of the Gironde but also numerous members of parliament from Southwestern France. In his invitations, Chaban-Delmas said that local communities had suffered serious restrictions to their freedoms which had thereby been "amenuisées qu'elles correspondent davantage à une clause de style qu'à une réalité tangible".[63] On this occasion there were shared objectives and action undertaken by Jacques Chaban-Delmas and André Voisin that were destined to become consolidated and develop further in the decades that followed.

Delegations from the *Comité National* were received by the Council of the Republic's Commission for National Affairs on March 30th, 1950, and by the Interior Minister on June 13th, 1950,[64] meetings that also resulted in the membership of the President of the National Assembly, Édouard Herriot, the mayor of Lyon. *Le Figaro* devoted a series of articles entitled *M. le Maire vous parle* to the issues proposed by the *Comité*.[65] The objective of this activism was addressed at overcoming the study period linked to the *Comités d'études* and the beginning of a campaign against "l'étatisme centralisateur, contre la tyrannie bureaucratique, pour la défense des libertés locales et régionales".[66] Initiatives promoted by *La Fédération* culminated in the organisation of the *États généraux des communes de France*, a very evocative name, which were attended by thousands of local administrators and were held in

62 AFCCRE Archives, Orléans, c. *Courrier nat. 1972*, f. *documents historiques CCRE. États-Genéraux des communes et départements de France. Conclusions générales* and a document dated 1950 entitled *Campagne pour la défense des libertés communales et départementales*, pp. 1-2. Protests were held between November 1949 and June 1950 involving a number of the most important cities in France, such as Rouen, Lyon, Nantes, Metz, Strasbourg, Lille, Bordeaux. About 6,000 local administrators attended the meetings.

63 AFCCRE Archives, Orléans, c. *Courrier national 1951*, letter from Jacques Chaban-Delmas dated May 30th, 1950.

64 ASUPv, Fondi aggregati, Fondo Fédération, c. *Fédération*. Provisional programme for the conference-debate *"Les citoyens face à la crise. Cinquantenaire du mouvement hommage à son fondateur André Voisin (1912-1990), Neuilly-sur-Seine 2 février 1995"*, p. 3.

65 Martin, "Bilan de dix ans d'efforts 1944-1954", p. 9.

66 *Idem*, "Défendons nos libertés locales".

Versailles, a symbolic location for the French Republic, on June 24th-25th, 1950.[67]

It is clear that the French political world was at least ready to discuss, if not totally accept, the proposal to create at a European level an association of local powers that could work for internal decentralisation and for a form of European union. As reported by Alain Poher, it is clear that for the politicians involved in the *États généraux des communes et départements de France* one of the objectives of this event was undoubtedly the creation of a European association of local communities.[68]

The initiative to found such a movement was not, however, French, although in France it found the necessary political-organisational support. It began instead with Alida De Jager,[69] a German trade-unionist

---

67 Marc, "Avant le congrès de La Haye". Marc had proposed the expression "States general" for the pro-European event to be held in The Hague in May 1948 that became known as the Congress of Europe. The wording implied that for federalists the creation of a united Europe was meant to be a revolutionary event. Therefore, this event was not only to include politicians, but was expected to mobilise all of European society's political and social forces. If the history of this Congress was to a certain extent different (Varsori, "Il Congresso dell'Europa dell'Aja 7-10 maggio 1948") the wording proposed by Marc became the legacy of *La Fédération.* According to Marc himself, the very project of a European Congress sanctioning the birth of the United States of Europe must be set at a preparatory meeting between federalists held in 1946. Only later did Winston Churchill's son-in-law, Duncan Sandys, take control of this project, thereby managing to partly run this event. See [Marc], "Un procès en paternité. La Haye 1948".

68 Poher, "L'Europe cette commune patrie à laquelle Jean Bareth a tant rêvé".

69 Alida De Jager (1890-1976), was born in Hamburg to a middle class family of Jewish origin and had a cosmopolitan education, attending schools in Switzerland and England. At a very young age she joined German socialist movements, becoming a member of Hamburg's Municipal Administration. As a councillor she was involved in the creation of a women's employment service and cooperated in the founding of the city's university. Between 1920 and 1924 she worked for socialist international organisations and for the League of Nations in Geneva. In 1924 she travelled to Moscow to establish personal contact with the Bolshevik movement. She returned from this journey with a profound admiration for those who had managed to overturn the tsarist regime, but also with an awareness that the Bolshevik route was not implementable in the rest of Europe. Between the end of the 1920s and the early 1930s she lived in the Netherlands and in Germany, where she carried out anti-Nazi activities until, in 1933, she was obliged to leave Germany for good and take refuge in the Netherlands, where she continued her internationalist activities. Faced with the Nazi occupation that spread in 1940 to the whole of Europe, Alida De Jager took refuge first in England in April 1940 and then in Mexico in 1942. When in 1945 the outcome of the war became clear, De Jager returned to London to try and resume her political work. In the British capital she suffered a serious heart attack that obliged her to rest for a long period, and in 1946 she joined her two daughters in Geneva. Thanks to the mediation of the Swiss socialist cultural environment she increased her knowledge of the country's federalism and gained awareness of the need to create a

exiled in Switzerland who believed that European unity and world peace would be achieved only thanks to an initiative started at the basis of the state organisation: the municipality. Between 1949 and 1950 De Jager travelled to Paris to set up direct contacts with *La Fédération* with the specific objective of creating an international organisation that would fight for the cooperation of local authorities and the creation of a united Europe. Her idea found the men of *La Fédération* in total agreement and guaranteeing their political support.[70]

The roots of this positive reception should be also searched for in the interest that Gasser's books and essays had aroused in the group of French integral federalists. After reading the Swiss historian's books, in 1948 Alexandre Marc, the main theoretician of integral federalism, felt the need to publish in the series of *La Fédération* a book entitled *Du communalisme au fédéralisme intégral* in which, emphasising the positive aspects of the "municipalist" idea identified in the critique of the centralised national state and in the positive role of municipalities, underlined a number of limits compared to integral federalism.[71] In fact, Marc emphasised how the ideas of the Swiss author were corrupted by a Swiss conservatism that led him towards "la dangereuse quiétude d'un 'provincialisme' quelque peu étriqué, alourdi d'illusions et de regrets, de moralisme et d'hypocrisie, de désirs refoulés et de 'bonne conscience'". He also concluded that in spite of "les défauts (...) de la thèse présentée par M. Adolphe Gasser, cette thèse reste orientée dans un sens prometteur, et c'est pourquoi elle mérite amplement d'être connue et méditée".[72]

---

federal society based on greater decentralisation. After participating in the foundation of the CEM she became its secretary general until December 31st, 1953. She continued to be involved in municipal autonomy issues, especially with the prospect of, as she herself described as utopian, a world federation of municipalities as the premise for achieving universal peace. As confirmed to me personally by her daughter Alida Ewald De Jager, her personal papers were not preserved, with a few exceptions, and hence this fundamental testimony of the events linked to the municipalist idea within a socialist framework is now lacking. Information reported here has been deduced from the Fondation Archives Européennes, in Geneva (from here on FAE, Geneva), AA6, c. *Alida de Jager*, from various documents found in a variety of CCRE archives, in particular those in Paris, and from the words of Umberto Serafini and Umberto Rossi, which, recorded on audio-cassettes, are now preserved at the ASUPv, Fondi aggregati, Testimonianze orali. Furthermore, the only biography of Alida De Jager is the one written in 1988 by her daughter Alida Ewald De Jager (typewritten text deposited with the FAE, Geneva, AA7, *Conseil des communes et des régions d'Europe*).

70 Bareth, "J'étais a Seelisberg".

71 Marc, *Du communalisme au fédéralisme intégral*. Of significance is the fact the book was published in the series of the French federalist movement *La Fédération*.

72 Ivi, p. 19 and p. 25.

The spreading of his ideas had also put Gasser in contact with Alida De Jager. Gasser and De Jager started to work together to sensitise to their ideas the political forces and movements that were being created at a European level. In particular, the interest caused in France also encouraged contacts between French personalities such as Jacques Chaban-Delmas, André Voisin, Jean Bareth and Alida De Jager and Gasser. It was from this meeting that the idea came to create at a European level a movement of municipalities that would work in favour of both administrative decentralisation and European unity.[73] At this point of our research, it is possible to say that the UIV's international experiences certainly contributed to providing if not a model, at least an outline to be worked on to create a new movement of local communities. On this subject, during the CEM's constituent conference on January 30th, 1951, Milhaud proposed the adoption, albeit with different percentages, of a system of UIV membership quotas to fund the new movement.[74]

The organisational and political responsibility for the creation of the movement of local European institutions was, however, entirely left up to De Jager, with *La Fédération*, and therefore the politicians linked to it, left to provide an overall direction. De Jager, in cooperation with Edgard Milhaud, organised a first meeting in Seelisberg, Switzerland in the autumn of 1950. Preceded by preliminary studies, this meeting established the association's name, the *Conseil des communes d'Europe*, and decided to exclude local institutions in Eastern Europe, which clearly set out the association's political position on the international stage. At the end of the meeting a decision was made to create a *Comité d'initiative européen*, which, helped by similar national committees, was tasked with organising the movement's constituent conference.[75] In France, seeing that the internal and international objectives of *La Fédération* coincided, it was sufficient to mobilise the by then well-tested mechanisms that allowed the *États généraux des communes et départements de France* to obtain the membership of significantly important political personalities and of the national organisations of those elected locally. In December 1950, the *Comité* became larger with the official arrival of Jacques Chaban-Delmas, Raymond Berrurier,

73 ASUPv, Fondi aggregati, Fondo Umberto Rossi, c. Riunioni di esecutivo del C.C.E., letter from the *Comité d'initiative pour le Conseil des communes d'Europe* dated December 15th 1950.

74 ASUPv, Fondi aggregati, Fondo Umberto Rossi, c. Riunioni di esecutivo del C.C.E, *Conférence costitutive du Conseil des communes d'Europe, Précis 30/1/1951.*

75 Archives d'État de la République et Canton de Genève (from here on AEG), Papiers Edgard Milhaud, c. XV 1948-1961, *Déclaration de principes. Réunion de maires de l'Europe occidentale, Seelisberg 1er octobre 1950.*

Émile Hamilius, Mayor of the City of Luxembourg, Joseph Lasalarié, Pierre Trémentin and other French and European personalities.[76]

A document stamped as "*confidentiel*", drafted before the assembly that created the CEM, reveals that the French delegation also included Édouard Herriot. It is therefore important to observe that in France, the second highest-ranking person in the state sided with the projects of *La Fédération.* Although he did not attend the constitutive meeting, Herriot effectively favoured the subsequent development of the CEM, becoming president of the *Association française du Conseil des Communes d'Europe* (AFCCE).[77]

The particular political and cultural atmosphere, favourable to Europeanist initiatives, which had developed in Western European countries between the end of the 1940s and the early 1950s, therefore allowed the drafting of a project that envisaged the creation of a large association of European municipalities working in favour of the creation of a democratic Europe. After the meeting in Seelisberg, the CEM's promoters decided to gain support for the constituent assembly planned for January 1951.

In Italy the situation was initially quite well structured. Thanks to an agreement between Adriano Olivetti[78] and Altiero Spinelli, the federalist

---

[76] ASUPv, Fondi aggregati, Fondo Umberto Rossi, invitation letter to attend the CCE's constituent assembly, dated December 15th 1950.

[77] AEG, Papiers Edgard Milhaud, c. XV 1948-1961, *Liste de la délégation française à la conférence constitutive.*

[78] Adriano Olivetti, was imprisoned in *Regina Coeli* because of his anti-fascist activities (the best known event was his cooperation in helping Filippo Turati leave the country) and released only before the arrival of the Germans. He then managed to take refuge in Switzerland where he joined the socialist party. Olivetti did, however, realise that it would be impossible for his highly revolutionary theories to be accepted by a party that had been reformed to face a political struggle according to the old rules of parliamentary democracy. He therefore embarked upon a complex and difficult proselytising process, which would lead him to found the *Movimento Comunità* in 1947. It was by using this movement that he hoped to influence local realities by creating social-economic workshops in Ivrea and the Canavese area, as well as a national one through the creation of "Centri Comunità". According to Olivetti it was necessary to create an organisation of society and the state capable of implementing, through a specific mechanism of technical-political representation, a made-to-measure human form of self-governance through the Christian integration of individual and collective values. At the basis of the state organisation, Olivetti placed his territorial "Communities", a social-economic synthesis of the needs of the basic community. At the beginning of the 1950s, the *Movimento Comunità* joined the political battle by running in the elections. While the Movement's success was astonishing in the Canavese region, where it was the strongest political party, at the national level the extremely harsh ostracism of all other political movements, worried about a possible flood of votes towards a movement not following political party rules, caused the failure of the *Movimento Comunità*'s electoral experience. Adriano

Umberto Serafini, at the time secretary of the Istituto italiano per i Centri comunitari in Rome,[79] was asked to organise Italy's participation at the CEM's constituent assembly.[80] Umberto Serafini was therefore tasked with directly supporting this initiative. Serafini worked on obtaining broader consensus by looking for support among politically committed Catholics.[81] He asked Luigi Sturzo for a meeting, which took place at the Roman Convent in Via Mondovì. Serafini's testimony clearly indicated how the exchange of ideas between the ederly Catholic leader and the young communitarian, although useful from the point of view of cultural in-depth analysis, only resulted in the involvement of two local administrators belonging to Sturzo's school of thought. They were the Mayor of San Donà di Piave and Christian Democrat Senator Celeste Bastianetto, a convinced federalist, and the Sicilian Regional Councillor, Giuseppe d'Angelo. A sign of a possible opening of the Catholic world to the initiative also came from a letter that Sturzo wrote to Celeste Bastianetto during the CEM's constituent assembly, which, translated into French, was made broadly available at an international

---

Olivetti's premature death, after being elected to parliament in 1958, marked the end of an unique political experience that, if understood, could have changed the country. To learn about Adriano Olivetti's ideas, see Olivetti, *L'ordine politico delle comunità* (the first edition was published in Ivrea by Nuove Edizioni Ivrea in 1945); Movimento Comunità, *Linee e mezzi d'azione. Punti programmatici e statuto (provvisorio)*; Olivetti, *Società, Stato, Comunità*; Movimento Comunità, *Tempi nuovi metodi nuovi*; Olivetti, *Per una libera comunità del Canavese*; *idem*, *Città dell'uomo*. On Adriano Olivetti, and in particular his relations with the European movement of local autonomies, the Council of European Municipalities and Umberto Serafini see *Ricordo di Adriano Olivetti*, published by the magazine *Comunità* in 1960; Serafini, *Adriano Olivetti e le dottrine politiche*; *idem*, *Adriano Olivetti: ci ha lasciato uno dei più grandi maestri del federalismo integrale*; *idem*, *Adriano Olivetti e il Movimento Comunità*; *idem*, *La comunità di Adriano Olivetti e il federalismo*; Caizzi, *Camillo e Adriano Olivetti*; Rotelli, *L'avvento della Regione in Italia*; Berta, "Fra centrismo e centro sinistra: Olivetti e il Movimento Comunità"; Pampaloni, *Adriano Olivetti: un'idea di democrazia*; Maggia (ed.), *Bibliografia degli scritti di Adriano Olivetti*; Ochetto, *Adriano Olivetti*; Sapelli and Chiarini, *Fini e fine della politica. La sfida di Adriano Olivetti*; Chiti-Batelli, "L'idea federalista nel pensiero di Adriano Olivetti"; Ricciardelli, *Olivetti: una storia, un sogno ancora da scrivere*; Soavi, *Adriano Olivetti. Una sorpresa italiana*; Gallino, *L'impresa responsabile. Un'intervista su Adriano Olivetti*; Mornese, *L'eresia politica di Adriano Olivetti*; Cadeddu, *Il valore della politica in Adriano Olivetti*, as well as my *Dagli enti locali all'unità europea: Adriano Olivetti e Umberto Serafini*, in the minutes of the AUSE's 15th Summer School *L'Italia e l'unità europea dal Risorgimento ad oggi. Un approccio interdisciplinare*, (Turin May 20th -21st, 2011), currently being published.

79 "Cronaca del Movimento".

80 Serafini, *Adriano Olivetti e il Movimento Comunità*, p. 215.

81 Serafini, *Quarant'anni di storia, X Congresso nazionale AICCRE, Roma 7-9 marzo 1991*.

level.[82] Together with the small Christian Democrat element, the Italian delegation was completed by the constitutionalist Massimo Severo Giannini, semi-officially representing the *Associazione Nazionale Comuni d'Italia* (ANCI).[83]

In Italy the initiative remained basically restricted to circles linked to the *Movimento Comunità*.[84] The movement itself did not consider it appropriate to send anyone to the constituent assembly who did not at that time hold a significant official position within the organisation. Not even Serafini attended the meeting. A very cautious position was effectively adopted regarding the new movement, of which the physiognomy and full potential was not totally understood.

Clarification within the Italian federalist movements began soon after the creation of the CEM. In an article published in the MFE's newspaper, *Europa Federata*, in February 1951,[85] the anonymous editorialist stated how it was necessary to think about a European federation that should, however, also promote local communities.

This resulted in emphasising the problem of the role of local institutions in the European unification process. The CEM presented itself as an element potentially capable of overcoming the dichotomy between infra-national autonomist tendencies and supranational federalism, and therefore represented an opportunity that should not be missed.

Between the end of July and early August 1951, Italian federalists, with the explicit consent of federalist leader Altiero Spinelli,[86] stated

---

82 Archives Association villes et communes luxembourgeoises, Luxembourg, c. *Conseil des Communes d'Europe 1951*, copy of the letter Luigi Sturzo sent to Celeste Bastianetto.

83 AEG, Papiers Edgard Milhaud, c. *DOC. EM. Procès-verbaux des six séances de la conférence constitutive du Conseil des communes d'Europe. Genève 28-30 janvier 1951. Deuxième séance plénière, dimanche 28 janvier*, p. 4. Massimo Severo Giannini himself stated in his keynote speech that, although representing the ANCI, he was attending the CCE's constituent assembly without having been able to previously consult the leadership of the Associazione dei Comuni Italiani. In addition to Massimo Severo Giannini, the other participants were Franco Ferrarotti and Alberto Quaroni.

84 According to Serafini's report, a brief manifesto was sent to about four hundred local institutions that had previously supported federalist initiatives. Of these, only fifty-seven expressed their interest (Paolini, "Il Consiglio dei Comuni d'Europa").

85 "The Council of European Municipalities".

86 Thanks also to the very positive work undertaken by the *Comitato nazionale per le celebrazioni del centenario della nascita di Altiero Spinelli*, his figure has been the subject of important research and conferences. Among other books see his unfinished autobiography, his diaries, his publications, many republished, and a number of biographies: Spinelli, *Come ho tentato di diventare saggio.* I. *Io Ulisse*; *idem*, *Come ho tentato di diventare saggio.* II. *La goccia e la roccia*, republished in a single volume in 1988 by Il Mulino; *idem*, *Diario europeo*; *idem*, *Il Manifesto di Ventotene*;

their readiness to adopt the innovative elements of the municipal association and added its creation to initiatives sponsored by the MFE.

Thanks to Umberto Serafini's work, two hundred and twenty-eight Municipal Councils, local governments and individual mayors joined the CEM's Italian Section by April 1952, compared to the aforementioned eleven thousand in France. The final objective of the two national associations also differed: the Italian one was European federalist, closer to administrative decentralisation, and the French one more involved in generic action in favour of European unity.[87]

The conflicting cultural positions did not, however, prevent the various elements in the movement of local autonomies from cooperating in order to promote the creation of the CEM. The participants' different political opinions did, however, result in a debate, at times bitter but always constructive, within the association of local European powers. Already at its constituent assembly the association had established its precise objectives, mostly set out by the French delegation, only after a complex series of speeches by all the delegations present. It was clarified how the exceptional international context justified the constituent meeting. The municipalities and people of democratic Europe should in fact unite to defend themselves not only from state centralism, but above all from communist totalitarianism. Europe, its role, its organisation, were all yet to be defined. The CEM therefore had to have two objectives. The first was to allow a debate among municipalities on real problems and to provide help in resolving them, thereby becoming part of the tradition of the associations, such as the immediate post-war UIV or the IFHP; the second was the creation of a united Europe. In this new Europe, local bodies were to be represented, and thus the organisation committee was to participate in the debate opened by the Schuman and Pleven proposals and within this framework address the problem of the representation of local communities. The charter also fully accepted Gasser's theories, stating in its first point the objective of achieving and defending municipal autonomy.

---

idem, *Il progetto europeo*; *idem*, *Discorsi al Parlamento europeo 1976-1986*; *idem*, *Una strategia per gli Stati Uniti d'Europa*; *idem*, *L'Europa tra Ovest e Est*; *idem*, *La crisi degli Stati nazionali*; Paolini, *Altiero Spinelli. Appunti per una biografia*; Paolini (ed.), *Altiero Spinelli e l'unificazione dell'Europa*; Graglia, *Unità europea e federalismo. Da "Giustizia e libertà" ad Altiero Spinelli*; Paolini, *Altiero Spinelli. Dalla lotta antifascista alla battaglia per la federazione europea 1920-1948*; Pasquinucci, *Europeismo e democrazia. Altiero Spinelli e la sinistra europea 1950-1986*; Graglia, *Altiero Spinelli*; Preda (ed.), *Altiero Spinelli e i movimenti per l'unità europea*.

87 On the creation of the AICCE see Zucca, "L'azione di Luciano Bolis per la costituzione dell'Associazione italiana per il Consiglio dei Comuni d'Europa".

The CEM also appointed a commission for municipal autonomy that was specifically tasked with drafting a European Charter of Local Freedoms, one of the movement's fundamental documents in which the organisation's theoretical work and political objectives were to be solemnly ratified. The Charter, the drafting of which saw the participation of Gasser as the CEM's scientific advisor, was approved in Versailles in October 1953 at the organisation's first States General. This also resulted in the definition of the international assemblies of European local administrators, within the framework of the political initiatives sponsored by *La Fédération.*[88] The text adopted was, however, the result of a lengthy debate between those who considered the European federation a natural ally for local demands and those, such as Gasser, who gave priority to an internal reorganisation of states in the most decentralised way possible.[89] If one excludes the preamble, in which the reference to European unity is clear, the Charter effectively adopted the ideas presented by Gasser during the 1930s and the 1940s.

After the approval of the European Charter of Local Freedoms, the CEM's work was to take place along two fronts; the constitutional reforms of states in Western Europe, aimed at guaranteeing administrative decentralisation and local autonomy, and along the international front support for the creation of a European federation, although as the years passed the international objective would prevail over that more strictly linked to promoting administrative reforms.

The new association did allow great freedom of action for the various cultural and political members who had accepted to participate in this initiative. Each individual member was in fact legitimised to valorise those parts of the charter most suited to them. While this pluralism would be the movement's strength, at times it was also an element of weakness, especially when the CEM experienced problems in finding internal leadership capable of understanding its different needs and prioritising these needs in one political objective. This did, however, mark the beginning of a new season of international relations between territorial institutions, one that was to have important consequences for the European Union's current international structure.

---

88 ASUPv, Fondi aggregati, Fondo Umberto Rossi, c. Riunioni di esecutivo del CCE, *Bureau du CCE les 14/15 avril 1951, Statuts adoptés par l'Assemblée constituante, p.* 5 and letter dated 20/12/1952 on the agenda of the second session of the CCE's board of directors (Palermo January 30th-February 1st, 1953); "Primo progetto di una Carta delle libertà comunali e regionali"; "Carta europea delle libertà locali"; *Ratificare la "Carta" e aderire al Consiglio dei Comuni d'Europa: questi sono i compiti immediati.*

89 "Autonomie e Stato".

CHAPTER 2

Twinning. Act One for an International Political Role for Municipalities

Research on twinning is not an easy task since source material and archives are hard to find and are dispersed across the continent. This consideration applies to an even greater extent to Italian public archives, which, in spite of very precise and ignored laws and good intentions, are often only accessible thanks to the goodwill of individuals, or in other cases intentionally made inaccessible.[1] State institutions, while on the one hand not complying with laws regulating the registration of documents with historical archives, and on the other often short of space and staff, have in some fortunate cases shown a marked sensitivity for research.

The primary source of material for this chapter was the previously mentioned CEMR documentation deposited with the Historical Archives of the European Union. This collection contains precious material for an initial overview of the subject of twinning, but it is not exhaustive with regard to references to the origins of the first international relations between local institutions, or to the entire complex issue of "fraternisations" as they were initially called. This has happened because each twinning had its own history linked to the political conditions experienced by the municipalities involved, to the work of the national sections of the movement of European local autonomies, to the national and international political situation in the context in which twinning was achieved, as well as to the role played by individual political and administrative figures.

There do not basically appear to be any historical studies available with very few exceptions, such as research by Antoine Vion on the *Constitution des enjeux internationaux dans le gouvernement des villes*

1 At Milan's Archivio Civico it was not possible to access the correspondence of former Mayor Aldo Aniasi or the minutes of municipal council meetings for the 1960s and 1970s, excluded from public consultation following an arbitrary decision taken by the municipality. One can only hope that the current administration, among the many problems to be addressed, will also resolve these absurd aspects clearly in conflict with current legislation.

françaises[2] or his essay *Superare i conflitti: il gemellaggio tra città europee dopo la seconda guerra mondiale*, in which, however, the author does not recognise the Europeanist political origins of the twinnings idea.[3]

The word twinning, described in the 1950s as a 'pairing of objects', is nowadays understood also in common language to mean "the symbolic act with which two cities or villages belonging to different nations decide to create and develop bonds of close brotherhood with one another for cultural, economic and political reasons".[4] The main player in this change was certainly the CEMR, which had already promoted at the beginning of this new millennium the twinnings of over eight thousand European municipalities[5] which have today reached the amazing figure of about twenty thousand[6], which, in sixty years of history largely coinciding with the European integration process, have led millions of citizens of different European nationalities to debate and become sensitised to the idea of a united Europe. By 2011, within the framework of activities sponsored by the AICCRE, in Italy alone 2,154 twinnings had been established, compared to the 2,223 recorded in 2006,[7] mainly involving municipalities that were members of the CEM, but with a growing tendency to set up new twinnings with local institutions in countries that over time joined the European Community

---

2 Vion, *La constitution des enjeux internationaux dans le gouvernement des villes françaises (1947-1995)*. Another bachelor degree thesis on twinning has been written by a French student who consulted documents preserved in the Florentine archives, but her thesis has not yet been deposited there (as reported to me by the director of the archives in Florence, Jean Marie Palayret). For a list of bachelor degree and PhD theses on this subject see Vion, "Europe from the Bottom Up".

3 Vion, "Superare i conflitti".

4 This definition is in the *Vocabolario della lingua italiana*, vol. II, p. 589. In an edition published in the 1950s, the *Nouveau petit Larousse* defined *jumelage* as "pairing pieces of wood longitudinally" or "cannons on a turret"; Bareth, "46 French municipalities are fraternised with other European cities".

5 Data refers to 2001 and the figure has risen further due to the policies promoting twinning in Eastern European countries that have returned to democracy (Giscard d'Estaing, "Prefazione. Il CCRE: cinquant'anni al servizio degli enti locali e regionali europei"; CEM Commission, *The Municipalities and Europe. A practical guide to twinning*, p. 10). One should bear in mind that by 1983 about 5,600 twinnings had been established between European municipalities. Of these, 2,000 involved municipalities in the Federal Republic of Germany, 1,700 French municipalities, 270 in Italy, 200 in Belgium, 180 in the Netherlands and about 250 in Austria, Luxembourg, Switzerland, Spain and Ireland (Logiou, *Mémoire sur le Conseil des communes et Régions d'Europe*, p. 20). The acceleration that took place between the early 1980s and the end of the 1990s is therefore evident.

6 "L'AICCRE, la cittadinanza europea e i gemellaggi".

7 "Cittadinanza europea e gemellaggi", p. 50.

and then the Union.[8] The initiatives undertaken have resulted in such successful contagion that, since the early 1950s, other associations or individual local institutions have organised twinnings between cities, provinces and regions all over the world.

Before addressing twinning from the perspective of the history of European integration, one must remember, in the context of the international activities of municipalities and in the broader one of the Cold War,[9] the twinnings sponsored by the association *Le Monde Bilingue* which, founded in July 1951 to promote an ideal of global understandding, created to organise cultural encounters, soon called linguistic twinnings, in the French-British area in 1953.[10] After an initial success that allowed linguistic twinning to spread to the United States of America and Canada, the association's wish to join together all municipalities with no particular political distinctions paved the way between 1955 and 1956 for work addressed at promoting French-American and French-Soviet twinnings, the latter encouraged by the Soviet government, in particular its embassy in Paris.[11] These policies led to the progressive clash between the association and local administrations linked to conservative, Catholic and socialist governments in power in Western Europe, to activities in North America being basically blocked, and to a clash with the CEM over the paternity and political management of twinnings. The clash resulted in a significant reduction in the number of twinnings sponsored by *Le Monde Bilingue* in Western European countries, and in democratic nations in general.

---

8 AICCRE, *Dossier gemellaggi. Autonomie locali e regionali per un Governo europeo federale*, a document presented to the 14th National Assembly of the AICCRE held in Rome on March 3rd-5th, 2011. This document indicates how twinnings established with French and German municipalities were more than half the total, but new countries such as Poland and Hungary are quickly receiving requests. The Italian regions with the highest number of twinned municipalities are Lombardy with 406 and Tuscany with 439.

9 On the Cold War see in particular the fundamental work of Fontaine, *Histoire de la guerre froide*. For a quick reference bibliography and to learn about the various periods and interpretations, see Calchi Novati, *Neutralismo e guerra fredda*; Denna, *Storia della guerra fredda (1917-1960)*; Catalano, *Europa e Stati Uniti negli anni della guerra fredda*; Ulam, *Stalin. The Man and his Era*; Boffa, *Storia dell'Unione Sovietica*. II. *Dalla guerra patriottica al ruolo di seconda potenza mondiale. Stalin e Cruscëv 1941-1964*; Yergin, *Shattered peace*; Barral, *Il y a trente ans. La guerre froide*; Di Nolfo, "La guerra fredda"; *idem*, *Storia delle relazioni internazionali 1918-1992*, pp. 601-876; Mammarella, *Storia d'Europa dal 1945 a oggi*, pp. 87-204; Dumoulin - Girauld - Trausch (eds.), *L'Europe du patronat. De la guerre froide aux années soixante*; Smith, *La guerra fredda 1945-1991*; Mantelli and Artico (eds.), *Ideologia e geopolitica all'ombra della guerra fredda*.

10 Vion, "Superare i conflitti", pp. 258-259.

11 Ivi, p. 262.

This type of twinning had in fact always been more perceived as an attempt by communists to enter the governments of NATO member countries by accessing lower levels. One must also bear in mind that the twinnings sponsored by *Le Monde Bilingue* did not envisage symbolic gestures, such as oaths sworn on the twinning, or political ones, such as motions approved by municipal councils, which instead formally characterised those created and promoted within the framework of the European integration process.

A number of twinnings were promoted by the UIV, which were more directly inspired by relations between this association and the CEM. The UIV promoted twinnings between municipalities all over the world, but its work did not thus assume precise political characteristics if not through a generic appeal for universal peace, unlike the CEM, which, as we shall see, had a well-defined Europeanist meaning. Relations between the two associations were inspired by an initial reciprocal and prudent relationship, if not a competitive one, in order to achieve political representation of local institutions at a European level. An UIV board meeting held in The Hague on May 13th, 1952, approved the proposal made by the recently created CEM to form a joint study commission aimed at "creating an atmosphere of trust between the two organisations" and developing reciprocal strategies to abolish eventual divergences and misunderstandings. Following these premises the UIV intended to study, together with the CEM, the possibility that the new organisation could soon join the more consolidated international association of local municipalities. After a series of meetings between their delegations, and thanks to the work of a specifically appointed commission, an agreement was approved in Basel on September 4th, 1953, on the basis of which "the UIV and the CEM" remained "free in their respective spheres of activity", allowing municipalities to be members of both associations while they committed to "regularly exchange documentation and publications, and maintain the most cordial relations." To achieve this, the *ad hoc* commission was made permanent, and it was hoped its work would lead to greater synergy if not unity.[12] Fully perceiving both the possible synergies and the problems in relations between the two associations, an editorial published by the magazine *Nuova Rassegna di legislazione, dottrina e giurisprudenza. Rivista amministrativa quindicinale per i comuni, le provincie e per gli altri enti locali*, one of the editors of which was Piero Calamandrei, stated that it did not share the preconceptions of some, among them Marrane, president of the French association that was a member of the UIV, that the UIV and the CEM's objectives were so

12 Ardy, "I rapporti del C.C.E. con l'Union International des Villes".

different that it would be difficult and inadvisable for them to become one organisation.

The article also emphasised how the UIV had become the world association of local administrations, while the CEM's main, if not priority, objective was to promote European unity. Both associations could therefore cooperate in the promotion and strengthening of local autonomies. It was proposed that the UIV was the basis of "an international movement for autonomy, instead of being satisfied with encouraging hopeless national efforts." The CEM should instead become, "without belittling itself," the UIV's "strongest" section at a European level.[13]

Confirming the many "eventual" divergences, the CEM's unification with the UIV was only progressively and with difficulty achieved in the 1990s. In 1988 Umberto Serafini still considered the International Union of Local Authorities (IULA) – the English name had by now prevailed over the older French one – a serious and dangerous problem for the CEMR. He remembered how for a very long time the IULA had prevented the creation of a national section of the Europeanist movement for local authorities in the Netherlands, as well as the fact that a merger between the two organisations was only proposed due to their serious crisis.[14] The most profound divergence was the two organisations' differing positions concerning Europe's federal integration, with the CEMR favourably active and proactive, and the IULA basically agnostic if not at times gently in opposition. After lengthy and difficult negotiations, the idea of a merger proposed by the IULA was dropped and the CEMR became the European section of the world organisation of local authorities. The agreement was signed in Brussels on December 11th, 1990, by the assembly of CEMR delegates, which became the European section of the UIV[15] about forty years after this was first proposed.

It was also due to these initial divisions that the word and implementation of twinning was certainly abused and tended to be applied well beyond the original political meaning that Jean Bareth, the aforementioned first international secretary of the CEM and an untiring promoter of twinning, described as:

13 Ardy, "Realtà nell'utopia".

14 Serafini, *Breve storia del Consiglio dei comuni e delle regioni d'Europa, p.* 143.

15 Only on October 1st, 1992, did the new charter of the CEMR, in attachment 1, establish the rights and duties of the CEMR-European Section of the IULA, in which the European movement of local autonomies committed itself to "supporting the global activity of the IULA within the framework of its charter" (Serafini, *Breve storia del Consiglio dei comuni e delle regioni d'Europa*, p. 197).

la rencontre de deux communes qui entendent proclamer qu'elles s'associent pour agir dans une perspective européenne, pour confronter leurs problèmes et pour agir et développer entre elles des liens d'amitié de plus en plus étroits.[16]

The twinnings, implemented first within the Community and then within the Union, did not always respect the Europeanist policy that should have and must characterise these initiatives in the spirit of its creators. The focus on Europeanism, but above all the invitation not to transform "fraternisation" into pleasant intercontinental holidays, of little political importance although undoubted tourist attraction, were part of the CEMR's internal and external political debate until twinning began. In particular the constitutional federalist wing within the CEM paid constant attention to maintaining and improving the political and Europeanist aspects of twinnings. It is in this context that one should understand the use federalists made of Pope Pius XII's words on the meaning and role of twinning. For the twinning of Rome and Paris, the Pope had invited local administrators to provide a constructive contribution "not only with pleasant courtesy and a real understanding of the twinned cities tastes and needs, but also with the will to pursue together the same objectives in spite of material conditions all too often excessively different." The Pontiff's words were used by the AICCRE's secretary general, Umberto Serafini, for a sensational headline, *Pio XII ammonisce a non far dei gemellaggi pure cerimonie esteriori*, for an article published by *Comuni d'Europa*, and to deliver harsh remarks about amounts spent on ceremonies for the twinning of Rome and Paris, thereby repeating a similar controversy started by Roman newspapers. In particular, Serafini reminded local administrators how twinnings should be used to promote a Europeanist spirit among citizens.[17]

The idea of promoting in an institutional form the international relations between individual European municipalities had been put forth

16 This quotation was also included in the *Rapport* presented by Michel Barnier, president of the AFCCRE, during a plenary session of the 7th European Congress of Twinned Cities held in Ferrara from November 12th to the 14th, 1998. Photocopies of the text were distributed to participants. Today there is one copy at Archivio Storico dell'Università degli Studi di Pavia (from here on ASUPv), Fondi aggregati, Fondo CEMR.

17 Serafini, "Gli europei adulti: le elezioni europee e i compiti politici dei poteri locali e regionali"; Pius XII, "Pio XII ammonisce a non far dei gemellaggi pure cerimonie esteriori"; [Serafini], "Le spese superflue di molti viaggi". On the Catholic world's attitude to the European integration process, among the vast bibliography, see Conte, *I papi e l'Europa*; Chenaux, *Une Europe vaticane?*; Vincent and Willaime (eds.), *Réligions et transformations de l'Europe*; Citterio and Vaccaro (eds.), *Quale federalismo per quale Europa*; Canavero and Durand (eds.), *Il fattore religioso nell'integrazione europea*.

by Jean Bareth in the second half of the 1940s. Bareth, a primary school teacher, had attended the *École normale d'Auteuil* and then devoted his life to teaching; during the 1930s he joined the corporativist Catholic movement that formed around *Justice sociale*. In 1939 he was drafted and fought in World War II. Encouraged by André Voisin, after France's defeat he became one of the founders of the French federalist movement, *La Fédération*. Bareth was the first representative of the French federalist movement to read the work of Adolf Gasser, which in 1946 inspired him to write an article and a brochure on municipalism. In 1947 he wrote a new leaflet in which he emphasised the importance of municipalities as the basic political community.[18] Between 1946 and 1948 he joined in the season of Europeanist conferences that led to the founding of the European Union of Federalists (EUF),[19] the European Movement (EM)[20], and the Council of Europe.[21] He then participated in

[18] See Jean Bareth, "Le fédéralisme c'est d'abord la commune"; *idem*, *Le fédéralisme par la commune; idem*, *Le fédéralisme: un principe, une action.*

[19] The EUF was founded after a series of meetings and International conferences, among them one held in Paris in March 1945 and one in Hertenstein in September 1946. At the end of the 1040s about eighty Europeanist and federalist movements from all over Europe joined the movement. On the EUF's role in relation to the history of European integration and compared to other Europeanist movements, see Rognoni Vercelli, "L'Unione europea dei federalisti"; Morelli, "L'Unione europea dei federalisti e il Movimento federalista europeo sovranazionale"; *idem*, "Il Movimento federalista sovranazionale e l'Unione europea dei federalisti".

[20] The EM has always been characterised by the heterogeneity of its members, who, although sharing a common Europeanist ideal, disagreed and were divided about the means, ways and time needed to achieve European unity. On the European movement see the essay by Caraffini entitled *Costruire l'Europa dal basso*, which not only perfectly reports the work done by the Italian Council, but also places it in the context of the international movement; see also Milward, "The International Committee of the Movements for European Unity"; Hick, "Il movimento europeo"; Palayret, "Il movimento europeo"; *idem*, "Il Movimento Europeo Internazionale e la battaglia per l'Unione Europea"; *idem*, "Le Mouvement européen 1954-1969"; Preda, "La commissione istituzionale del Movimento europeo".

[21] The Council of Europe, created in 1949, was initially joined by "the governments of the Kingdom of Belgium, the Kingdom of Denmark, the French Republic, the Irish Republic, the Italian Republic, the Grand Duchy of Luxembourg, the Kingdom of the Netherlands, the Kingdom of Norway, the Kingdom of Sweden and the Kingdom of Great Britain and Northern Ireland" (Charter of the Council of Europe). Iceland, the Federal Republic of Germany, Greece, Austria and Turkey joined later. The Council of Europe consisted of a Parliamentary Assembly and a Committee of Ministers and resulted in the broadest and most advanced expression possible of intergovernmental cooperation on the subject of European unity. The British and Scandinavian presence significantly influenced the Assembly, denying it effective powers, while the Committee of Ministers, committed to deliberating unanimously, turned out to be the guardian of the absolute sovereignty of national states. The Assembly did, however, play an important role in clarifying the different positions of governments, political parties and movements, more or less favourable to real European union, as well as, to

the preparatory phases and was one of the founders of the CEM, which would become the means through which Bareth attempted to merge the struggle for local governments with the one for European unity. He first became the Secretary for European affairs and then the secretary general of the organisation of local European institutions, a position he held until he died. Together with Umberto Serafini, he directed the association of European municipalities' international activities and was responsible for the movement's organisation and its political activity.

On the subject of the international 'fraternisation' of municipalities, Bareth almost immediately realised that to achieve his objectives he could not ignore the international situation and, in particular, a new European order that presupposed the creation of a European federation guaranteeing the security of western European states. Within this framework, municipalities could have implemented international activeties as well as promoted reforms of a federal nature within the individual states.

The ideas presented by Bareth were also able to rely on the political experience developed by André Voisin,[22] leader of the French federalist movement, who at the end of World War II had already sponsored relations between French and British municipalities. In those years Voisin's objective was to create a network of solidarity among municipalities that were to help one another rise from the destruction of the ongoing war; thus the issue of creating permanent international relations between territorial institutions was only outlined. After these

a certain extent, acting as a stimulus for reflection on the institutions real unity would require. On the Council of Europe see in particular the not always identical testimonies of Dehousse, *L'Europe et le Monde*; Spinelli, *L'Europa non cade dal cielo*; Adenauer, *Erinnerungen 1945-1953*; Monnet, *Mémoires*; see also Duclos, *La réforme du Conseil de l'Europe*; *idem*, *Le Conseil de l'Europe*; Robertson, *Le Conseil de l'Europe*; Leone, *Le origini diplomatiche del Consiglio d'Europa*; Segretariato generale del Consiglio d'Europa, *Il Consiglio d'Europa*; Bitsch, "Le rôle de la France dans la naissance du Conseil de l'Europe"; Burban, *Le Conseil de l'Europe*; Greppi, "Il Consiglio d'Europa: l'istituzionalizzazione della cooperazione politica tra Stati sovrani"; Bitsch, (ed.), *Jalons pour une histoire du Conseil de l'Europe*; Bitsch - Loth - Poidevin (eds.), *Institutions européennes et identités européennes*.

22 A biography of André Voisin, pseudonym for André Bourgeois (1912-1990), has yet to be written; it would be particularly useful to study in depth his role as the "éminence grise", if he really was one, of a number of French governments, as well as the role he played within the framework of federalist and Europeanist movements. Historians will not, however, be able to consult his personal archives because supposedly they do not exist, nor do those of *La Fédération*, which have been lost. It will be necessary to draw on documents preserved by other personalities and movements that were in close contact with him, such as Jacques Chaban-Delmas or Antoine Pinay. For biographical information see "1912-1990"; Richard, "Soixante années de connivence"; *La Fédération, mouvement fédéraliste français*.

first experiences, *La Fédération* sponsored the first "unions" between the municipalities of Orléans and Dundee in 1946, Bordeaux and Bristol, and Velettes-sur-mer and Greenock in 1947.[23] In this phase no forms were envisaged for institutionalising and rendering stable international relations between municipalities, but the determination to resume past direct relations between local institutions was now evident.

Simultaneously, on April 26th, 1948, within the framework of activities for supporting the Benelux, a meeting was held between the municipalities of Amersfoort in the Netherlands and Esch-sur-Alzette in Luxembourg. This encounter was sponsored by Hubert Clément[24], the mayor of Luxembourg City. Clément was a convinced supporter of solidarity between European municipalities and as such had participated in the 1930s in the founding of the *Fédération des conseillers communaux socialistes*, becoming one of its most active members. After the war he was a determined supporter of the need to create a European union, the only remedy against frustrated nationalisms that had caused so much suffering to humankind. He joined the *Mouvement socialiste pour les États-Unis d'Europe* (MSEUE)[25] and became president of Luxembourg's section, attending the 1948 congress in The Hague. He founded Luxembourg's section of the EM and became a member of its international executive committee and vice-president of the Grand

23 Association française du Conseil des Communes et Régions d'Europe, *L'art du jumelage*.

24 Hubert Clément (1889-1953), a socialist from Luxembourg, played a key role in the creation of the CEM. He carried out his political activities at a European level, taking part in the congresses of the *Union interparlementaire* from 1937 to 1948; in August 1939 he was one of the promoters of the resolution with which the *Union* condemned the annexation of Czechoslovakia. During the war he led the vast exodus of his compatriots to France. After France was defeated and the Vichy Republic invaded, he escaped the Nazi police, taking refuge in Switzerland, where he represented Luxembourg's government. He was mayor of Esch-sur-Alzette, the Grand Duchy's main industrial town, from 1935 to 1945; Municipal Councillor from 1929 to 1935 and from 1946 to 1953; a member of parliament from 1928 to 1948; and Councillor of State from May 1952 until he died. For his many activities Clément received accolades including the Legion d'Honeur. For the moment no one has written an exhaustive biography of Clément, and for the information provided in this book the author consulted documentation preserved in the Archives Association villes et communes luxembourgeoises, Luxembourg (from here on AVCL Archives, Luxembourg), c. Hubert Clément as well as accounts published in *Hubert Clément. Un humaniste du travail*.

25 Il *Mouvement socialiste pour les États-Unis d'Europe* (MSEUE) was founded in London in 1947. The movement did not officially join the Socialist International but was considered a supporting group that individual socialist militants could join. The movement's objective was to form a European Left favouring the idea of a united Europe. On the MSEUE see Loth, "Il Movimento Socialista per gli Stati Uniti d'Europa".

Duchy's section. He created Luxembourg's section of the EUF and thus participated in the international federalist congresses that, among other events, led to the creation of the Council of Europe. He was one of the supporters of his country joining the European Coal and Steel Community (ECSC) and the European Defence Community (EDC). In order to promote the European ideal, every week he devoted an editorial in his newspaper, the *Tageblatt*, to European issues. Involved with Milhaud's magazine *Annales*, and invited and encouraged by him, he organised the Luxembourg delegation that participated in the founding of the CEM. He then created the Luxembourg section of the association of European local authorities, ensuring that almost all the Grand Duchy's municipalities joined it. This massive membership resulted in the mayor of Luxembourg, Émile Hamilius,[26] being appointed president of the CEM.

Clément strongly believed in the need to resume international relations between municipalities as an active element in achieving peace in Europe. He therefore sponsored the initiative between the municipalities of Amersfoort, in the Netherlands, and Esch-sur-Alzette, as a step towards the union of Belgium, the Netherlands and Luxembourg, and, in a more advanced perspective, of Europe. Clément believed that it was necessary to work at the level of local administrations so as to organise and encourage "les échanges d'idées entre citoyens, commerçants, employeurs, ouvriers".[27] The idea that municipalities should and could accompany the reconciliation of European countries and therefore promote peace on this continent and in the world was beginning to take shape.

---

26 Émile Hamilius (1897-1971), although a citizen of Luxembourg, was born in Esch-sur-Alzette on May 16th, 1897, and attended the Military Academy of Saint-Cyr, where he was one of Charles de Gaulle's students. Commissioned at the end of 1922, the following year he joined the Luxembourg Army, from which he resigned in 1930. That same year he became a partner in one of Luxembourg's most important commercial companies. Elected municipal councillor in 1933, he became a member of parliament from 1936 to 1963, a career interrupted during the Nazi occupation. On June 20th, 1946, he was appointed mayor of the city of Luxembourg, an appointment he held until December 31st, 1963, when he was made *bourgmestre honoraire*. Hamilius was a member of the promoting committee for the Council of European Municipalities but did not attend the meeting held for its founding. During the first States General of European municipalities (held in Versailles in October 1953) he was acclaimed the movement's president. He held this appointment until April 22nd, 1959, when he was appointed the associations' honorary president. Although there is no reference biography for Hamilius, as is the case for many other leading players in the history of European local institutions, information was taken from AVCL Archives, Luxembourg, c. *Notices biographiques*, *Notice biographique de Monsieur Émile Hamilius*; see also "Émile Hamilius président d'honneur du C.C.E., ancien bourgmestre de Luxembourg".

27 "Rapprochement entre deux villes du Benelux Esch-sur-Alzette et Amersfoort".

As mentioned, in January 1951 the CEM was founded in Geneva. The debate clarified that the organisation's main objective was to:

> Développer l'esprit européen dans les communes et collectivités locales pour promouvoir une fédération européenne, baseé sur l'autonomie de ces collectivités.[28]

One of the objectives the movement adopted, as proposed by the French delegation, was therefore to promote *jumelages*. *La Fédération* and its members provided a fundamental contribution both in defining the political project of twinnings and in the CEM's organisation. Jean Bareth and André Voisin therefore played decisive roles, the former organisational and the latter political, within the movement of European local institutions, with the objective of also promoting *jumelages* as a political deed through which local administrators could involve their citizens in the European integration process. The word *jumelage* was chosen to identify:

> une telle association de communes, durable et étendue à l'ensemble des activités humaines, avec d'une part, certaines relations intercommunales plus limitées telles que les "parrainages" qui ont pour but d'aider une commune éprouvée et d'autre part avec certains échanges spécifiquement économiques, universitaires et autres, de caractère limité, qui résultent souvent d'initiatives privées et qui échappent à la direction des communes.[29]

Twinnings thus became the instrument used by federalist and Europeanist public relations for sensitising first the local administrators and then the citizens. The position assumed by French federalists was also able to rely on the support and experience provided by Hubert Clément, who, as seen, had previously organised one of the first international meetings of municipalities, though initially he received a tepid welcome from the then national secretary of the AICCE[30] Umberto Serafini, the reference figure for constitutionalist federalists within the CEM.

---

28 Archives d'État de la République et Canton de Genève (from here on the AEG), Papiers Edgard Milhaud, c. Doc. EM 2 A 1936-1956 B 1907-1948, *Procès verbaux des six séances de la Conférence constitutive du Conseil des communes d'Europe, Genève 28-30 janvier 1951*, p. 16.

29 "Comment organiser un jumelage!".

30 Serafini, convinced of the priority of the struggle for European integration, did not initially grasp the Europeanist potential of twinnings; see Serafini, "Convertito ai gemellaggi".

It was also the need for French-German reconciliation that led French federalists to find a unifying formula that, in a context involving a search for new political instruments, Jean Bareth called *jumelage.*[31]

In 1947, the *Union internationale des Maires pour le rapprochement franco-allemand et la compréhension entre les peuples* was created, which, after organising a round table for French and German mayors in Mont Pèlerin that same year, experienced a period of stalemate until the establishment of the Federal Republic of Germany. In 1950 a new congress of French and German mayors was held in Stuttgart, followed immediately by the first official visit by a German mayor to France thanks to an agreement between the municipalities of Montbéliard and Ludwigsburg. *La Fédération* in some ways also claimed the paternity of this first meeting, described, probably in an intentionally derogatory manner, as "apparentement" in an article published in the magazine *Le Bulletin fédéraliste*, in which the genesis of this visit was reported on at length.[32]

In this phase a document was prepared to be approved by municipal councils and signed by the mayors involved. The text, which would become known as the *serment du jumelage*, explicitly stated the wish to "maintain permanent bonds between the municipalities" to encourage exchanges between citizens in all sectors and to "develop with better reciprocal understanding sentiments of European brotherhood." Municipalities also committed to undertake action in favour of "founding European unity."[33] Twinning, with its symbolism and rituals, reintroduced to European history stable and, at the time, partially free international relations between municipalities, in order to encourage the continent's integration and peace.

---

[31] Umberto Serafini attributed this merit to Bareth both in a letter to the CEM's secretary dated December 3rd, 1954, in which on the subject of twinning he wrote: "c'est à vous le mérite d'avoir commencé" (Historical Archives of the European Union in Florence, CCRE fond, c. 172, f. 1954), and in his political report presented during the meeting of one thousand twinned cities held in Magonza in 1978 (Serafini, "Gli europei adulti: le elezioni europee e i compiti politici dei poteri locali e regionali"). Consultation of documents preserved in the CCRE fond of the Historical Archives of the European Union in Florence, and in the Archives of the *Association française du Conseil des communes et régions d'Europe* in Orléans, provide further information that supports Serafini's testimony.

[32] "Jumelages Troyes-Tournai, Montbéliard-Ludwisburg". Traces of later relations between the *Union* and the CEM are preserved in the CCRE fond of the archives in Florence. See also Vion, "Superare i conflitti", pp. 249-272, which does not, however, mention the role played by French federalists.

[33] Associazione italiana per il consiglio dei comuni d'Europa, *Statuto e documenti fondamentali*.

The first official *jumelage* sponsored by the CEM was between the cities of Troyes and Tournai,[34] but one must underline how, in reality, it had been wanted and organised by *La Fédération* as a means of public relations to be implemented at the same time the federalist movement's National Congress was held in Troyes on November 4th, 1951.[35] The twinning ceremony was held in Troyes in front of the monument to the fallen, in the presence of the mayors of both cities who, for the first time, spoke the words of the twinning oath. The ceremony was also attended by political and economic authorities, representatives of the French and Belgian governments, the president of the *Association des Maires de France*, and the president of the CEM's European *Comité d'action*. The twinning's objective included that of "coordenner les effors économique des deux centres et notamment de développer les échanges des jeunes apprentis et ouvriers".[36]

Immediately after this initiative, the AFCCE organised a study conference in Paris on twinnings between local communities in European countries. This conference was held at the International Chamber of Commerce in Paris on January 9th and 10th, 1952. It was attended by delegations from the CEM's national sections in Austria, Belgium, France, West Germany, Great Britain, Italy, Luxembourg, the Netherlands, Saarland and Switzerland. During this important debate, the objectives and forms of twinning were outlined for the first time at an international meeting. The conclusions of this conference, summarised by Umberto Serafini, who presided over the final session, clearly indicated how, by creating stable relations between municipalities, twinnings would encourage both the development of local authorities within centralised national states in Western Europe and the struggle for a European federation, which was a priority according to Serafini.[37]

These principles were implemented during the second important and politically significant *jumelage* between the cities of Metz and Luxembourg. The two cities' approval of the CEM's proposals was no coincidence, since Raymond Mondon,[38] mayor of the French city, was

34 "Jumelages Troyes-Tournai, Montbéliard-Ludwisburg".

35 Testimony provided by Jacques Jira, one of *La Fédération's* most active militants, now preserved on tape at the ASUPv, Fondi aggregati, Testimonianze orali; see also AVCL Archives, Luxembourg, c. *jumelage 1952-56, Association française pour le Conseil des communes d'Europe. Commission des affaires européennes, Documents sur les jumelages.*

36 AVCL Archives, Luxembourg, c. *jumelage 1952-56, Documents sur les jumelages.*

37 "Jumelages".

38 Raymond Mondon, an MP and on various occasions a minister of the French Republic, Mayor of Metz, was also one of the CEM's founders, also becoming vice-

close to *La Fédération*, while his colleague from Luxembourg, Émile Hamilius, had been a member of the CEM's promoting committee and, as mentioned, was to become its president in 1953. He was also in close contact with his colleague Clément, which represented a precursor of international relations between municipalities. The forms established for this twinning, its organisational model, and the Europeanist spirit that characterised events were to become the model for future twinnings organised by the CEM at least throughout the 1950s and 1960s. One must also underline how the forms encoded at the time and the wording used are identical to those still used today. The objectives established by the promoters can be summarised in the pedagogic work done to sensitise citizens regarding the need for internal federalism in European construction in order to establish permanent relations between cities within an administrative, commercial, industrial, educational, associative framework, as well as that involving local management and social policies.[39]

Encouraged by the press and the appeals from local administrators, citizens attended the ceremonies held in both cities, in Metz on March 23rd, 1952, and in Luxembourg on June 21st, 1953, in extraordinarily large numbers. In the main squares of their cities the mayors read the *serment du jumelage* that sanctioned the commitment to maintain "des liens permanents entre les municipalités" as well as to "favoriser en tous domaines les échanges" between citizens to develop "par une meilleure compréhension mutuelle le sentiment vivant de la fraternité européenne". The mayors also swore to "conjuguer" their efforts to support "l'unité européenne". The *serment du jumelage* was made in the presence of representatives of the French government, among them Robert Schuman,[40] and of the Luxembourg government, such as Hamilius, who, commenting on this twinning, wrote:

---

president of the French section of this movement. For notes on his work within the movement of local institutions, see "Raymond Mondon". It is interesting to observe that, like other members of the French association of European local institutions, Mondon too was a government under-secretary for *Affaires départementales et communales*.

39 AVCL Archives, Luxembourg, c. *jumelage 1952-56, IIe États généraux des communes d'Europe. Les jumelages. Rapport de M. Henri Jaquet, maire du Locle (Suisse)*, p. 4.

40 To understand Schuman's Europeanist ideas see his political testament, *Pour l'Europe*, and also his personal account of the evolution of the plan named after him, "Origines et élaboration du Plan Schuman". See also Pennera, *Robert Schuman, la jeunesse et les débuts politiques d'un grand europeen de 1886 a 1924*; Poidevin, *Robert Schuman. Homme d'État*; Lejeune, *Robert Schuman, une âme pour l'Europe*; Comité pour la commémoration du 100e anniversaire de Robert Schuman, *Les racines et l'œuvre d'un grand Européen. Robert Schuman 1886-1986*; Beyer, *Robert*

> Quant à l'idée européenne, elle a, pour tout Messin, pour tout Luxembourgeois, perdu son caractère abstrait: elle est maintenant une concception raisonnable et concrète, conforme aux intentions de son principal promoteur. En commun, nous travaillerons à sa réalisation, sous l'égide de celui qui, enfant de Luxembourg, citoyen de Metz, nous appartient en commun, et nous donne un lumineux exemple d'européanisme, je veux dire M. Robert Schuman.[41]

In summary, twinning marked the beginning of real relations both between the two cities and between the mayors of the Moselle and Luxembourg region, in order to address shared problems concerning the use of the waterways and the control of industrial development. In particular, the Europeanist objective was broadly achieved, to the extent that Robert Schuman said, "ce jumelage constituait une initiative sans précédent"[42] emphasising how similar initiatives could "rendre plus populaire encore l'idée d'unification européenne."[43] It is obvious how, during the 1950s, the direct role played by municipalities in forming public opinion was of fundamental importance compared to current means of information,[44] so much so that Schuman also emphasised how no city in Europe or France had been so "largement et aussi intimement touchéè par l'idée européenne que ne le fut celle de Metz."[45]

Apart from this initial success, it was necessary to export the twinning formula from the French-speaking region to ensure it became really European. Jean Bareth, whose work was at this point mainly addressed at organising the newly created movement of European local institutions, was the first to warn that this was necessary and began to work on the CEM's Italian and German sections, which needed to take action to sensitise a number of important cities to the need to establish twinnings with municipalities in France or in the Benelux area.

The issue of twinning was also posed during the first States General of the Council of European Municipalities held in Versailles from October 16th to the 18th, 1953, effectively winning the support of the entire association, which at the time already had about twenty thousand

Schuman; Monnet and Schuman, *Correspondance 1947-1953*; Fondation Spaak, *Les pères de l'Europe. 50 ans après.*

41 Hamilius, "Préface".

42 Bareth, *L'Europe des Communes*, p. 22; this book has been translated and published in English with the title *The Municipality and Europe. Twinning and Intermunicipal Encounters.*

43 "Le Discours de M. Robert Schuman". On the Metz-Luxembourg twinning, also quoted in the CEM's informative publications on twinning, see in particular AVCL Archives, Luxembourg, c. *jumelage 1952-56*, *Documents sur les jumelages.*

44 Zucca, "L'organisation du consensus parmi les administrateurs locaux européens".

45 Bareth, *L'Europe des Communes*, p. 22.

municipalities as members. It was again in Versailles that the first international conference of twinned cities was held, which later led to the international conferences of municipalities.[46]

To support and complete his work, at the end of 1953 Jean Bareth wrote ra book with the meaningful title, *La Commune et l'Europe. Jumelages et rencontres intercommunales.*[47] Bareth emphasised the priority need to involve public opinion in the ongoing European integration process. To achieve this objective it was necessary to act within the "cadre des réalités de chaque jour"[48], establishing relations between citizens of all the nations involved in the process through the municipalities, the basic cells of western democracy. Twinning should, and must, promote "liens permanents entre les cités en même temps qu'une action généralisée et cohérente en vue de promouvoir une fédération européenne basée sur l'autonomie des collectivités locales."[49] According to Bareth, twinnings would also be useful in broadening the political horizons of local administrators, leading to new administrative and political perspectives by comparing different experiences. He also provided political-organisational advice, on the basis of which the twinning ceremony had to have solemn characteristics also involving the use of previously experimented symbolic gestures such as an oath and playing the national anthems. The population should be involved because signatures by the mayors were of no meaning if not executed in the presence of citizens. To achieve these results, following the example set by the Metz-Luxembourg twinning, it was necessary to develop a programme studied at preliminary meetings held by the mayors and administrators of the cities involved. The choice of municipalities was not to be a random one, but interested municipalities were to present "une similitude de vocation", an element that was not indispensable since twinnings could also be promoted for great events such as international fairs or cultural encounters. Twinning was not to remain restricted to large cities but also involve medium-sized and small municipalities rich in historical and cultural traditions, thereby bringing all citizens closer to the idea of a united Europe. To strengthen and make permanent the exchanges between municipalities, twinning committees were also to be organised, formed by citizens not involved in local administration, who would be the driving force in promoting the European idea and understanding between citizens.

Bareth ended his essay stating:

---

46 Serafini, *Breve storia del Consiglio dei comuni e delle regioni d'Europa*, p. 179.

47 Bareth, *La Commune et l'Europe.*

48 Ivi, p. 10.

49 Ivi, p. 18.

Les jumelages sont sans doute l'expression la plus frappante et la plus facilement compréhensible de la tâche immense enterprise pa le Conseil des Communes d'Europe. Leur développement servira à la fois les libertés communales et l'esprit européen.[50]

The idea that municipalities should and could play a role in the reconciliation of European countries, thus helping to bring peace to the continent and the world, was discovering its first ways of being implemented.

We have seen that during the 1950s twinnings were mainly used as a means for Europeanist public relations; however, since these were complex events some also assumed an important moral significance. In this regard, the twinning organised by Jean Bareth himself between the municipality of Boulogne Billancourt, of which he was *maire adjoint*, and a district in West Berlin was exemplary. It was feared that there would be clashes at the ceremonies between French workers and the German delegation, still perceived by the working classes as representing the Nazi regime. However, when the delegation arrived led by its mayor, who bore the signs of the Nazi concentration camps and of torture, it became understood that the whole of Europe had fought and defeated fascism. Within the context of the reconciliation of European peoples, twinnings were organised, as were meetings between the municipality of Marzabotto and German municipalities, which commemorated together the massacre perpetrated by Nazi troops and the murder of the young Germans of the *Weisse Rose*.[51]

Since there were men capable of ensuring that events moved in this direction, twinnings were useful for Europeans to get to know one another and for some categories, in particular local administrators, to compare experiences. Twinnings were, and still are, an instrument and thus can be useful or not, depending on the manner in which they are used. One should not forget that in a significant number of cases they were used, as Umberto Serafini had reported from the very beginning, to cover a degree of recreational spontaneity. They had very little to do with the struggle to achieve European unity, but nevertheless they did over the decades contribute to interpersonal exchanges that would probably never have taken place if twinning had not been enacted.

After 1954, acknowledging the positive potential of twinning, the AICCE changed its initial prudence providing well-informed support. In February 1954 an unsigned article, and consequently attributable to the editorial staff, appeared in the *Comuni d'Europa*, the aforesaid

---

50 Ivi, p. 26.

51 Serafini, *Breve storia del Consiglio dei comuni e delle regioni d'Europa, pp.* 177-178.

magazine published by the Italian section of the CEM, emphasising for the first time the importance of "inter-municipal fraternisations" being implemented thanks to the CEM. The anonymous editorialist remembered how twinnings had taken place when "two or more municipalities, or groups of municipalities, of different European nations" decided to meet due to "chosen affinities, similar or complementary economic or cultural characteristics, shared problems addressed, or a desire for reciprocal knowledge or understanding, after centuries of clashes that were condensed in explosions of national hatred."[52]

Alongside the various possible individual initiatives that resulted from twinnings, the CEMR tried, at times successfully, to coordinate the increasingly large number of twinned municipalities by creating an important network of twinned cities, on each occasion sensitising them to the importance of the Europeanist struggle undertaken. On the basis of the experience of the States General, created and organised both as an opportunity for internal debate within the world of local authorities as well as an opening to the international political world, the CEMR organised the conferences of twinned municipalities, not on a twice-yearly basis like the States General, but on certain particular occasions or to address important issues concerning the European integration process.[53]

In view of the first elections of the European parliament, the CEM had prepared an extremely complex and organised Europeanist public relations programme.[54] The programme envisaged international conferences of elected local and regional authorities open to other social and political elements, the organisation of training seminars for local administrators, who would have then autonomously done public relations work, a summons of States General with an agenda that included the democratisation of communitarian institutions, as well as the mobilisation of twinned cities that were to be informed and rendered participants in an effort to provide Europe with its first parliament elected by direct universal suffrage.

It was with this in mind that the 12th States General was held in Lausanne on June 8th-11th, 1977, followed by another in The Hague in May 1979, intentionally close to the date of the first European elections. The Lausanne States General was considered by federalist forces as the

52 "Fratellanze intercomunali".

53 On the political role of twinnings see AICCE, *Il ruolo dei gemellaggi per l'Unione europea*; Associazione Italiana per il Consiglio dei Comuni e delle Regioni d'Europa, *I gemellaggi per l'unione europea e per la pace.*

54 Zucca, *La contribution du Conseil des communes d'Europe à la première élection du Parlement européen.*

beginning of the European campaign to sensitise the political classes, also represented by local authorities, on the profound constituent and unitary meaning of the European elections.[55] Within the framework of agreements entered into with the Commission, the CEM received community financing that allowed it to embark on capillary political public relations work.[56] The various initiatives sponsored by the movement included the European Conference of Twinned Cities held in Lucca on May 19th-20th, 1972,[57] and the meeting of the one thousand twinned European cities held in Magonza on September 28th and 29th, 1978, which turned out to be the most significant event organised by the CEM in the context of the campaign for the European elections. This meeting was attended by two thousand local administrators as well as by the Speaker of the European parliament Emilio Colombo, the president of the Bundestag Karl Carstens, and the Federal Republic of Germany's (FRG) interior minister Gerhart Rudolf Baum.[58] In his report, Serafini emphasised that the CEM, the great European political parties and the governments should address three interdependent issues. The first concerned the need to create monetary and economic union that would "replace the snake in the tunnel." The creation of such unity assumed the resolution of the second issue, which required the presence of an effective political and democratic Community government. In order to form a European government, it would be necessary for the democratically elected European parliament to assume the right to draft a European political charter in which a Community Cabinet was envisaged, with limited but real powers, that would answer to both the Community's Council of Ministers – the future European Senate – and to the elected parliament – the Lower House. If events had developed in the manner proposed, the Community would not have been able to hesitate in allowing three new countries (Spain, Portugal and Greece) to gain membership after acquiring democratic regimes. On this subject, it

55 "La mobilitazione del CEM per le elezioni del Parlamento europeo"; Philippovich, "I nuovi compiti del CEM per le elezioni del Parlamento europeo"; "Il dibattito politico generale".

56 Archives of the Conseil des communes et des Régions d'Europe, Paris, *armoire G*, c. *Parlement européen*, f. *Réunion de travail. Campagne du C.C.E. pour l'élection du Parlement européen au suffrage universel direct. Plan d'utilisation des subventions communitaires*. The Commission had established the allocation of 1,950,000 Belgian Francs for 1977; this amount would be increased by about 50% in 1978. Should the elections have been postponed to the autumn of 1978 or the spring of 1979, the Commission would have doubled its contributions.

57 Giuseppe Bufardeci, "Il significato politico dei gemellaggi e le elezioni dirette del parlamento europeo".

58 Serafini, "Gli enti locali e le elezioni europee"; "Incontro delle città europee a Magonza".

is necessary to emphasise how, in spite of progress made in integration especially on the monetary front, the political proposal presented about twenty years ago is still extremely current in addressing the profound crisis experienced by Europe today. Without a federal government it is obvious that it is impossible to govern a single currency. At the time, however, Serafini's proposal gave rise to opposition from those who saw in Europe the creation of a technocracy and rejected the presenter's political approach.[59]

The final resolution in Magonza reiterated literally that the Community needed to "address three great changes. Economic and monetary union, its political charter and its enlargement to include three new countries in southern Europe".[60] In this manner the CEM sided with European federalists, and in particular with the MFE, which had launched its Campaign for Europe in which the creation of economic-monetary union was demanded as the premise for implementing the irreversible process that was to lead to a European Union.[61]

Twinnings, European and extra-European municipal relations, the struggle for a United States of Europe, and peace in the world are issues that clearly can be addressed starting from an initiative invented by a Catholic French primary school teacher that resulted in an international association of municipalities that, although heterogeneous, had, and to a certain extent still have, the objective of promoting the continent's unity through the valorisation of local governments.

The Maastricht Treaty marked a fundamental stage in this process, introducing European citizenship as the founding symbol of a European identity. The Amsterdam Treaty further strengthened these symbolic elements, introducing the principle that European citizenship complements national citizenship. With decision 1904/2006/CE dated December 12th, 2006, the European Parliament and Council adopted the Europe for Citizens programme for the 2007-2013 period, thereby creating the legal framework to support a wide-ranging series of activities and organisations aimed at promoting active European citizenship and involving citizens in the European integration process. In its first point in Action 1, Active Citizens for Europe includes twinnings between cities that envisage "direct exchanges between European citizens through participation in activities involving the twinning of

---

59 Serafini, "Gli enti locali e le elezioni europee".

60 "Le risoluzioni dell'incontro di Magonza del Consiglio dei comuni d'Europa".

61 Paolini, "Pensiero e azione dei federalisti europei". On July 3rd, 1977, the UEF's federal committee adopted the manifesto for the European elections in which the political guidelines for the Campaign for Europe were outlined (Albertini, "Far partecipare le basi dei partiti alla elaborazione dei programmi elettorali europei"; "I lavori del Comitato federale a Monaco").

cities and encouraging the creation of networks and cooperation between twinned cities."[62] The Commission has financed this programme with a total of 18,674,000 Euros, of which 11,500,000 have been allocated to support and promote twinnings also through the creation of an IT network between twinned cities.[63] In this manner, in further developing the original Europeanist spirit the *jumelage* formula enters the third millennium with one yet uncompleted task: the creation of the United States of Europe.

62 Patriciello, *European twinning. Speciale dossier "gemellaggi europei"*.

63 "Cittadinanza europea e gemellaggi", p. 51.

Part II

International Action

CHAPTER 3

Twinnings for European Unity

The Case of Florence[1]

The AICCE was created in January 1952 thanks to the work of Umberto Serafini, the decisive support of the MFE, especially Luciano Bolis[2], and Adriano Olivetti's *Movimento Comunità*. By April that year, two hundred and twenty eight municipal councils, mayors and governments, including the city government of Florence, had joined the Italian section of the movement of European local institutions.[3] The constituent assembly was attended by the engineer Menotti Riccioli, the Tuscan capital's Councillor for Demographic Services. He was then elected to the *interim* executive council of the new association of European local institutions,[4] the first of many appointments the Tuscan administrator was to hold within the CEM at a national and international level.

Menotti Riccioli role is essential for understanding the genesis of Florence joining the newly-created CEM and of the city's first twinning. He was born in 1882 and died in 1969, and graduated in industrial engineering in Turin in 1907. Born to a family inspired by Mazzini and

---

1 With reference to this chapter, I must express my most heartfelt thanks to Lando Conti, a descendent of Menotti Riccioli, one of the leading Florentine players in this historical reconstruction; to Gianfranco Martini, a federalist director of the AICCRE and for many years politically responsible for the twinnings of the *Conseil des Communes et des Régions d'Europe;* to Gastone Bonzagni, always a federalist militant; and to the Giorgio La Pira Foundation for having opened to scholars their archives or their memoires, without which the few faded documentary traces left would often be useless. Thanks also to Eugenio Giani, the Municipality of Florence's former Councillor for Sport and for Twinnings, who allowed me to consult current and municipal archives, as well as to the staff at the Archivio storico del comune di Firenze. I must also mention Giancarlo Zoli (1917-2007), a Florentine politician and an important representative of the AICCRE, who granted me an important interview.

2 On the role played by Bolis in founding the AICCE see Zucca, "L'azione di Luciano Bolis per la costituzione dell'Associazione italiana per il Consiglio dei Comuni d'Europa". On Bolis also see Rognoni Vercelli, *Luciano Bolis dall'Italia all'Europa.*

3 "Regolari adesioni scritte e sottoscritte ricevute entro il 24-IV-1952".

4 "Il Convegno costitutivo dell'Associazione italiana per il Consiglio dei comuni d'Europa", p. 1.

the Freemasons,[5] he secretly joined the republican movement after 1897 and then volunteered for service in World War I, which he perceived as the last deed of the national Risorgimento. Immediately after the war he returned to politics, having actively participated in defending the Florentine headquarters of the Republican Party from attacks by Fascist paramilitary squads. In this clash in 1922, thirty two republicans fought against three hundred fascists. Twenty eight of the Republicans were seriously injured, among them Riccioli, who only survived the clash because the body of an equally badly-injured companion protected him from the last shots fired by the Fascists. When Mussolini came to power he refused, despite frequent encouragement, to take out Fascist party membership, and when possible he devoted himself to clandestine activities to keep alive the republican ideal. During World War II he edited and published, along with a number of friends and with his brother Ernesto, the clandestine leaflet *La voce del popolo*.[6] He actively joined the Resistance, involving his entire family while simultaneously attempting to reorganise the Republican Party. He took part in a secret conference of Italian republicans in Milan and assumed organisational and political responsibility for the party in Florence and its province.[7] In October 1944 he wrote a book in which he provided the guidelines for a

---

5 See Menotti Riccioli's private archives preserved by Lando Conti on the *Attestato rilasciato dal Collegio dei venerabili dei Liberi muratori d'Italia "Al carissimo fratello Menotti Riccioli della rispettabile Loggia L. Bezzoni. Da oltre cinquanta anni attivo e fedele Libero Muratore".*

6 Ernesto Riccioli (1880-1955) joined the Republican Party's youth movement at the age of sixteen and then became a member of its university group. He later became the Republican Party's secretary for the Tuscan section and, from 1908 to 1909, was a member of the municipality of Florence's administration. Graduating in medicine in 1905, he became a volunteer aid worker after the earthquake in Calabria, and as such he also travelled to Serbia to set up a field hospital. When Italy entered the war he returned home to leave for the front. In 1921 he was the Republican candidate in the general election and, following the abolition of political parties, he started his own personal resistance to the Fascist regime, which led him to join *Giustizia e Libertà* and the *Partito d'Azione*. He then participated in the Resistance and was the *Partito d'Azione*'s candidate after liberation. Having rejoined the Italian Republican Party, he left it to join the *Movimento di Alleanza Democratica* against the so-called fraud bill. He held a number of appointments. In 1944 he was head of the administration of Santa Maria Nuova, a member of Florence's provincial delegation, and subsequently the president of the *Commissione per il recupero delle Opere d'Arte e della Fratellanza Militare*, Menotti Riccioli's private archives, c. *Ernesto Riccioli*; *Istituto storico della Resistenza* in Tuscany, *Ernesto Riccioli* fond, envelope 17, ff. 1 and 2.

7 Biographical information was taken from *Riccioli Menotti curriculum vitae (end of November 1956)* and the *Volantino di propaganda del Partito repubblicano italiano per l'elezione dell'Ing. Menotti Riccioli al Senato della Repubblica*, preserved in Menotti Riccioli's private archives, and from the "Prefazione", to Conti Riccioli (ed.), *Scritti di Menotti Riccioli.*

Profilo programmatico del Partito repubblicano italiano.[8] In this book he referred to Mazzini's idea of a brotherhood of free peoples as a means for overcoming wars, and for the future organisation of the Italian state he proposed not only a republican form of government, but also great decentralisation and administrative autonomy for municipalities. During that same period, his brother Ernesto first joined the *Giustizia e Libertà* movement, attending meetings at Rosselli's home, and then the *Partito d'Azione.* One should not therefore be surprised that for Menotti the ideal of Mazzini's brotherhood of peoples was soon influenced by the idea of European unity. On January 27th, 1945, he participated in the foundation of the *Associazione federalisti europei* (AFE), becoming a member of its executive committee.[9] He was then one of the founders of the MFE's Florentine section and a member of its executive committee, and he was later appointed president as well as secretary of the movement's municipal and regional headquarters.[10] His conversion to supranational federalism was firm. He devoted himself in part to intense political activity as well as to writing many articles in favour of European unity in local and party newspapers.[11]

In the first free local elections he was elected a municipal councillor in Florence, representing the Italian Republican Party (PRI), becoming a member of the local government led by the communist Mario Fabiani.[12] The Cold War and the party's national policies resulted in him siding with the centrist majority governing the city. After being re-elected to the municipal council in 1951, he was a member of the first La Pira[13]

---

8 Riccioli, *Profilo programmatico del Partito Repubblicano Italiano.*

9 Graglia, "L'Associazione Federalisti Europei di Firenze (A.F.E.) ed il I Congresso Federalista di Venezia".

10 Menotti Riccioli's private archives, *Volantino di propaganda del Partito repubblicano italiano per l'elezione dell'Ing. Menotti Riccioli al Senato della Repubblica*, p. 3. On Riccioli's work within the MFE's Florentine section there are important reports in the MFE's *Quaderno del Comitato direttivo* preserved by Gastone Bonzagni in Florence, now photocopied and also held in the *Archivio Storico dell'Università degli Studi di Pavia.*

11 A number of documents on Europe have been collected in the aforementioned book *Scritti di Menotti Riccioli* published in 1979. Europeanist articles published in Prato's bi-weekly republican *Il cittadino* had been published in Riccioli's book, *La federazione europea in marcia.*

12 Innamorati, *Mario Fabiani. Il sindaco della ricostruzione.*

13 Giorgio La Pira is a figure of fundamental importance for understanding the international role played by the city of Florence during the 1950s and the first half of the following decade. There is no doubt that the idea of the first twinning came from Menotti Riccioli. In this initial phase, La Pira followed preparations for the event from a distance, subsequently realising its great potential and using this instrument in the framework of his international political activity. To seize the European aspects of twinnings, and those linked to international peace, enacted during the La Pira

council (June 10th, 1951-May 27th, 1956), receiving from the mayor a full mandate to deal with European issues and also acting as an advisor and a stimulus for La Pira himself.

After the creation of the AICCE, Riccioli's objective was the municipality of Florence's membership in the newly-created association. The problem was above all a political one since centrist parties, as we shall also see in the following chapters, had based their local electoral campaign also on the principle that the only debates permitted during municipal council meetings should be those concerning purely administrative issues. This choice had been made to prevent the Left from placing on the agenda subjects concerning international politics.[14] The adoption of this policy at a national level had resulted in a small number of municipalities joining the AICCE based on decisions made following a debate in the municipal council,[15] which was also the only method of authorising local administrations to pay their membership fees to the association. It was only in councils in which the centrist politicians were particularly attentive to European issues that there was a bitter clash with communist and socialist minorities, which considered the new organisation of municipalities a "NATO surrogate."[16] Riccioli's work to persuade people was not easy even with his colleagues in the municipal council. However, on October 16th, 1952, following a proposal made by the municipality, the municipal council's agenda included Florence's membership in the Council of European Municipalities. The debate that followed developed during the October 18th and 20th sessions. The minutes clearly indicate an attempt made by representatives of the Communist and Socialist Parties to seize this opportunity to

administrations, see his papers and speeches now collected in De Siervo - Giovannoni - Giovannoni (eds.), *Giorgio La Pira sindaco. Scritti, discorsi e lettere*.

14 This analysis was presented during a meeting of the AICCE's interim executive council held in Rome on February 16th, 1952. The debate was attended by represent-tatives of the Christian Democratic, Liberal, Republican, and Social Democratic parties as well as federalist and communitarian representatives, among whom the secretary of the AICCE Umberto Serafini. (Archivio Storico dell'Università degli Studi di Pavia – from here on ASUPv – Fondi aggregati, Fondo Umberto Rossi, c. *Consiglio direttivo A.I.C.C.E. Roma 24 giugno 1958).* On the political system of Italian political parties and its comparison to that of other western European countries, see the recent Ordina (ed.), *Partiti e sistemi di partito in Italia e in Europa nel secondo dopoguerra*.

15 At the AICCE's constituent assembly, out of the 228 memberships received only 50 had been approved following a debate in the municipal councils. The others were personal memberships of mayors (84) or municipalities (94). The difference was a significant one. Only a resolution from a municipal council could in fact commit administrations to paying membership fees ("Regolari adesioni scritte e sottoscritte ricevute entro il 24-IV-1952").

16 "Forlì e Firenze nell'AICCE".

draw the majority into a debate on the pros and cons of Italy choosing the West. Opposition parties also posed a series of prejudicial techniques, among which the important supposed impossibility for an Italian municipality to join a European association. If this last objection had been accepted, it would have blocked not only Florence's AICCE membership but probably the existence of the new association. In order to overcome this obstacle, the resolution was amended during the debate to clarify that the Florence Municipality was joining an Italian association of municipalities which, in turn, belonged to the European movement of local institutions. During the debate, Riccioli and his colleagues accepted the political clash, stating that in the field of popular democracies the need was not felt for municipalities to be "free and autonomous" and that the European federation should be the main objective pursued precisely in order to consolidate democracy against communist and dictatorial regimes, whose representatives in Italy would certainly not be in favour of an association of free municipalities.[17] At the end of this lively debate, Florence's municipal council approved a resolution allowing the municipality to join the AICCE, indicating among the objectives of this membership that of:

> sviluppare lo spirito europeo nei Comuni e nelle collettività locali allo scopo di promuovere una federazione di Stati europei basati sull'autonomia di queste collettività; assicurare la partecipazione e la rappresentanza dei Comuni e collettività locali negli organismi europei e internazionali; integrare le future istituzioni europee con l'Assemblea rappresentativa dei Comuni e collettività locali.[18]

In the meantime, having become the CEM's secretary general, Jean Bareth applied pressure on the AICCE's secretary Umberto Serafini, to complete at least one twinning between important cities in both countries. Bareth also reported the availability of the city of Reims,[19]

---

17 Archivio storico del Comune di Firenze (from here on ASCFI), Atti del Consiglio comunale di Firenze anno 1952, vol. II, seduta del 18 ottobre 1952, pp. 979-980 and seduta del 20 ottobre 1952, pp. 986-1000.

18 ASCFI, Atti del Consiglio comunale di Firenze anno 1952, vol. II, seduta del 20 ottobre 1952, p. 1000 (transl. "developing the European spirit in municipalities and local communities in order to promote a federation of European states based on the autonomy of these communities, the guarantee of a participation and representation of municipalities and local communities in European and international institutions, and the integration of future European institutions with the assembly representting municipalities and local communities").

19 Historical Archives of the European Union in Florence, CCRE fond, Italy, c. 172, f. 1954, letter dated February 19th, 1954, in which Bareth announced to Serafini that the cities of Lezoux, Bougie, Limoges, Reims, Lille and Fains La Folie had expressed the wish to be twinned with Italian towns of the same size and importance. Bareth emphasised how twinning "permettent de *concupire* une action européenne" and

whose mayor, René Bride, was close to *La Fédération.*[20] After overcoming his own doubts concerning the usefulness of twinning in the struggle for European unity, Serafini contacted Menotti Riccioli to find out whether Florence might be available. The answer by a convinced Europeanist such as Riccioli could only be a positive one, and in the course of 1953 he debated the proposed twinning with the Florentine administration.[21] Contacts were established between the administrators of the two cities, initially during a meeting of the CEM's international executive council in Palermo held from January 31st to February 1st, 1953,[22] and then again during the first States General of European municipalities held in Versailles from October 16th to October 18th of that year. The Palermo meeting was attended by Menotti Riccioli, the bearer of a message from Mayor La Pira, and the mayor of Reims,[23] while the second event was attended once again by the mayor of Reims and Riccioli, who represented the municipality of Florence together with his party and council colleague Enzo Giacchetti.[24]

Contacts continued during the final months of 1953. During this period Riccioli travelled at least once to Reims to address in depth the preliminaries of *jumelage* and agree on a series of events to be held for

therefore should be implemented. The letter reveals how the availability of French cities had been previously announced, receiving no reply from the Italians.

20 As the *adjoint au maire* of Reims and councillor general for the Marne, René Bride participated in the preliminary commissions for the *Journées d'études nationales pour la mise en valeur des régions de France* organised by *La Fédération* in 1952. He was then elected president of the *Centre d'études et d'action fédéraliste de la Marne*, a body set up by the French federalist movement to organise a link between local communities and the federalist association (Historical Archives of the European Union in Florence, CCRE fond, Secrétariat général, c. 30, *Journées d'études nationales pour la mise en valeur des régions de France*; photocopied sheet without date but probably 1952 or 1953, signed by René Bride as *Président du Centre d'études et d'action fédéraliste de la Marne*).

21 Archivio corrente del Comune di Firenze, Ufficio relazioni esterne, c. Reims 1954, reports on the Florence-Reims twinning, p. 5.

22 Archives Association villes et communes luxembourgeoises, Luxembourg (from here on AVCL Archives, Luxembourg), c. *Jumelage 1952-56*, *Association française pour le conseil des communes d'Europe. Document sur les jumelages.* This document clearly states how the origins of the twinning between the cities of Reims and Florence dates back to a first meeting between Menotti Riccioli and René Bride in Palermo during a meeting of the CEM's executive council. On the importance of Palermo for the history of the movement of local communities see Zucca, "Il Conseil des communes d'Europe e il rilancio europeo di Messina".

23 Ardy, Silvio (ed.), *Il Consiglio dei comuni d'Europa.*

24 *Idem*, pp. 921, 923 and 938. Menotti Riccioli participated in the work group that drafted the report on *I comuni e le istituzioni europee.*

the twinning,[25] although an analysis of the small amount of correspondence indicates that the final decision was only taken by the Florence municipality thanks to the interest shown in this initiative by the Italian Ambassador to Paris, Pietro Quaroni,[26] and to the pressing insistence from the French.[27] In March 1954 Councillor Riccioli was at last able to write to the mayor of the French city stating that, having overcome all the political problems within the majority governing Palazzo Vecchio, the city of Florence was particularly delighted to be joined to the city of Reims in a *jumelage*. According to the Florentine city councillor, twinning only made sense if perceived within the framework of encouraging European unity.[28] The event's organisation was delegated by the Florence municipality to Riccioli, who in April informed La Pira that the twinning with Reims was making progress "with a following wind".[29]

An international press conference organised by the Italian Ambassador Pietro Quaroni was held in Paris on June 14th to illustrate the meaning of the proposed twinning between Reims and Florence. The press conference was attended by the mayor of Florence, his colleague from Reims, and Riccioli, as well as by many representatives of French local institutions and the CEM.[30] On that occasion the programme for the events that would sanction the twinning of these two cities was outlined. On July 3rd the first twinning ceremony was held in Reims, presided over by the mayor of Florence and Menotti Riccioli. The occasion was attended by large crowds, with the symbolic rituals respected and the local, national and Italian press extensively reporting the events.[31] On that occasion La Pira made an important speech, and,

[25] Archivio di deposito del Comune di Firenze, c. 311, f. gemellaggio Firenze Reims 1954-1955, copy of a letter from Giorgio La Pira to Luciano Sibille dated March 24th, 1954.

[26] Archivio di deposito del Comune di Firenze, letter from Pietro Quaroni to Giorgio La Pira dated October 8th, 1953, and the mayor's answer dated October 31st.

[27] Archivio di deposito del Comune di Firenze, letter from Luciano Sibille to Giorgio La Pira dated February 4th, 1954, and letter from Jean Bareth to Giorgio La Pira dated March 9th, 1954.

[28] Archivio di deposito del Comune di Firenze, copy of a letter from Menotti Riccioli to René Bride dated March 5th, 1954. Letters soliciting a reply sent by the French probably crossed paths with Riccioli's positive reply.

[29] Archivio di deposito del Comune di Firenze, letter from Riccioli to La Pira dated April 7th, 1954.

[30] AVCL Archives, Luxembourg, c. *Jumelages 1952-1956, Association française pour le conseil des communes d'Europe. Document sur les jumelages;* Archivio corrente del Comune di Firenze, Ufficio relazioni esterne, c. Reims 1954, review of the Florence-Reims twinning p. 5.

[31] The mayors pronounced the *serment du jumelage* from the Town Hall's balcony in front of "la foule massée en demi-cercle" (AVCL Archives, Luxembourg, c.

addressing twinnings, he did not conceal his initial doubts concerning the initiative, stating that in the beginning he had been concerned that twinning would be understood as merely "folkloristic, tourist and sentimental" events, instead of being a "singular moment of community life" with historical meaning and a "universal content." The mayor of Florence said he had overcome these doubts, reflecting on how the celebrations had a meaning deeply-rooted "in the mysterious germination of current and future history." He then added that this twinning would have allowed the integration of

> l'officina con la cattedrale, l'economia con la grazia, la cultura con la rivoluzione, la politica con la bellezza, lo stato con la città, l'Europa col mondo. Integrando – attraverso la storia presente – la storia di domani alla storia di ieri. Ecco signori, il significato proprio, simbolico, delle cerimonie odierne: esse sono come uno stendardo elevato in Europa: segno di una civiltà che si edifica, di una speranza che fiorisce, di una pace che viene.[32]

In reporting to the city council on the first twinning of the city of Florence, Menotti Riccioli, though emphasising the "grandiosity of the event" and its success, acknowledged regretfully that the rest of the municipal council had underestimated the political, social and economic implications of this initiative, considering it almost "his personal affair". He also underlined how the city of Reims had experienced this twinning in an intense manner, while Florence had sent to Reims a "pathetic" representation of just a few politicians.[33] Riccioli did, however, point out that the Tuscan city could redeem itself in organising an equally intense and important ceremony in Florence the following year. He planned to

Jumelages 1952-1956, Association française pour le conseil des communes d'Europe. Document sur les jumelages); a plane left Reims that morning for Florence, where it dropped leaflets bearing "messages of greetings as a sign of the new bonds of friendship between the two cities", while the French Post Office issued a commemorative stamp (Archivio corrente del Comune di Firenze, Ufficio relazioni esterne, c. Reims 1954, review of the Florence-Reims twinning, p. 7).

32 La Pira, "Discorso per il gemellaggio di Firenze con Reims" (transl.: "Workshops with cathedrals, the economy with grace, culture with the revolution, politics with beauty, the state with the city, and Europe with the world, through present history integrating yesterday's history with tomorrow's. This, ladies and gentlemen, is the real and symbolic meaning of today's ceremonies. They are like a standard raised over Europe, the sign of a civilisation being created, of hope rising, of peace to come").

33 The Florentine delegation consisted of the Mayor, Riccioli himself, a priest representing the Cardinal of Florence, and three other people representing the Istituto Statale d'Arte in Florence, Florence University and the *Associazione dei donatori di sangue*. It was therefore obvious that Riccioli was completely right to emphasise the initial lack of enthusiasm with which the Florentine institutions had reacted to this initiative he cared so deeply about (Archivio corrente del Comune di Firenze, Ufficio relazioni esterne, c. Reims 1954, review of the Florence-Reims twinning).

follow the example set by Reims by "holding a public press conference in Florence to publicise the event and set up a citizens' committee for the twinning which had obtained such excellent results in Reims." He also added that it was necessary to acknowledge how the twinning of "immensely important cities in these two countries" would lead to a "sense of brotherhood between the two populations that was destined to result in jewels of peace, wealth, commercial, industrial and cultural development."[34]

Riccioli also reported to the MFE's Florentine executive committee, of which he was a member, emphasising on this occasion only the positive aspects of the initiative which, in summary, were correctly set in the framework of international activities aimed at promoting the idea of European unity among the citizens of the various nations.[35]

As Riccioli had hoped, the protocol now envisaged that the French ceremony would be followed the next year by a similar event in Florence. As the event drew near, on April 4th, 1955, the municipal council approved the allocation of appropriate funds "considering the symbolic and spiritual importance of the *jumelage* that had and continued to ideally bring closer together two great and noble European cities, sharing very high historical and cultural traditions, as well as its meaning of an ever-increasing fraternal solidarity between the Italian and French people".[36] The Florentine ceremonies, held on May 3rd at Palazzo Vecchio, were attended *en masse* by citizens and important personalities alike. The local and Italian press reported the event extensively.[37]

The two cities thus established stable cultural, sporting and political relations thanks in part to the creation of two permanent twinning committees,[38] which have lasted until now following the renewal of the

---

34 Archivio di deposito del Comune di Firenze, c. 311, f. gemellaggio Firenze Reims 1954-1955, Menotti Riccioli's report to the mayor, to councillors and to the secretary general on July 7th, 1954.

35 Gastone Bonzagni's private archives, the Executive Committee's notes, book of minutes of the meetings of the Executive Committee of the MFE's Florentine section, p. 72.

36 ASCFI, resolutions approved in Apri/May/June 1955, and 4/4/1955 on Jumelages Florence-Reims.

37 Ufficio Stampa del commune di Firenze (ed.), *Firenze. Rassegna del comune 1951-1960.*

38 For example, when organising events for *Firenze, capitale europea della cultura* in 1986, the task involving the proposal of initiatives shared by both cities was entrusted by the French to the president of the twinning Committee (Archivio corrente del Comune di Firenze, Ufficio relazioni esterne, c. Philadelphia 1964, report on the first meeting held at Palazzo Vecchio on November 10th, 1986, with the mayors and

twinning in 1985 by Mayor Lando Conti,[39] later brutally murdered by the Red Brigades. Lando Conti had, by marrying a Riccioli, become a member of the family, continuing Menotti's work and ideals.

The twinning with Reims and the idea of the city's international political role, at the basis of the promotion of all twinnings, influenced a number of initiatives implemented later by La Pira. The conference of the mayors of capitals all over the world, held in the 16th-century hall in October 1955, also attended by Umberto Serafini representing the AICCE,[40] as well as the other twinnings sponsored directly by the mayor of Florence, such as the one with Fez in 1961 and the one with Philadelphia in 1964, were to a certain extent influenced by that first experience and by the Catholic Tuscan administrator's later reflections.

What was significant in the meeting of the mayors of the world's capitals was the fact that it was preceded by a vote in the municipal council which, as proposed also by Riccioli, invited the mayor of Florence to take all appropriate initiatives to develop "a love of peace among the people" so as to associate to the vote of Florence's municipal council all its "sister" cities in the world.[41]

There is no doubt that in the twinning with Fez the dominant issue was that of dialogue between the Islamic and Christian worlds;[42] in the twinning with Philadelphia, the American Federal Constitution was often evoked as an example to be followed for European unity and to achieve peace in the world.[43] In both twinnings all the formats and rituals for twinnings created by Jean Bareth were rigorously respected. In summary, La Pira's intuition was that Western Europe, as the highest expression of Christian Europe, had a mission to bring unity first of all to the continent's Christian family and then to the world. The driving force to set in motion this process could come from cities that, faced with the real danger of a death sentence for humankind due to new weapons of mass destruction, had the right to defend their lives and those of their citizens.[44] The mayors were to undertake basic diplomatic

---

representatives of twinned cities for "Florence, Europe's capital of culture" for 1986).

39 Archivio corrente del Comune di Firenze, Ufficio relazioni esterne, c. Reims 1954, renewal of twinning pact on February 16th-17th, 1985.

40 Ufficio Stampa del comune di Firenze (ed.), *Convegno a Firenze dei Sindaci delle Capitali, 2-6 ottobre 1955.*

41 *Ibidem.*

42 Archivio corrente del Comune di Firenze, Ufficio relazioni esterne, c. Fez 1961, speech by Mayor Giorgio La Pira.

43 Archivio corrente del Comune di Firenze, Ufficio relazioni esterne, c. Philadelphia 1964.

44 La Pira, "Il valore delle città"

work, implementing the unity of cities which were to be culturally and spiritually enriched before being handed over to future generations. Local administrators were to create a bridge between united cities and united nations. La Pira therefore agreed to attend the second States General of European Municipalities in Venice in 1954, where he made a speech with Europeanist contents in which he stated that:

> l'obiettivo del consiglio dei Comuni è quanto mai valido su questo punto determinante della storia umana: l'unità d'Europa vista attraverso le città d'Europa (...) l'Europa vista quale tessuto solidale delle sue città è una sola realtà culturale, sociale, spirituale e storica: perché non deve essere una sola realtà politica? E' il vero ponte fra l'Oriente e l'Occidente: un ponte di amicizia e di bene![45]

The Catholic politician therefore continued to cooperate with Umberto Serafini and the CEM with the objective of involving the association of local European institutions in his initiatives for peace.[46]

During the States General in Venice, a motion was approved in which the Europeanist organisation was invited to increase twinnings to develop consensus around the idea of a united Europe.[47] In Florence this invitation was welcomed in particular by the Christian Democrat, Giancarlo Zoli,[48] born in 1917 and the son of Adone Zoli.[49] After graduating in law from Florence University in July 1939, Giancarlo Zoli was a member of the *Movimento Fucino* and then an active participant in the Resistance. In Tuscany he was among the founders of the clandestine Christian Democratic Party. Arrested twice by the Fascists and Nazis, his life was saved only by the intervention of Cardinal Elia Dalla Costa.[50] In the early post-war period his attention was initially concentrated on the republican choice, and then after 1948 on the

---

45 La Pira, "Nuova Europa" (transl. "The objective of the Council of Municipalities is all the more valid on this fundamental point in the history of man, with European unity seen through the cities of Europe (...) Europe considered as the fabric of solidarity of its cities is a single cultural, social, spiritual and historical reality. Why should it not become a single political reality? It is the real bridge between the East and the West; a bridge of friendship and goodness!").

46 Oral report preserved on tape at the ASUPv, Fondi aggregati, Testimonianze orali, provided by Umberto Serafini.

47 "Jumelages et échanges intercommunaux".

48 Giancarlo Zoli's biographical data was reported to me by him in a taped interview granted on September 23rd, 2002, now preserved at the ASUPv, Fondi aggregati, Testimonianze orali.

49 The figure and work of Giancarlo and Adone Zoli were outlined by Danilo Veneruso during the conference *Europeismo e federalismo in Toscana 1945-2001* (Siena November 15th-16th, 2002), the minutes of which were published in 2005.

50 Zoli, "Testimonianza".

decisive struggle. De Gasperi's decision[51] to support European unity and the struggle for the EDC[52] sensitised him to the subject of a European federation, leading him to also reconsider his experience as a "European resistance fighter."[53] In December 1953 he joined the MFE's Florentine section with the specific objective of defending positions in favour of the EDC against a number of Tuscan federalists who only saw the Community's negative military aspects. In 1956 he was elected a municipal councillor in Florence and after September that year started to participate in the activities of the AICCE; he was still a member of the AICCRE executive council in 2002.[54] He was a councillor in the second

---

51 On De Gasperi see the recent works by Canavero *et. al.*, *Alcide De Gasperi.* I. *Dal Trentino all'esilio in patria (1881-1943)*; Malgeri, *Alcide De Gasperi.* II. *Dal fascismo alla democrazia (1943-1947)*; Ballini, *Alcide De Gasperi.* III. *Dalla costruzione della democrazia alla "nostra patria Europa" (1948-1954)*. On the positions assumed by De Gasperi on foreign policy, and in particular on Europeanist policies, see Catti De Gasperi, *La nostra patria Europa*; De Gasperi, *De Gasperi scrive*; Petrilli, *La politica estera ed europea di De Gasperi*; Catti De Gasperi, *De Gasperi e l'Europa* (Brescia, 1979); Pastorelli, "La politica europeistica di De Gasperi"; Poggiolini, "Europeismo degasperiano e politica estera dell'Italia"; Brunello Vigezzi, "De Gasperi, Sforza, la diplomazia italiana e la percezione della politica di potenza dal trattato di pace al Patto Atlantico (1947-1950)"; Pastorelli, *La politica estera italiana del dopoguerra*; Varsori, "De Gasperi, Nenni, Sforza e il loro ruolo nella politica estera italiana del secondo dopoguerra"; Melchionni, "Genèse de la proposition européenne avancée par Alcide De Gasperi en 1951"; *La politica estera e di sicurezza di Alcide De Gasperi: il valore di quelle scelte ieri e oggi*, a conference organised in Rome on July 2nd 1998 by the *Fondazione Alcide de Gasperi per la Democrazia, la Pace e la Cooperazione Internazionale*. As emphasised by Ottavio Barié (in his "Presentazione" for the text by Guido Formigoni, *La Democrazia Cristiana e l'alleanza occidentale (1943-1953)*), it is remarkable to observe the lack of systematic studies on the DC's NATO choice and therefore of De Gasperi's foreign policy, aspects that, even after the Roman conference on his foreign and security policies, still leaves scholars much in terms of future research. To fill this void a book on de Gasperi's Europeanist policy has been published by Preda, *Alcide De Gasperi federalista europeo* along with one by Canavero entitled *Alcide De Gasperi. Cristiano, democratico, europeo.*

52 On the EDC's political hopes and its links to the history of European integration see in particular research by Preda, *Storia di una speranza*; *idem Sulla soglia dell'Unione*. See also Aron and Lerner (eds.), *La querelle de la CED*; Fursdon, *The European Defence Community*; Breccia, *L'Italia e la difesa dell'Europa*; Pastorelli, *La politica estera italiana del dopoguerra*; Varsori, "L'Italia fra Alleanza Atlantica e CED (1949-1954)"; Clesse, *Le project de C.E.D. du Plan Pleven au "crime" du 30 août*; Vial, "Jean Monnet, un père pour la CED?"; Deighton (ed.), *Western European Union 1954-1997*; Del Vecchio, "Dalla CED all'UEO"; Dumoulin and Remacle, *L'Union de l'Europe occidental*; Dumoulin (ed.), *L'échec de la CED (1954)*; Catala (ed.), *Histoire de la construction européenne.*

53 Zoli, "Non poteva esistere la sola libertà del villaggio".

54 Zoli, was also a DC council leader, often appointed councillor for Town Planning and Legal Affairs in the Tuscan capital. From September 4th to October 28th, 1974, he was the mayor of Florence at the head of a DC-PSDI coalition. For about twenty

and third La Pira municipal administrations, 1956-1957 and 1961-1965, playing the federalist and Europeanist role previously played by Menotti Riccioli. After resigning from the second La Pira municipal administration, between 1957 and 1961 he was appointed by the Prefecture's Commission as the municipality of Florence's representative in Europe and in associations of European municipalities. During those years he intervened at various levels and on numerous occasions, always expressing his convinced Europeanism, involving the administration in these issues, and using Florence's international prestige in the struggle for European unity.[55] He was a strong supporter of twinnings as a means for federalist and Europeanist campaigning. To achieve this he has worked at a local and international level until the present. In his work he was constantly supported by the federalist Gastone Italo Bonzagni who, although born in Bologna, had since the 1960s fought a coherent and brave battle in Florence in favour of European unity. Bonzagni also became a member of the AICCE's executive councils.[56]

The Municipality of Florence is now twinned with 19 cities all over the world and has established friendship pacts with another ten, as well as having regular relations with an equal number of local institutions. The days in which municipalities could not establish institutional relations with one another are over, although the limits of some twinnings established for no specific political reasons remains obvious, and these are destined to be restricted to the initial ceremonies.[57] On this subject, one should bear in mind that Florence is now twinned with Aiun (1996), Asmara (1978), Dresden (1978), Edinburgh (1965), Esfahan (1998), Fez (1961), Philadelphia (1964), Kassel (1958), Kiev (1967), Kyoto (1965),

---

years he was a member of the EEC's Economic and Social Committee as the representative of local institutions. Following in his father's footsteps, he continued his legal work while simultaneously performing his political and administrative tasks.

55 On April 22nd, 1958, the European Communities' Council of Ministers appointed him the representative of European local powers. He attended the CEM States General in Liège in 1958 and the one in Cannes in 1960, also becoming the vice-president of a commission. He was appointed vice president of the second commission of the European conference of local powers at the Council of Europe, playing an active role in both the first and the third conferences. In 1957, as the representative of the municipality of Florence, he became a member of the AICCE's executive council, while in 1958 he was appointed a member of the CEM's executive council. In this dual role he undertook intense Europeanist work in favour of European local institutions ("Il comune di Firenze e l'Europa"). On the Tuscan administrator's Europeanist and municipalist ideas see in particular Zoli, "Il nostro messaggio".

56 On Gastone Italo Bonzagni, who worked at both a local and a European level, see his own paper in the minutes of the conference on *Europeismo e federalismo in Toscana 1945-2001* (Siena, November 15th-16th, 2002).

57 Archivio corrente del Comune di Firenze, Ufficio relazioni esterne, Twinned cities. See also *La Toscana per la pace. I gemellaggi in Toscana.*

Kuwait City (1991), Nanking (1980), Nazareth (1996), Reims (1954), Riga (2000), Salvador Bahia (1991), Sydney (1991), Tirana (2001), and Turku (1992). The following have been declared friendly cities: Cracow, Gifu, Istanbul, Malmo, Tel Aviv, Cannes, Sarajevo, Olomouc, Providence, and Leon.

After reconstructing the history of twinnings of the city of Florence, the implicit question arises concerning the work done. Were and are the twinnings of Florence in some way useful in the struggle for the creation of European unity?

We have seen that in the 1950s twinnings were used as a means for Europeanist sensitisation. The men capable of ensuring that events moved in this direction were of use to Europeans, who thereby got to know one another, and to some specific categories, such as local administrators in particular, who exchanged experiences. Twinnings were and still are an instrument and therefore can be useful or not, depending on the use they are put to. One must not forget how in quite a significant number of cases, as reported by Umberto Serafini from the start, they also involved a degree of tourist opportunism that has little to do with the struggle for European unity. The twinning between another Tuscan and a French city remains exemplary as far as the usefulness of twinning is concerned.

On May 24th, 1984, François Mitterrand,[58] at the time president of the European Council, made a speech to the European parliament that has gone down in history both for its Europeanist coherence and its unexpected contents. As one can imagine, that stand did not appear from nowhere, but among the many reasons that led the president to make this speech, one was very probably unknown to most people. Like most French politicians Mitterrand had been a mayor. The city he administered for a long time, Château-Chinon, was twinned in 1962 with the Tuscan city of Cortona. The twinning ceremonies held in

[58] On Mitterrand's political-cultural path, some of his papers are of the greatest importance: Mitterrand, *Aux frontières de l'union française. Indochine, Tunisie*; *idem*, *Le coup d'État permanent*; *idem*, *Ma part de vérité. De la rupture à l'unité*; *idem*, *Ici et maintenant. Conversations avec Guy Claisse*. On the role played by Mitterrand in the European integration process see Lathière, *François Mitterrand et l'unification européenne 1945-1957*. At the end of the 1940s, Mitterrand was linked to André Voisin and to *La Fédération*, and he attended the Congress at The Hague after being invited by the French federalist movement. In the archives of *La Fédération* there are a number of photographs portraying Voisin and Mitterrand both before the congress and after it. Some of these photographs were published by the movement's magazine in a special issue dedicated to the commemoration of Voisin (*XXe siècle fédéraliste. Pouvoir européen*. See also the oral report provided to me by Jacques Jira in Paris on December 2nd, 1994, and preserved on two tapes deposited with the ASUPv, Fondi aggregati, Testimonianze orali).

Château-Chinon on July 15th, 1962, and in Cortona on August 12th were attended by Mitterrand and by the then mayor of Cortona, Italo Petrucci.[59] When Europeanist movements organised events to support Altiero Spinelli's constituent work at the European parliament, the idea was to use inter-municipal relations to ensure the French president received useful suggestions. The Château-Chinon-Cortona twinning was renewed in 1982, with solemn ceremonies held in the presence of the French ambassador to Italy. On that occasion, remembering the pact of fraternal friendship he had signed, President Mitterrand sent a message in which he remembered that event and the subsequent shared initiatives.[60] This was another opportunity for reaching the French president and sensitising him, obviously not to twinning, but to the project for European unity. Umberto Serafini and the mayor of Marseille, the socialist Gaston Defferre,[61] assumed and achieved this task.[62]

---

59 *La Toscana per la pace. I gemellaggi in Toscana*, pp. 106-107.

60 "Il ventennale di un gemellaggio". During 1982 many events were held in Tuscany to support European union, among them a number were held in Cortona. See "Manifestazioni in Toscana per il XXV dei Trattati di Roma".

61 Gaston Defferre fought for European unity since the end of the 1940s, and within this context predicted the integration of French overseas territories within a European common market. Appointed by Guy Mollet as the socialist representative responsible for local institutions, he was the president of his party's association of local administrators, vice-president of the AFCCE, and then in the 1960s president and later honorary president of the French association of local communities. In 1981 he resigned as Speaker of the National Assembly and as president of the socialist group to become Minister of the Interior and of Decentralisation (1981-1984). In this role he achieved the first real decentralisation of administrative power in French history (laws dated March 1982 and November 1983). Defferre had government responsibility over territorial planning, housing and professional training moved to the local authorities and ensured the approval of the transformation of Regional Councils into local institutions elected directly by citizens. With this the mayor of Marseille crowned a life devoted also to the struggle of the affirmation of the principle of administrative autonomy for local institutions. There are currently many studies underway on Gaston Defferre, being written above all by students and post-graduate students at Aix-en-Provence University. The studies that have been published so far appear modest. See Suffert, *De Defferre à Mitterrand, la campagne présidentielle*; Olivier, "Entre Europe et Afrique: Gaston Defferre et les débuts de la construction européenne" and the more recent Unger, *Gaston Defferre*, in which, however, references to Defferre's international policies are almost non-existent. Primary sources for an overall research can be found in the archives of the city of Marseilles, but the papers deposited by his wife Edmonde Charles-Roux with this archive as well as with the archives of the Bouches-du-Rhône Department, are certainly incomplete, since, for example, there is no trace whatsoever of his work for the AFCCE and the CEM, while there are instead references to this in the archives of both associations. (Archives de la ville de Marseille, Archive de Gaston Defferre, c. 100 II 274, f. *Union interparlementaire européenne* and f. *Mouvement socialiste pour les États-Unis d'Europe*; c. 100 II 721, f. *articles et textes d'interviews de G. D. sur la régionalisation*).

Florence, Tuscany, European and non-European municipal relations, the struggle for a United States of Europe, and world peace where the issues that, when local institutions re-appropriated for themselves delegated political power, wrote the history of international relations.

[62] Oral report made to me by Luigi Vittorio Majocchi and confirmed by articles in *Comuni d'Europa*, 6 (June 1984).

CHAPTER 4

The City of Turin's International Initiatives and the First Twinning

Turin was one of the first Italian municipalities to join the AICCE.[1] The political gesture of joining the constituent assembly of the newly created movement of local autonomies in Italy is understandable when one considers the priority given by the mayor of Turin and politician Amedeo Peyron (1903-1965)[2] to the importance of his position and the international role he assigned to the city.

Amedeo Peyron was not by training a Europeanist or a federalist, but slowly and gradually he opted for Europe, fully aware of the cost and commitment involved in this decision. This was not an easy option then or now, something that the former president of the Piedmont Region, Mercedes Bresso, has been a excellent example of in her dual role as president of one of the most important European regions and of AICCRE, an appointment making her an ideal successor to President Peyron himself. Peyron did not allow himself to be discouraged. A prudent, cautious and realistic man, to quote Umberto Serafini, he brought to the federalist struggle for a united Europe "the moral capital

1 "Regolari adesioni scritte e sottoscritte ricevute entro il 24-IV-1952".

2 There has been a rise in recent years in the number of research projects concerning Amedeo Peyron, both within the framework of research on federalist and Europeanist movements and for anniversaries such as the celebration of the city of Turin's first twinnings. See "Amedeo Peyron. Un sindaco federalista", pp. 265-284; Rosboch (ed.), *L'opera del sindaco Amedeo Peyron: la dimensione europea di Torino*; Rosboch and Sabatino (eds.), *Atti del seminario Torino città europea*; Rosboch, "La figura di Amedeo Peyron dalla ricostruzione alle celebrazioni di Italia '61". Among previous studies, see Grosso, *Commemorazione dell'avvocato Amedeo Peyron ex sindaco di Torino*; Serafini, "Amedeo Peyron", pp. 1-4; Bareth, "Uno dei più esemplari sindaci europei"; [Bareth], "Mort d'Amedeo Peyron"; Occhiena, "Amedeo Peyron, un sindaco europeista"; Scalfaro and Porcellana, "Amedeo Peyron un uomo, una città", pp. 51-53; Petrella, "I due Peyron". There is also a brief biography written by his family, which is now also preserved in the Archivio Storico dell'Università degli Studi di Pavia (from here on ASUPv), Fondi aggregati, c. Amedeo Peyron. Documentation concerning his work for Europe instead unfortunately "vanished" during its "mysterious" transfer from Turin to Rome after Peyron left the presidency of AICCRE.

and authority deriving from long years in the important position of mayor of Turin,"[3] an appointment he held from 1951 to 1962.

The origins of Peyron's political, administrative and Europeanist commitment was not doctrinal, but as happened to many in his generation, the drive to work in favour of European unification first in a social and then in a political perspective came from the war and the profound rift resulting from the "pointless massacre" denounced by Pope Pius XII.[4] In 1942 Peyron accepted an appointment to the presidency of the High Council of the Società di San Vincenzo de' Paoli,[5] and immediately after the war he joined the Christian Democratic Party (DC), as a representative of which he was elected Municipal Councillor in Turin in 1946.[6]

The June 1951 elections in Turin were won by the centrist coalition led by the DC and were a personal success for Amedeo Peyron, who was to be elected mayor in July that year.[7] His Catholic culture, a stated desire to be totally committed to creating, as a Christian, "a people's city, on a human scale"[8] resulted in his election being perceived as that of a "mayor of the Curia".[9] Peyron instead immediately proved he was the mayor of the entire city, representing with dignity and pride the local institutions as a fundamental part of the Italian state and of the future European state. As Scalfaro and Porcellana said, "Peyron was Turin," managing to lead this city above all during difficult times.[10] He led a number of different majority coalitions, among them an alliance with the Movimento autonomista of the Piedmont Region led by Michele Rosboch and Rodolfo Sacco, while also obtaining the best election results of those years for the DC, with up to 34.8% of the votes in the 1956 local elections.

---

3 Serafini, "Amedeo Peyron", pp. 1-4.

4 On Pius XII's position in favour of the European Union, see Murgia, "I cattolici e l'Europa"; *S.S. Pie XII parle de l'Europe (1948-1957)*; Mayeur, "Pie XII et l'Europe"; Chenaux, *Une Europe vaticane?* In general, on the Catholic Church's attitude, see Di Nolfo, *Vaticano e Stati Uniti 1939-1952 (dalle carte di Myron C. Taylor)*; Citterio and Vaccaro (ed.), *Quale federalismo per quale Europa*.

5 Gagliano, "Amedeo Peyron", p. 156.

6 ASUPv, Fondi aggregati, c. Amedeo Peyron.

7 After the Liberation, Turin was governed by a left-wing coalition. Peyron, although not heading the list of Christian Democrat candidates, won about 18,000 preferences, the result of his work while in opposition in the Municipal Council and of he guaranteed support of the ecclesiastic hierarchy (Gagliano, "Amedeo Peyron", pp. 156-157).

8 Scalfaro and Porcellana, "Amedeo Peyron un uomo, una città", pp. 51-53.

9 Petrella, "I due Peyron".

10 Scalfaro and Porcellana, "Amedeo Peyron un uomo, una città", p. 51.

Amedeo Peyron is therefore a fundamental figure for understanding the genesis of the decision by the Municipality of Turin to join the newly-created association of European local institutions and the city's first twinnings.

Turin is today twinned with seven European cities and nine non-European ones. This may seem a small number if compared, for example, to Florence, twinned with 19 cities, which has also entered friendship pacts with another ten locations and entertains regular relations with an equal number of local institutions all over the world. One should not, however, judge the figures but the political work behind them. Of Turin's seven European twinnings, six were established while Peyron was mayor and had a profound political meaning. The seventh European twinning was established with the Scottish city of Glasgow in 2001, although initial approval and the beginning of procedures by the Turin municipal council started in 1982.

All this work was closely linked to the activity promoted at an international level by the CEM and, at a national level, by its Italian section. Turin sent a representative to the AICCE's constituent meeting,[11] a gesture which was not insignificant. In fact, the governing parties, and in particular the DC, although acknowledging the validity of the Europeanist cause, had not yet obtained the full and staunch support of all their members for the AICCE's federalist and Europeanist demands.[12] These requests can be summarised in the objectives of "organising pro-European action in Italy, in cooperation with those associations interested in various countries", as well as "promoting in municipalities and in other local communities action addressed at supporting the creation of a federation of European states based on local autonomies".[13] At a local level, the DC had therefore based its propaganda on the principle that the debates allowed in the Municipal Councils should concern "only the Council's administrative activities". The choice had been adopted, as seen in Florence, to prevent left-wing parties from placing international political issues on the agenda. In his programme for governing the city Peyron himself had stated as a

11 "Il convegno costitutivo dell'Associazione italiana per il Consiglio dei comuni d'Europa", p. 1 and p. 8.

12 It is significant that, although a member of the association's board of directors, the mayor of Turin was systematically represented by a delegate. When Peyron decided to unreservedly support the ideas of the movement of European local institutions, "he personally started to show an interest in the AICCE and to personally represent the municipality" at meetings. This change occurred between the end of 1952 and the beginning of 1953 (Serafini, "Amedeo Peyron", p. 2).

13 "Il convegno costitutivo dell'Associazione italiana per il Consiglio dei comuni d'Europa", p. 2.

priority the need to address the municipality's administrative and financial problems, eliminating "all sterile discussion."[14] Moreover, at a national level, in spite of the fact that De Gasperi's position was now openly in favour of the federalist idea,[15] as previously mentioned a number of representatives of the DC and of the Catholic world remained sceptical about a European choice, which they considered abstract compared to Atlantic solidarity.

However, although acknowledging modest membership levels in the AICCE, revealed after a debate in the Municipal Council,[16] one must emphasise how Piedmont was the region with the most members in the new association, thanks both to the almost complete affiliation of municipalities in the Canavese area, close to Adriano Olivetti's Movimento Comunità, and to the incisive work of federalists. Alberto Cabella,[17] at the time the MFE's regional secretary, had been entrusted

---

14 Cagliano, "Amedeo Peyron", p. 157.

15 De Gasperi matured his Europeanist ideas between 1948 and 1953. During this period the Christian Democrat statesman clarified his idea of a community of European peoples and, also thanks to Altiero Spinelli's support, proposed and supported the idea of the need for a European political community (Preda, *Storia di una speranza*, pp. 123-131).

16 "Regolari adesioni scritte e sottoscritte ricevute entro il 24-IV-1952".

17 Alberto Cabella (1927-) was born in Turin and received a classical education. During the war, to help his family following his father's death in a German prisoner-of-war camp in February 1944, he worked in a factory in Turin as a chemical technician. In February 1945 he became the leader of the factory's internal commission, undertaking intense anti-fascist and federalist activities. On April 25th, for the first time on the streets of a liberated Turin, he distributed copies of the MFE's clandestine newspaper *Unità europea*. In 1946 he became secretary of the MFE's Turin section and in 1947 secretary of the Piedmont regional section, simultaneously writing for the *Unità Europea*. In August 1947 he took part in the founding assembly of the European Union of Federalists in Montreux, where he was the youngest delegate. From 1948 to 1956 he was continuously elected a member of the central committee of the international organisation of federalist movements. In 1948 he participated in the founding of Adriano Olivetti's *Movimento Comunità* and was the MFE's adjunct national secretary with Altiero Spinelli from October 1951 to December 1952. In this role he took part in the foundation of the AICCE. After the fall of the European Defence Community, he participated in the organisation of the Congress of the European People, becoming at first the secretary general of the Initiatives Committee and then of the Congress itself from 1956 to 1958. From 1958 until 1962 he was the president of the Congress of the European Peoples' Piedmont Regional Committee. When his experience with the Congress came to an end, Cabella decided that it was necessary to work on founding a federalist party, becoming a member of the Initiatives Committee for a federalist party from 1963 to 1965. Having abandoned the militant struggle, from 1982 to 1992 he was an officer, the deputy director and then the director of the *Istituto Italiano di Cultura* in Paris. During this period he also taught at the Sorbonne Nouvelle university. After 1993 he held seminars and conferences at universities and cultural institutions on "the concept of nations and nationalism in European history." On Cabella see his autobiography at

with the task of sensitising local administrators in the Piedmont capital, in particular the mayor of Turin, on federalist ideas.[18] Cabella's work was a resounding success. According to Umberto Serafini, in December 1952 Peyron had already offered Turin's cooperation in organising the MFE's 5th Congress. On that occasion he made a speech to delegates in which Europeanist contents went well beyond merely formal positions.[19] During the Congress a motion was approved stating that the policies of the newly-founded association of local institutions were addressed at encouraging a stable relationship between "local territorial" administrations and European federalism, "in the prospect of overcoming the monopoly of central state bureaucracy in the interest of the integral preservation of national sovereignty." This document ended by launching an appeal to "all federalists, in particular those serving in local administrations, to unreservedly work to ensure the support of municipal, provincial and regional councils – where this was lacking – for the Associazione Italiana per il Consiglio dei Comuni d'Europa".[20]

However, between December 1952 and October 1953 Peyron's increasingly staunch commitment within the AICCE had forestalled the appeal contained in the motion. The mayor of Piedmont's capital had in fact presented to the Municipal Council a resolution for Turin's official membership in the movement of local institutions, faced a difficult debate, and obtained the votes of the majority in the Council.

To achieve these objectives the mayor of Turin also agreed to work in synergy with Turin's Centro Comunità[21] in order to promote the Piedmont Regional Committee for the AICCE, which was then founded in February 1954.[22] The decision to cooperate with Olivetti's movement

---

the ASUPv, Fondi aggregati, Fondo Alberto Cabella; see also "Alberto Cabella segretario nazionale aggiunto del M.F.E.".

18 In a letter dated July 1953 Umberto Serafini spoke of Peyron as a "federalist mayor", convinced of this thanks to Cabella (Magda Da Passano's private archives, Letter from Umberto Serafini to Magda Da Passano, s.d., dated July 1953).

19 [Serafini], "Il MFE per i comuni d'Europa. Due risoluzioni del Congresso di Torino"; Serafini, "Amedeo Peyron", p. 2.

20 ASUPv, Fondi aggregati, Fondo Alberto Cabella, Resoconto del V Congresso nazionale del MFE, Torino 6-8 dicembre 1952, allegato n. 5, Consiglio dei comuni d'Europa.

21 In the second half of 1953 the *Movimento Comunità* had reopened a "Cultural Centre in Central Turin". This new organisation in Turin, together with the "Centro di Borgo S. Paolo", was meant to be the starting point for increasing the movement's political influence in Piedmont's capital. The movement's best electoral results had in fact been achieved where community centres existed ("Cronaca del movimento. Riunione della D.P.E. del Movimento Comunità").

22 "Il lavoro dell'AICCE. Un comitato regionale piemontese". Peyron participated personally in the foundation of the Committee, of which the deputy mayors of Turin,

proved Peyron's ability to not allow himself to be conditioned by the party's political prejudice or by dominant rigid social-economic ideas[23] in order to achieve the lofty objectives that were envisaged.

The positive potential of the federalist "conversion" of a local administrator as important as Peyron did not escape Umberto Serafini, at the time secretary general of the AICCE, who, for the first States General of European Municipalities (as the association's great international assemblies were called) proposed to add Peyron to the list of "Italian speakers".[24] During the States General held in Versailles from October 16th to October 18th, 1953, the mayor of Turin was entrusted with the task of presiding over "l'Assemblée pionnière" on "18 octobre", attended by about one thousand two hundred delegates.[25] In the opening speech to the session, Peyron spoke of how the contribution of municipalities "à la réalisation de l'unité européenne" was "au delà des contacts et des pourparlers entre les Gouvernements, une action (...) à même de toucher et d'orienter l'opinion publique" and therefore "absolument nécessaire". He committed to intensifying the work of the Italian section to achieve the CEM's objectives, doing so while fully aware "des problèmes quotidiens, souvent très pressants et difficiles" that mayors had to address and resolve in order to guarantee acceptable living standards for their citizens.[26] The awareness that European unity should first of all be of use to citizens resulted in the social democrat Senator Alessandro Schiavi, the AICCE's first president, presenting a motion, during the session presided over by Peyron, in which he expressed the hope that "an International Institute of Credit for European Municipalities" would be created. This institute was to guarantee homes for European citizens who had survived the catastrophic war, raising funds by issuing bonds guaranteed by states

---

Guido Secreto and Emilio Bianchi, and many of Peyron's city councillors also became members.

23 Competing in the elections with government parties, the *Movimento Comunità* also had very innovative social and economic programmes that openly clashed with the dominant ones (Berta, "Fra centrismo e centro sinistra: Olivetti e il Movimento Comunità").

24 Magda Da Passano's private archives, Letter from Umberto Serafini to Magda Da Passano, dated July 1953. Seventy-eight Italian delegates attended the States General of European Municipalities, with Piedmont's thirteen local administrators, led by Amedeo Peyron and Adriano Olivetti, playing a lead role (Historical Archives of the European Union in Florence, CCRE fond, List of those attending the general assembly of the Council of European Municipalities).

25 Historical Archives of the European Union in Florence, CCRE fond, Letter dated November 10th, 1953, from Amedeo Peyron to Jean Bareth.

26 Historical Archives of the European Union in Florence, CCRE fond, c. 227, *Discours de Mr. le Maire de Turin*.

and by the municipalities. European local administrations would in this way obtain "low interest and long-term capital, encouraging (...) the construction of council houses".[27] After a lively debate, the assembly decided to create a study commission that was to present a detailed project on this subject. This marked the beginning of a first brave attempt to set up a financial institution at a European level that, had it succeeded, would have forestalled and integrated the work of some of the European Union's current institutions.[28] The importance of this proposal did not escape Amedeo Peyron, at the time busy dealing with Turin's serious housing problems, which was to be made dramatic by future massive migratory flows.[29] He assimilated the elderly socialist administrator's proposal and later made it one of the primary objectives in his European political work. The documents bearing witness to Amedeo Peyron's work, initially for the European Institute for Municipal Credit and later in favour of the European Community of Municipal Credit, which scholars believed had been lost forever, have instead been found in the municipality of Turin's historical archives. These documents are contained in various files and will allow scholars to better understand the work of this politician from Turin as well as the genesis of current European economic-financial institutions.

On August 30th, 1954, the French National Assembly failed to ratify the treaty for the European Defence Community (EDC) along with the one for the European Political Community (EPC) due to changed international conditions following Stalin's death and the evolution of the internal political situation in a number of countries.

This led to a new debate at an international level on possible European solutions. The different views regarding a possible re-launching of European unity were addressed soon after at the second major assembly of mayors belonging to the CEM,[30] organised in Venice in October 1954.[31] On that occasion the movement's federalist elements

27 "Terza seduta plenaria al Palazzo municipale di Versaglia".

28 A project similar to the one presented by Schiavi had also been approved by the Council of Europe's Advisory Assembly, but the cabinet, although acknowledging the importance of the assembly's recommendations, had sent it back to a study commission, in practice putting an end to the project ("Terza seduta plenaria al Palazzo municipale di Versaglia").

29 It is well known that after the mid-1950s Turin experienced great and frantic industrial growth that brought to the Piedmont capital a large migratory flow, initially from northern regions and then from southern ones. In 1961 the city had over one million inhabitants.

30 On the CEM's role after the fall of the EDC see Zucca, "Il Conseil des Communes d'Europe e il rilancio europeo di Messina".

31 Archives of the Conseil des Communes et Régions d'Europe, Roissy (from here on ACCRE, Roissy), c. 16, f. *Deuxième États Généraux Venise 1954*. Following its

planned to take action addressed at strengthening their presence within the CEM, so as to provide federalists with an international stage "at this delicate time"[32] to support the call for the election "au suffrage universel (...) d'une Assemblée Constituante".[33] This position, devised by Umberto Serafini in agreement with Altiero Spinelli, was unanimously supported by the Italian municipalities in the movement.[34] After a bitter debate within the commission, the CEM's various elements drafted a series of summary documents with Europeanist characteristics. Peyron also was involved in this debate, but renounced all official roles to direct the work of the Commission for European Municipal Credit, which, on September 26th, 1954, in Geneva, approved the creation[35] of the *Communauté européenne de crédit communal* (CECC).[36]

Further evidence of Amedeo Peyron's progressive and total support for federalist and Europeanist ideas comes from his acceptance in March 1955 of the vice-presidency of the AICCE[37] and the presidency of the CECC, from which position he helped the association later move to Turin[38] and establish headquarters at the Royal Palace.[39]

---

recovery from a *garde meuble* at Charles de Gaulle Airport in Paris, the ACCRE, Roissy has been added to the Historical Archives of the European Union in Florence, creating the aforementioned CCRE fond, but these new shelf-marks have maintained the previous index order which is the one used in this book.

32 The archives of the Movimento Federalista Europeo, Turin (from here on AMFE, Turin), c. Ass. int., f. ass. int. 4, Confidential letter from Umberto Serafini and Altiero Spinelli dated September 1st, 1954. In order to emphasise the federalist position, Serafini invited Spinelli to speak "following a statement from the enemy, the Gaullist Chaban-Delmas".

33 AMFE, Turin, c. Ass. int., f. ass. int. 4, Letter from Umberto Serafini to Dieter Roser dated October 1st, 1954.

34 As mentioned, the municipalities that initially joined the AICCE were mostly managed by local administrators who were at least sensitive to the MFE's ideas.

35 "The Venice resolutions".

36 Historical Archives of the European Union in Florence, CCRE fond, c. 223, Report by Alessandro Schiavi, dated May 10th 1955.

37 "Un primo resoconto del Congresso di Forlì".

38 Historical Archives of the European Union in Florence, CCRE fond, c. 223, *Procès verbal de la réunion de l'assemblée générale du comité directeur de la Communauté européenne de crédit communal*, Geneva December 1st, 1956, p. 2. The CECC's transfer from Geneva to Turin came after a period of heated discussions between the Italian presidency, held by Alessandro Schiavi, and the Swiss secretariat. The debate concerned articles of the charter, into which the Italians had introduced all possible supranational elements, including the need for the institution to be recognised by the Swiss authorities (Archives of the Conseil des Communes et Régions d'Europe, Paris – from here on ACCRE, Paris – c. *archives 1955 membres de la Communauté européenne de crédit communal*, Letter from Jean Bareth to Robert Mossé dated January 31st, 1956; ACCRE, Paris, Letter from Lucine Sergent to Erwin Freiburghaus

According to the Mayor of Turin, local and European perspectives were now organically linked. During the election campaign for the 1956 local elections he used the subject of European unity and the CEM's struggles to indicate to citizens in Piedmont's capital a new path for the city's political and economic development at a continental level.[40]

Peyron was elected vice-president during the AICCE's first congress, held in Forlì on May 14th and 15th, 1955. Alessandro Schiavi was appointed president of the association, and a second vice-presidency was conferred on Umberto Rossi, Mayor of Ivrea, with Umberto Serafini confirmed as secretary general. Revealing the political importance and the quantitative support of Piedmont municipalities, two local administrators from this region were appointed to important positions in the movement of local institutions. With his election in January 1957 to the presidency of the AICCE,[41] Peyron's Europeanist political work assumed a new political impulse since, as he himself said, "currency unification and the creation of a common market" would have contributed in providing mankind with freedom and dignity if founded on a "European political Community".[42] It was for this community and for the CEM that he worked, holding the position of president of the AICCE and member of the international board of the association of European local powers. His political position provided the association with broad institutional visibility, as shown, for example, by the attention paid by the President of the Italian Republic, Antonio Segni, to the AICCE's various initiatives, thanks in part to the efforts of its president.[43]

In this stage of his political work, Peyron also started to work on completing the first twinning for the city of Turin. As mentioned

---

dated June 22nd, 1956; ACCRE, Paris, Letter from Alessandro Schiavi to Erwin Freiburghaus dated June 21st, 1956).

39 The CECC's proactive role is mostly still unknown. Research is now possible thanks to the author having discovered in the Archivio storico della città di Torino (from here on AST) a number of large files that could provide an important basis for the work to be done.

40 Peyron, "Torino e l'Europa".

41 Peyron was elected president of the AICCE on January 3rd, 1957. He succeeded Alessandro Schiavi, who was too old to hold such a demanding international position ("A.I.C.C.E. provision dated January 3rd").

42 Peyron, "Il discorso del sindaco Peyron alla Paulskirche".

43 "Antonio Segni interviene al direttivo dell'AICCE"; news reported in bold on page 2, in the *Comuni d'Europa* in June 1962, about the private meeting between AICCE's president, Amedeo Peyron, and President Segni in Rome on June 26th, 1962. On this occasion, Segni expressed words "of great appreciation for the Association", describing it as "one of the most useful and valid means of spreading the European idea".

regarding the twinnings of the city of Florence, for some time Jean Bareth had applied pressure on Umberto Serafini to complete at least one twinning between important cities in France and Italy.

Following informal contacts, on September 28th, 1956, Chambéry's Municipal Council deliberated the jumelage with the city of Turin. The motivation was both historical, the French city's bonds with its ancient capital, and political, to implement the "new spirit of solidarity created between the municipalities of various European nations under the aegis of the Council of European Municipalities".[44] In October, Mayor Peyron immediately informed the city's Municipal Council to obtain the political-administrative council's opinion on a possible twinning with Chambéry. His prudent and capable work persuaded the entire Municipal Council to express a generally favourable opinion, leaving aside bitter divergences concerning the beginning of the European integration process, and on November 10th, 1956, it unanimously approved,[45] "voting by standing or remaining seated," the twinning with the ancient Savoyard city.[46]

The first ceremony sanctioning the twinning of Turin and Chambéry was held in Turin on May 19th, 1957. The event was celebrated at Palazzo Madama and attended by the highest-ranking Italian and French municipal authorities and councillors, as well as by economic and political delegations. The ceremony's solemnity was intended to emphasise the unanimous commitment to reconciliation between the European peoples. The excellent success of Turin's initiative encouraged Peyron to contact the Italian railroads to organise "a carriage reserved for the municipality's administrators and councillors and all the city's authorities and personalities" who would have attended the second official ceremony, to be held in Chambéry on September 15th of that same year.

Following the Turin municipality's now constant Europeanist activity, on April 19th, 1957, in Strasbourg, Amedeo Peyron was presented with the *Prix de l'Europe*, which, assigned by the Council of Europe, was at the time in its third edition.[47] The award was presented to the cities of Turin and Bordeaux, whose Mayor, Jacques Chaban-Delmas, had been both one of the CEM's founders and a leading player

44 AST, Atti Consiglio comunale, f. 60, p. 87. Consiglio comunale del 10 novembre 1956.

45 AST, Atti municipali Consiglio comunale del 22 ottobre 1956.

46 AST, Atti Consiglio comunale, f. 60, p. 87. Consiglio comunale del 10 novembre 1956.

47 AST, c. 815, Affari gabinetto del sindaco, "Il sindaco Peyron riceve a Strasburgo il "Premio Europa" per la nostra città".

in the history of European integration, although not always in a way useful to the federalist cause, as in the case of his vote against the EDC.

An analysis of documentation clearly indicates that the award was presented to Turin also for political reasons within the Strasbourg Assembly.[48] In fact, Peyron was the leader of the Italian delegation of local institutions at the advisory Assembly, while Chaban-Delmas was a leading player in the Strasbourg parliament.[49] Assigning this award to these two cities was also a way of "compensating" the two mayors' Europeanist political work and acknowledging their international roles.

In any event, the documentation presented by Turin to support its candidacy was without doubt extremely important and provided evidence of a lucid Europeanist policy. Among the various initiatives listed to support its candidature was the successful twinning with the city of Chambéry.

At the presentation of the award, Peyron said that, as a person who had for many years been a convinced Europeanist and as Mayor of Turin, he had fought for a European agreement, above all to spread the Europeanist idea and because of the contribution that local institutions can and effectively do provide for the creation of tomorrow's Europe.

Confirming the close bond between Europeanist work and local administrations, on March 22nd, 1958 Peyron proposed to the Municipal Council that half of the money won with the *Prix de l'Europe* should be given to the *Istituto universitario di studi europei*, which had "significantly contributed to making the name of Turin known in the field of juridical studies", while the rest should be given to the Department of Sport and Youth Problems, which, with a recent provision, had "created many foreign travel awards for Turin's workers".[50]

The CEM's fourth States General was held in Liège in July 1958. The assembly of local administrators acknowledged the Treaties of Rome, but strongly emphasised how the common market was only a "stage" in the European integration process that should be achieved with the "creation of a political authority, the only one capable of allowing Europe to regain its position in the world".[51]

---

48 AST, c. 815, Telegrammi e lettere augurali per il Conferimento del Premio Europa, *Conseil de l'Europe. Assemblèe consultative, Commission despouvoirs locaux*, 25 ottobre 1957.

49 AST, c. 815, Mayor's Cabinet, f. Affari gabinetto del sindaco, f. Discorsi trilingue nelle diverse edizioni, Discorso pronunciato dal sindaco di Torino, avv. Amedeo Peyron in occasione del conferimento del Premio d'Europa alla città di Torino.

50 AST, c. 815, f. *Prix de l'Europe*, Verbale Consiglio comunale del 22 marzo 1958.

51 Serafini, *Breve storia del Consiglio dei comuni e delle regioni d'Europa nel quadro di due secoli di lotta federalista*, p. 75.

In Liège the local European institutions also strongly affirmed that "the municipalities and regions are the natural birthplace of the European spirit".

It was in this spirit that in this Belgian city one of the most important multiple twinnings in European history was organised between the cities of Lille (France), Cologne (Germany), Esch-sur-Alzette (Luxembourg), the aforementioned city of Hubert Clément, co-founder of the CEM, Rotterdam (the Netherlands), Liège itself, and Turin.

The idea of a twinning between Turin and Liège had been presented by the Mayor of the Belgian city during a meeting of the CEM's International Department held in Cannes on July 7th and 8th, 1957. The proposal had been readily accepted by the AICCE's president, who, reporting to the Turin Municipal Council, spoke of how the city of Liège had been encouraged to present this proposal "following the recent conferral of the *Prix de L'Europe* on Turin" to Piedmont's capital "for its merits in the field of European unity". Peyron went on to state how the ceremony would be held during the States General of European municipalities, convened for July 1958 in Liège. The Mayor added that on that occasion three thousand European local administrators would be present in the Belgian industrial city, and "in view of the elevated meaning and spirit" that invested this initiative, as well as the "already existing sentiments of affinity between two large Belgian and Italian industrial cities", he suggested this request should be agreed to. Thanks to the ground work done earlier by a special commission, the Municipal Council unanimously approved the initiative that was to become a multiple twinning between European industrial cities, as wished by the CEM's international secretariat.[52]

Peyron presided over the twinning ceremony, but this did not prevent him from also playing an important political role within the framework of the States General. He was appointed vice-president of the Second Commission on Le Marché commun et l'avenir des communes et régions d'Europe. On this occasion, as always, he played a political role in leading the commission towards a final resolution in which, acknowledging the advent of the Common Market, local authorities asked to "faciliter les rapports des collectivités locales et des institutions europèennes, en tenant compte de l'immense contribution qu'elles peuvent mutuellement s'apporter et de mettre en place la partecipation des collectivités locales au fonctionnement de ces institutions". The commission also asked governments to sponsor internal decentralisation policies, while the new Community organisations were invited to

52 AST, Atti Consiglio Comunale città di Torino, f. 210, Consiglio comunale del 22 luglio 1957.

implement regionalisation policies,[53] an opportunity that would be achieved after a number of decades thanks specifically to the work done by the CEMR.

In this manner, Peyron played the political role of the mayor of a great European city, opening Turin even more to a continental debate that was intended not only as a cultural and economic debate but as one that was deeply-rooted in policies for the creation of a United States of Europe.

---

53 "Les IV États Generals des communes d'Europe".

CHAPTER 5

Milan as a European City

Federalist Activities and Twinning[1]

As Norberto Bobbio said, the novelty of the *Manifesto di Ventotene* was that of bringing federalism into history, transforming what in European political practices was considered utopian, a doctrine, into real political action.[2] The path that led to this political and historical awareness began with the ideas and work of the men who, through their experiences in prison and with the anti-Nazi and anti-fascist resistance, gave life to the federalist ideas and movements, of which the *Manifesto di Ventotene* is a fundamental building block. Its first political

---

1 The contents of this chapter are the result of earlier research on Milan's twinnings and international relations. This research was carried out in the framework of a broader context of studies that followed the conference entitled *Europeismo e federalismo in Lombardia dal Risorgimento all'Unione europea*, the minutes of which were published in a book with the same title, edited by the author and published by Il Mulino in 2007. One must emphasise that although this research addressed many issues, the papers available to the scholar turned out to be few, albeit providing a "central thread" for reconstructing relations and political processes that a possible future recovery of new documentary sources could enrich. In this context, the Aldo Aniasi Archives at the *Circolo De Amicis* in Milan were of fundamental importance, and, although not yet totally indexed, turned out to be a precious source (thanks to the great help provided by Fiorella Imprenti, who accompanied me by opening the doors to the Archives and whom I must therefore thank). The Archives of the Municipality of Milan, which for the period addressed here are still in the archive storage section, turned out instead to be incomplete. In particular, there was no trace of files on the twinnings of the city of Milan or on the municipality's international relations during the 1950s, 1960s and 1970s; these files had indeed existed, as proved by other sources. This deficiency was to a certain extent compensated for by the city's *Ufficio Servizio internazionalizzazione* (to which I am extremely grateful), which made available all its documentation. It is, however, indicative of differing sensitivities on the subject of preserving documentation that the municipality of Milan, one of Europe's capitals, has not as yet provided a real archival service (also required by current legislation) that is at least concerned with preserving documentation. The fact that the *Ufficio estero e città gemellate* had moved, and was then closed in 2007, with all competences moved to the *Settore relazioni internazionali* and now to the new *Servizio internazionalizzazione*, is no excuse for justifying the loss, one hopes a temporary one, of documents that should have been preserved, and not only for historical reconstructions.

2 Bobbio, *Il federalismo nel dibattito politico e culturale della Resistenza*.

achievement was the secret meeting held in Milan on August 27th and 28th, 1943, to found the MFE at the home of the Waldesian Mario Alberto Collier.[3] The contents of the document drafted on the island of Ventotene by Altiero Spinelli, Ernesto Rossi[4] and Eugenio Colorni,[5] who also consulted Ursula Hirschman,[6] at the time married to Eugenio

---

3 On the movement's constituent meeting see Levi and Pistone (eds.), *Trent'anni di vita del Movimento federalista europeo*, pp. 66-71. On Rollier see: Rognoni Vercelli, *Mario Alberto Rollier*, pp. 85-112; Gagliano (ed.), *La personalità poliedrica di Mario Alberto Rollier*.

4 Federalism was an essential and constant element in the ideas and the work of Ernesto Rossi. As proved by Antonella Braga, his federalist ideas began to emerge during his youth and then developed throughout his life. Even when the co-author of the *Manifesto di Ventotene*, following the fall of the EDC, lost all hope of achieving European federation over a reasonable period of time, Europeanist and federalist ideals remained constant elements in his thoughts and his work. On Rossi, see Rossi, *Un democratico ribelle. Cospirazione antifascista, carcere, confino: scritti e testimonianze*; *idem*, *Guerra e dopoguerra. Lettere 1915-1930*; *idem*, *Miserie e splendori dal confino di polizia*; Ignazi (ed.), *Ernesto Rossi, una utopia concreta*; Fiori, *Una storia italiana: vita di Ernesto Rossi*; Franzinelli (ed.), *Nove anni sono molti. Lettere dal carcere 1930-1939*; Braga, "La collaborazione con Ernesto Rossi nel lavoro di organizzazione e propaganda del Movimento federalista europeo in Svizzera"; *idem*, "Nazionalismo, federalismo e autonomie nel pensiero politico di Ernesto Rossi"; *idem*, *Un federalista giacobino. Ernesto Rossi pioniere degli Stati uniti d'Europa*; Franzinelli and Braga (eds.), *Ernesto Rossi. Una vita per la libertà (1897-1967). Bio-bibliografia*; Braga and Michelotti (eds.), *Ernesto Rossi. Un democratico europeo*.

5 In 1991 an edition of the *Manifesto* was published with only Altiero Spinelli's name on the cover (Spinelli, *Il Manifesto di Ventotene*). While some tend to even forget the name of the co-authors of the *Manifesto* (about whom Luigi Vittorio Majocchi wrote, "We know almost everything about this anti-fascist, stubborn, caustic and docking, unyielding and radical figure Rossi. As an aside it was also said that, obviously in a subordinated position, he assisted Spinelli and Colorni in drafting the *Manifesto di Ventotene*, but this is whispered rather than proclaimed", in Majocchi, "Prefazione", p. 12.) It is all the more important that Eugenio Colorni's role must, whenever possible, be constantly remembered to ensure it is not forgotten as some, consciously or not, have often done. On Eugenio Colorni see Degl'Innocenti (ed.), *Eugenio Colorni: dall'antifascismo all'europeismo socialista e federalista*; Cerchiai and Rota (ed.), *Eugenio Colorni e la cultura italiana fra le due guerre*; Zucca (ed.), *Eugenio Colorni federalista*; and also the collection of philosophical essays recently re-published, *La malattia della metafisica. Scritti filosofici e autobiografici*.

6 Ursula Hirschmann (Berlin 1913-Rome 1991), the daughter of a doctor of Jewish origin, joined socialist youth movements while still at high school. She met Eugenio Colorni at Berlin University where she attended the Faculty of Political Science. With the advent of Nazism in Germany, she emigrated to Paris with her brother Albert, where she continued her studies and took part in political activities. In 1936 she joined Colorni in Trieste where he was teaching and there they married. In 1938 Colorni was arrested and exiled to Ventotene, while as the wife of a an intern and as a foreigner, Ursula was able to visit the island quite freely. This allowed her to become a "precious" go-between for federalists interned on this Island. On Ventotene Ursula met Altiero Spinelli whom she was to marry after Colorni's death. For the rest

Colorni, were drafted at a historical moment that saw individual choices often fade away in the shared struggle against fascism, with its constant and at times compulsory cultural and political exchanges; these documents are still fully alive and current, because the objectives they proposed for Italy and for a federal Europe have not yet been achieved.

The debate between the various political fronts had extraordinarily fruitful results, which the Milanese context in which the founding event was held contributed to enrich and expand by drafting the *Tesi politiche federaliste*, which provided the theoretical guidelines for the creation of a federal Europe, as well as the programming and organisation required to achieve this objective.

The *Manifesto*'s theoretical guidelines included a growing awareness of the crisis experienced by the national sovereign state, a crisis that in federalist theory played a fundamental role, the same represented in liberalism by the concept of the crisis experienced by absolute monarchies, and in Marxist theory by capitalism's crisis. This allowed the authors to identify the basic contradiction in the contemporary world, formulating an overall historical judgement and consequently drafting a new political theory compared to the dominant political schools of thought of the times.

This perspective allowed the three authors to analyse in-depth the causes of nationalism, imperialism and fascism, observing how at the basis of nationalism there was a symbiosis between state and nation, which, creating an explosive mix, had developed authoritarian tendencies within states and aggressive ones at an international level. Fascism was defined as the arrival point in the national state's historical evolution, the expression of increasingly simmering warlike and authoritarian tendencies within the closed and centralised organisation of the national state that exploded when the battle for power in Europe deteriorated.

The reaction to this existing situation was the idea of a federal form of government, capable of guaranteeing unity within diversity, following the achievement of permanent peace between a group of democratic states. Federalism on the one hand envisaged a new form of international organisation, suited to the size of the economic and social problem, while on the other simultaneously presented a new form of

---

of her life she actively shared with Spinelli his federalist commitment also founding in Brussels in 1975 the movement *Femmes pour l'Europe*. On Hirschmann see Spinelli, *Come ho tentato di diventare saggio. Io Ulisse*; Hirschmann, *Noi senza patria*; and also the important introduction written by Maurizio Degl'Innocenti for the minutes of the conference on Eugenio Colorni held in Rome in 2009: see Degl'Innocenti, "Introduzione a Eugenio Colorni".

state capable of contributing in a fundamental manner not only to peace on the European continent but to the world.

Spinelli remembers that during the MFE constituent meeting in Milan those present, who culturally belonged to different political schools of thought and were mostly part of the Lombard capital's political-social fabric,[7] had indeed read and approved the outline of the documents that accompanied the invitation, both the *Manifesto di Ventotene* and the *Tesi politiche federaliste*, but considered themselves more like a choir than the real leading players in creating this movement, leaving Colorni, Rossi and himself the responsibility of accepting or rejecting their advice.[8]

What did emerge from this meeting and became consolidated among those present was the perception of the topicality as well as the need for a European federation as a political objective, which had become possible in the historical context of World War II and the Resistance, as well as the necessary reconstruction of Europe on new foundations moving beyond the concept of the sovereign nation state. Centralised national states, having exposed the problem of security and expansion as the priority in their international policies, had been forced to relegate to a lower level the needs for internal freedom and decentralisation, favouring instead militaristic, centralistic and authoritarian tendencies, which had led to the totalitarianism of the Nazi-Fascist regimes as well as the politics of power.[9] A European federation could permanently resolve the problem by changing the international picture and therefore allowing a different approach to the problem of security in order to achieve continental and potentially global peace.

During the Resistance the MFE therefore found a fertile environment in Milan for political debate and propaganda. The DC's programme for Milan hoped for the creation of a federation of European states "based on free systems", with a "direct representation of the people added to that of governments," the creation of international armed forces, as well as the adoption of European citizenship in addition to the national one.[10]

---

7 On those gathered for the MFE's constituent meeting see Rognoni Vercelli, *Mario Alberto Rollier*, pp. 100-110.

8 Ivi, p. 95.

9 On the politics of power see the fundamental work of Dehio, *Equilibrio o egemonia*; *idem*, *La Germania e la politica mondiale del XX secolo*; and Pistone's essay entitled *Ludwig Dehio*.

10 "Programma del Partito democratico cristiano". The programme quoted by the federalist newspaper was the one drafted between 1942 and 1943 by the group promoting the new party and published with the title *Idee ricostruttive della Democrazia cristiana*. One must, however, emphasise that a position in favour of European unity would be less outlined in the next programme drafted by Alcide De

Clandestine newspapers such as *Democrazia*, published in Milan after February 1944, and *L'uomo. Giornale degli uomini d'Italia* published a number of articles in favour of European federation thanks in part to the influence of federalist militants who had participated in founding the MFE.[11]

Between 1944 and 1945, the newspapers of the Milanese Republican Party supported the federalist supra-national theses that indicated a United States of Europe as the political objective in the continent's reorganisation.[12]

The Milanese Partito d'Azione (PdA), which basically represented the heart of the party in northern Italy, was the political movement that had the closest relations with the MFE, in part because many of the federalist movement's founders had belonged to it.[13] Later additional federalist conversions resulted in political and organisational mingling.[14]

Gasperi in November 1943, published by the clandestine edition of the *Popolo* on December 12th, 1943, signed Demofilo [Alcide De Gasperi]. In this article the author restricted himself to hoping that "the Anglo-Saxon world" would promote "also in Old Europe, a region of peaceful solidarity among equal peoples" based on the model provided by the British Commonwealth or the Pan-American Union (Damilano (ed.), *Atti e documenti della Democrazia cristiana 1943-1967*, pp. 9-11and pp. 32-33).

11 Frosio Roncalli, "La segreteria nazionale del MFE a Milano: la gestione Umberto Campagnolo", p. 274.

12 *Ibidem*.

13 Among the founders of the MFE who also joined the PdA one should remember Arialdo Banfi, Alberto Damiani, Vittorio Foa, Giovanni Gallo Granchielli, Leone Ginzburg, Enrico Giussani, Alberto Mortara, Dino Roberto, Mario Alberto Rollier, Ada Rossi, Manlio Rossi Doria, Ernesto Rossi, Altiero Spinelli, Gigliola Spinelli and Franco Venturi. PdA members who joined the MFE during the war and played an important role later on included Giulio Bergman, Luciano Bolis, Bruno Caizzi, Mario Dal Pra, Franco Formiggini, Egidio Reale and Guido Rollier (these lists were made comparing names of those who participated in the founding of the MFE reported by Rognoni Vercelli in *Mario Alberto Rollier*, p. 89, and those of PdA members quoted by De Luna in his *Storia del Partito d'Azione 1942-1947*).

14 The level of organisational cooperation became clear immediately after the Liberation when the men and offices of the PdA and the MFE were in many cases one and the same (Colombo, *Per una storia del federalismo italiano: il dibattito interno del Movimento Federalista Europeo dal 1945 al 1948*, pp. 99-100). The book analyses a number of cases concerning cities in northern Italy, although research should be completed with a broader analysis of the territory. Objective cooperation led some to describe the PdA as the "federalist party par excellance" (Collotti, *Solidarietà europea e prospettive di un nuovo ordine internazionale nel pensiero della Resistenza italiana*, p. 45); others are instead more cautious in sharing this assessment (speech made by Giovanni De Luna at the conference on *Émile Chanoux et le débat sur le fédéralisme*, held in Aosta on November 24th and 25th, 1995); unfortunately, this speech, like many others, was not added as an appendix to the minutes. See Louvain *et al.*, *Emile Chanoux et le débat sur le fédéralisme*). For the moment there is no paper that has analysed this subject in depth.

After initial hesitations, Spinelli himself had joined the PdA to permeate it with the federalist vision and to ensure that, through converted members, the federalist ideas would reach the *Comitato di Liberazione Nazionale*, which, in his opinion, was to become "il nucleo della futura classe politica democratica".[15]

Relations with the Resistance's socialist and communist elements were more complex. Both Lombard and Milanese reformists had, over time, already addressed the issue of a reorganisation of Italy and Europe in a federal or confederate manner,[16] especially through the debate that had taken place in magazines such as *Critica sociale*,[17] as the political context of those years was not initially fertile for widely spreading federalist ideas within the Milanese socialist party. On the other hand, the more rigorously Marxist socialists and those who fully approved of the pact for united action with the Communists entered upon in September 1943 rejected the federalist programme.[18] This did not mean

15 Spinelli, *Come ho tentato di diventare saggio. La goccia e la roccia*, p. 71.

16 On relations between socialism and Europeanist federalism see Zucca, "Il riformismo socialista lombardo e la questione dell'unità europea", and the essay by Ragusa, "Eugenio Colorni dall'antifascismo all'Europeismo socialista e federalista". In the vast bibliography on the history of the socialist party, its international policy, and relations with the PCI, see among others Benzoni and Tedesco, *Il movimento socialista del dopoguerra*; Galli, *Storia del socialismo italiano*; Ciuffoletti *et al.*, *Storia del P.S.I.*; Felisini, *1943-1957. Il Partito socialista italiano e l'integrazione europea*; *I socialisti e l'Europa. Annali della Fondazione G. Brodolini e della Fondazione di studi storici Filippo Turati*; Benzoni - Guitti - Landolfi (eds.), *La dimensione internazionale del socialismo italiano*; Lizzadri, *Il socialismo italiano dal frontismo al centro sinistra*; Amato, *Il PSI tra frontismo e autonomia*; Arfè, *Intellettuali e società di massa*; Canavero, "Pietro Nenni, i socialisti italiani e l'Internazionale socialista tra Est e Ovest dopo la seconda guerra mondiale". On relations between Socialists and Communists on the subject of European unity see Maggiorani and Ferrari (eds.), *L'Europa da Togliatti a Berlinguer*.

17 *Critica sociale* was the most important Italian socialist magazine between the end of the 19th century and the first decades of the 20th. Banned by fascism in 1926, publication was resumed the day after the country was liberated. Initially it was the expression of the only Italian socialist party, to later become the voice and the cultural workshop for the reformist school of thought. On the magazine's foundation and early years see Turati's personal opinion expressed in Turati, *Trent'anni di Critica sociale*, pp. 1-4.

18 On the socialist's attitude to action taken in favour of a European federation, that of Sandro Pertini was exemplary. The future President of the Italian Republic initially expressed his support for the *Manifesto* only to then withdraw it. In receiving Italian members of the European parliament on October 7th, 1982, Pertini turned to Spinelli and publicly explained that gesture: "Ero completamente d'accordo con te, ma quando i miei compagni all'interno seppero che avevo firmato il Manifesto, mi fecero sapere che non erano d'accordo con questo mio gesto che complicava i rapporti del partito socialista con gli altri. Ed io, per restare fedele al partito, ho obbedito" (Spinelli, *Come ho tentato di diventare saggio. Io Ulisse*, p. 313. Transl. "I was completely in agreement with you, but when my fellow party members learned

that individual militants did not join the movement, providing a fundamental contribution to the socialist work and ideas, with men such as the Milanese Eugenio Colorni, Guglielmo Usellini,[19] future secretary of the Union of European Federalists (UEF), or groups such as the one led in Zurich by Ignazio Silone.[20] Their position was linked to the experience of the Socialist Party's *Centro Estero*, which, in searching for new paths for socialism, had identified federalism and autonomy as possible answers for the reconstruction of democracy in Italy and in Europe. In November 1944 the Italian Socialist Party for Proletarian Unity (PSIUP) had, thanks to the work done by Eugenio Colorni, adopted a motion in which it expressed the hope that a federal organisation of European states could be achieved as the premise for a Union of Socialist Republics. In this sense the socialists were committed to providing their support to movements working in favour of a Federation of European Peoples, founded on the people's need to establish economic and political unity at a higher level than states and all forms of national autarchy.[21] Membership was, however, conditioned by two preliminary issues previously expressed by the party, which for years were to influence official relations between the future Italian Socialist Party (PSI) and the MFE. The first concerned the political, economic and social homogeneity of the peoples and the states that would have joined the federation, while the second was the binding need for the

that I had signed the Manifesto, they made it known that they did not agree with what I had done and that due to that gesture relations between the socialist parties and others had become complicated. Out of loyalty to the party, I obeyed"). Pertini concluded this speech adding, "Oggi non lo farei" (transl. "I would not do the same today"). On the subordinated position assumed by some European socialist parties with regards to Communist parties, and therefore the obligation not to accept federalist ideas, see Arfè, "Presentazione".

19 On Colorni and Usellini as socialist federalist militants see Zucca, "Eugenio Colorni, Guglielmo Usellini e l'Unità europea".

20 The debate with federalists exiled in Switzerland, especially with Ernesto Rossi, persuaded Silone to be among the first to sign the *Manifesto di Ventotene*. He did, however, feel the need to set the federalist idea within a socialist framework. On Silone's federalist position, see Signori, *Ignazio Silone nell'esilio svizzero*; Landuyt, "Un tentativo di rinnovamento del socialismo italiano. Silone e il Centro estero di Zurigo"; Napolitano, *Il socialismo federalista di Ignazio Silone*.

21 "Adesione socialista". The MFE's clandestine newspaper commented with great satisfaction the resolution adopted by the PSIUP's congress, because it perceived in this the firm support of socialists for the ideas presented, above all in that it recognised that the objective involving European unification should not be subordinated to the implementation of socialism "integrally and everywhere in all its classic postulates." The extent to which this perception was unfounded would become clear immediately after the liberation. On Colorni's work see Fabio Zucca, "Eugenio Colorni, Guglielmo Usellini e l'Unità europea".

United States of Europe to join the Union of Soviet Socialist Republics (USSR).[22]

The merit of the debate concerning the problem of European unity was that of having stimulated a political and ideological debate within socialist circles, which allowed, on the one hand, the widespread and strong support of the social-democratic elements, and on the other the reciprocal enrichment with the mainly orthodox socialist elements that allowed the foundations for the later development of the federalist ideal to be established.

Communists perceived the *Manifesto di Ventotene* as an anti-Marxist and intrinsically reactionary document. Thus, starting with the spreading of federalist ideas in Ventotene[23] the Manifesto was supported only by Marxist intellectuals on the verge of heresy[24] or by occasional groups of Communist militants who later abandoned the MFE.[25]

The birth of the PSIUP sanctioned both the reconstruction of a socialist movement in Italy, broken up during the Fascist period, and an attempt to bring into the same fold the groups that identified with all

---

22 Signori, *La* Svizzera *e i fuorusciti*, p. 181.

23 On the manner in which Communists reacted to the *Manifesto* see Spinelli's account in his *Come ho tentato di diventare saggio. Io Ulisse*, pp. 312-313. For a comparison between the federalist and the Marxist ideas see Levi, "Internazionalismo marxista e federalismo", *Mondo Operaio*, 7-8 (July-August 1976) and *Mondo Operaio*, 10 (October 1976); Monteleone, "Le ragioni teoriche del rifiuto della parola d'ordine degli Stati Uniti d'Europa nel movimento comunista internazionale". As is well known, Palmiro Togliatti blamed the Marshall Plan for being the first step towards a division of Europe into two blocks by creating an indissoluble connection between all possible political and economic integration of non-soviet Europe and American imperialism (Togliatti, "Il Piano Marshall"). On the PCI's attitude regarding the European integration process, see a number of papers written at the time of those events, such as Sereni, *L'europeismo, l'Italia e la CED*; *idem*, *Argomenti per l'Europa*; as well as the essays by Galante, *Il Partito comunista italiano e l'integrazione europea*; *idem*, *L'autonomia possibile*; Galli, *Storia del PCI*; Gualtieri, *Togliatti e la politica estera italiana*; Maggiorani, *L'Europa degli altri*; Maggiorani and Ferrari (eds.), *L'Europa da Togliatti a Berlinguer*.

24 One of the very few Communist intellectuals who in some way did not prejudicially reject the federalist ideas was Umberto Terracini (Terracini, *Al bando dal Partito*, p. 109; *idem*, *Intervista sul comunismo difficile*).

25 In Turin, for example, just after the war a number of Communist militants joined the MFE section, certainly one of the most active together with Milan, but later federalist work in favour of a European union, which would only include countries in Western Europe following the Marshall Plan, resulted in them leaving the movement (Paper presented by Gustavo Malan, at the conference *Europeismo e federalismo in Piemonte tra le due guerre mondiali. La Resistenza e i Trattati di Roma (1957)*, held in Turin on October 9th and 10th, 1997; and Pistone, "Il contributo del movimento Federalista Europeo del Piemonte alla lotta per l'unità europea negli anni 1945-1957", p. 62).

socialist and reformist policies. The continuous debate between the various elements marked the party's brief history until the split at Palazzo Barberini in January 1947.

In addition to the fundamental subject of socialism's autonomy from the Italian Communist Party (PCI), the internal debate that led to the split was characterised by the various positions on the subject of socialist commitment to a united Europe. Militants who gathered around *Iniziativa socialista*, empowered in part by the federalist teachings of Eugenio Colorni, and those close to *Critica sociale*, inspired by the ideas of Filippo Turati implemented by the Milanese Ugo Guido Mondolfo,[26] perceived the federalist and Europeanist commitment from a 'third force' perspective as a reaction to the creation of international blocks.[27] Militants who joined the social-democratic element of Italian reformism had therefore been mainly sensitive to the subject of a European federation since the end of the 1940s, while for most socialists it would take a few more years to achieve a Europeanist position.

At the end of the war, Milan continued to be the main centre for federalist propaganda, strengthened by the presence in the city on September 9th and 10th, 1945, of the movement's organisational conference,[28] which gathered together the representatives of regional sections in the Valle d'Aosta, Piedmont, Lombardy, Veneto, Tuscany and Emilia Romagna. *L'Unità europea*, the MFE newspaper,[29] was published in

---

26 Ugo Guido Mondolfo, who was born in Senigallia in 1875 and died in Milan in 1958, joined the PSI at a very young age and was elected Municipal Councillor in Milan and then appointed Town Planning Councillor in 1919 by the socialist administration in the Lombard capital. During the 1930s he became a director of *Critica sociale*. A high school history teacher, he was dismissed from his job in 1938 because he was Jewish. Two years later he was sent into internal exile. In 1943 he managed to flee to Switzerland. After World War II he became editor-in-chief of *Critica sociale* and a member of parliament in the first republican legislature. After the Palazzo Barberini rift he joined the Italian Socialist Democratic Party (PSDI). On Mondolfo's Europeanism see Cofrancesco, "La battaglia federalista di U.G. Mondolfo"; *idem*, "La 'Battaglia per il socialismo' di U.G. Mondolfo"; Alfassio Grimaldi, "Il federalismo della 'Critica' mondolfiana".

27 In the vast bibliography available on the subject of a United States of Europe see in particular, Masini, "Filippo Turati e gli Stati Uniti d'Europa"; Cialdea, "Presupposti di un'Unione Europea"; Alfassio Grimaldi, "Il federalismo della 'Critica' mondolfiana"; Valeri, "L'idea federalista e l'Internazionale nella 'Critica' turatiana"; Decleva, "I socialisti fra unità europea e politica dei blocchi"; Solari, *I giovani di "Rivoluzione socialista"*; Punzo, *Dalla Liberazione a Palazzo Barberini*; Solari, "Colorni e il federalismo socialista"; Decleva, "La politica estera: dal frontismo alla riscoperta dell'Europa"; Sebastiani, *Laburisti inglesi e socialisti italiani*; Taddei, *Il socialismo italiano del dopoguerra*; as well as the previously mentioned book about Eugenio Colorni.

28 Levi and Pistone (eds.), *Trent'anni di vita del Movimento federalista europeo*, p. 39.

29 Rognoni Vercelli, *Mario Alberto Rollier*, p. 186.

Milan, where it had its offices, although publishing was temporarily suspended in August 1945 due to a lack of funds. The movement's first national headquarters were also opened in Via Montenapoleone in Milan,[30] while the Milanese managerial group took leadership of the MFE, basically until 1948, bringing one of its own members, Umberto Campagnolo,[31] into the national secretariat.

The work of Milanese federalist forces also received economic and political support from Milanese and Lombard industrial circles, which were attentive to international political change and also to financing a movement the objective of which was to create a new Europe perceived both as a barrier against the Communist threat and as a possible opportunity for economic development.[32]

In this sense the Europeanist rally organised at Milan's *Teatro Lirico* on June 1st, 1947, was exemplary. The event was an extraordinary success, filling the theatre's two thousand seats. The objective of this great mobilisation was achieved also thanks to careful public relations financially supported, among others, by sponsors such as the Falck steelworks, the publishing house Rizzoli and Snia Viscosa.[33]

The Milanese MFE thus continued to become consolidated within the city fabric, acquiring the support of the socialist mayor Antonio Greppi, one of the promoters of the revival of the magazine *Critica sociale* and a future president of the MFE's Milanese section,[34] and that of the Rector of the University of Milan, Felice Perussia, the Rector of the *Politecnico di Milano*, as well as the future Social Democratic mayor, Gino Cassinis.[35] Cassinis was the advocate of the *Manifesto*

---

30 *L'Unità europea*, 10 (May 6th, 1945), p. 2: addresses of the movements headquarters in Milan and Turin are provided at the bottom of the page.

31 On Umberto Campagnolo, a controversial figure in federalist circles who led the MFE from October 1946 to April 1947, see the quoted essay by Moris Frosio Roncalli and also Bobbio, "Un uomo del secolo: Umberto Campagnolo"; Mancuso, "Il federalismo democratico di Umberto Campagnolo" and the file named "Pour commémorer Umberto Campagnolo", in the 1978 vol. 43-44 of the magazine *Comprendere*, published by the Società Europea di Cultura, founded and edited by Campagnolo until his death in 1976.

32 Petrini, "Gli industriali lombardi, la Confindustria e l'Europa negli anni Cinquanta".

33 Archives of the Movimento federalista europeo, Turin (from here on AMFE, Turin), c. 1947.

34 Antonio Greppi (1894-1982), a member of the Italian Socialist party's executive committee since 1920, was obliged to take refuge in Switzerland on December 26th, 1943, settling in Mendrisio. After hearing of the death of his son Mario, who died fighting for the Resistance in August 1944, he returned to Italy to actively participate in the Resistance, joining the Matteotti VIII brigade. He became the first mayor of a liberated Milan, continuing his militancy in the socialist party. See Greppi, *La coscienza in pace. Cinquant'anni di socialismo.*

35 Frosio Roncalli, "La segreteria nazionale del MFE a Milano", p. 286.

degli universitari italiani per la federazione delle nazioni d'Europa signed by 266 Italian university professors.[36] This *Manifesto* proposed for the first time the constitution of a united Europe as a juridical instrument capable of fully implementing the federalist European objective. Both Greppi, won over to federalist ideas while exiled in Switzerland,[37] and Cassinis[38] were thus fully integrated in the process involving reciprocal enrichment between the Social Democrats and Milanese federalists.

Following the federalist movement's second national conference, on June 6th, 1948, acknowledging the new political prospects presented by the Marshall Plan,[39] together with Ernesto Rossi, Altiero Spinelli took over the leadership of the MFE, replacing Umberto Campagnolo as the movement's secretary general. Spinelli moved the movement's headquarters from Milan to Rome.[40] The federalist leader's new objective was to induce the Italian government, in particular De Gasperi, to move on the path towards European federal integration.

The MFE's new secretariat sent Luciano Bolis to Milan,[41] effectively placing under compulsory administration the Milanese section, which had partly opposed the new federalist policies, which were less revolutionary and more attentive to the evolution of national and international politics and the political opportunities linked to this. Between the end of the 1940s and the early 1950s, the MFE's activism and consequent reinforcement at a local and national level[42] were able to

---

36 *Mondo europeo. Rivista di civiltà europea*, 7 (July-August 1946); *L'Unità europea*, 17 (September 1948); *L'action fédéraliste européenne*, 3 (November 1946).

37 Frosio Roncalli, "La segreteria nazionale del MFE a Milano", p. 286.

38 On Gino Cassinis' political and administrative activities see in particular: Punzo, "Gino Cassinis, sindaco di Milano"; Landoni, *Il laboratorio delle riforme*, pp. 445-514; *idem*, "L'attività dell'Amministrazione Comunale da Cassinis ad Aniasi".

39 To set the Marshall Plan in the context of European integration, among the many books written see Melandri, *Les États-Unis face à l'unification de l'Europe 1945-1954*; Aga Rossi (ed.), *Il piano Marshall e l'Europa*; Bossuat, *L'Europe occidentale à l'heure américaine*; *idem*, *La France, l'aide américaine et la construction européenne 1944-1954*; Ellwood, *L'Europa ricostruita*; Mammarella, *Europa-Stati Uniti, un'alleanza difficile 1945-1985*; Mammarella and Cacace, *Storia e politica dell'Unione europea (1926-2005)*.

40 Pistone, "La lotta del Movimento Federalista Europeo dalla Resistenza alla caduta della Comunità Europea di Difesa nel 1954", pp. 22-33.

41 On Luciano Bolis see Preda and Rognoni Vercelli (eds.), *Dalla Resistenza all'Europa. Il mondo di Luciano Bolis*; Rognoni Vercelli, *Luciano Bolis dall'Italia all'Europa*.

42 At that time the MFE was a movement experiencing fast expansion and with important political links to the parties in power. In 1951 there were 264 officially registered sections, which in 1952 became 350 and by June 1954 about 1,000; membership rose from 20,000 in 1952 to 50,000 in 1954. Two parliamentary groups

benefit from further momentum due to a favourable context in which Italy participated in the creation of the European Coal and Steel Community (ECSC) and in political negotiations for the creation of the first EDC and then the EPC, which led to public opinion and the political parties in power having a favourable attitude to Europeanist subjects.

In this context, particularly sensitive to Europeanist and federalist initiatives, the founding of the CEM in 1951 and its Italian section the following year did not attract particular attention from the Milanese political class linked to the MFE. This may also be attributable to the initial perplexities experienced by Spinelli, who was convinced of the need to focus all energy on the creation of a United States of Europe, to be achieved by influencing the governments in smaller European countries. This resulted in delays in support for the initiative from the MFE, which, only following pressure from Luciano Bolis,[43] who in the meantime had moved to Genoa, took initiatives addressed at encouraging the creation of a movement of European local autonomies in Italy.

On October 16th, 1951, a circular letter signed both by the MFE and by Adriano Olivetti's *Istituto italiano per i Centri comunitari*, was sent to a number of centrist mayors known for their Europeanist militancy.[44] In this letter, mayors were asked to join the movement of local autonomies. To persuade other local administrators to join the CEM's new Italian section, specific action was taken that involved directly contacting political representatives close to the MFE, whatever their political inclinations may have been.

In Milan of significance was the letter with which the MFE invited Pietro Bucalossi, at the time a Milan municipal councillor representing the Socialist Party of Italian Workers (PSLI), to take an initiative similar to the one that Bolis, who in the meantime had joined the Social Democratic Party, had successfully accomplished in Genoa with the

---

for European Union had been created, joined among others by Alcide De Gasperi, the group's president in the House of Representatives, Ugo La Malfa, Mariano Rumor, as well as by federalists such as Natale Santero, president of the group in the Senate, Giuseppe Caron, Celeste Bastianetto (Comitato direttivo nazionale del MFE, "Verso il IV Congresso del MFE"; "Relazione organizzativa del Segretario aggiunto per il VI Congresso nazionale del MFE, Genova 11-13 giugno 1954", p. 1 and pp. 18-20).

43 Zucca, "L'azione di Luciano Bolis per la costituzione dell'Associazione italiana per il Consiglio dei Comuni d'Europa".

44 AMFE, Turin, c. 1951, G, f. g 34, 1951, copy of a letter to the mayor of Ancona dated November 8th, 1951, in which this circular letter is mentioned.

city's mayor.[45] Bucalossi was asked to persuade the mayor of Milan to join the CEM, by ensuring the municipal council or government approved a motion on this initiative or, if necessary, by joining the movement as an individual member.[46]

The Social Democratic councillor's initiative had no effect on his fellow party member and mayor, Virgilio Ferrari, since at the AICCE's constituent meeting in January 1952 no request for membership, in any form whatsoever, had been sent by the municipality of Milan.[47] The only sign of attention was the participation in a private capacity of the Social Democratic Municipal Councillor Lamberto Jori, who was invited to preside over the opening session of the constituent conference.[48]

Federalist work on the municipality of Milan did not stop, and in January 1953 it led to Mayor Ferrari and many other mayors of cities that were provincial capitals to support the MFE's appeal for a European "constituent assembly".[49]

In December 1952 the MFE's 5th national conference was held in Turin at Palazzo Madama. On that occasion the movement approved a motion – presented among others by Luciano Bolis, Umberto Serafini, Ursula Spinelli Hirschmann and Mario Alberto Rollier – which, as mentioned in previous chapters, overcame the initial diffidence of constitutionalist federalists regarding the newly-created association of European local autonomies,[50] stating:

> la formula giuridico-politica dell'Associazione Italiana per il Consiglio dei Comuni d'Europa (AICCE) (...) si è rivelata quella che, senza ostacoli formali inerenti alla legislazione italiana sugli enti locali, può legare stabilmente le amministrazioni territoriali locali al federalismo europeo,

---

45 Zucca, "L'azione di Luciano Bolis per la costituzione dell'Associazione italiana per il Consiglio dei Comuni d'Europa". Bolis had joined the Social Democratic Party convinced that the new party would become a useful instrument in the federalist struggle for a United States of Europe (Rognoni Vercelli, *Con Spinelli alla testa del MFE*, p. 233).

46 AMFE, Turin, c. 1951, G, f. g 34, 1951, copy of a letter to Pietro Bucalossi dated October 4th, 1951.

47 "Regolari adesioni scritte e sottoscritte ricevute entro il 24-IV-1952".

48 "Il convegno costitutivo dell'Associazione italiana per il Consiglio dei comuni d'Europa (Rome January 26th-27th, 1952)", p. 1.

49 "Sindaci di capoluogo firmatari dell'impegno per la Costituente". On federalist initiatives taken during those years, see Pistone, "La lotta del Movimento Federalista Europeo dalla Resistenza alla caduta della Comunità Europea di Difesa nel 1954".

50 Zucca, "L'azione di Luciano Bolis per la costituzione dell'Associazione italiana per il Consiglio dei Comuni d'Europa".

> nella prospettiva del superamento del monopolio della burocrazia centrale statale, interessata alla integrale conservazione della sovranità nazionale.[51]

The motion therefore committed:

> il nuovo Comitato centrale e tutti i federalisti, particolarmente quelli che risiedono nelle amministrazioni locali, a dare la loro opera senza riserve per l'adesione dei Consigli comunali, provinciali, regionali – che ancora non l'avessero fatto – all'Associazione Italiana per il Consiglio dei Comuni d'Europa.[52]

This clear stand finally led socialist and federalist Lamberto Jori, at the time Councillor for the Arts and Entertainment of Milan (led by Mayor Virgilio Ferrari, who was his fellow party member), to attend the first States General of European Municipalities held in Versailles in October 1953. Here he was elected a member of the CEM's International committee,[53] thereby also becoming a member of the AICCE's executive council[54] presided over by Senator Alessandro Schiavi.

While the participation in a personal capacity of Jori – an authoritative member of the Milan Resistance and co-signer for the PSIUP of the *Comunicato di Assunzione dei poteri* issued by Lombardy's *Comitato di Liberazione Nazionale* on April 26th, 1945[55] – did not yet lead to that of the municipality of Milan, his work paved the way for a dialogue between the AICCE and the Lombard capital that took place on April 5th, 1956, when the Municipal Council at last deliberated that it would join the association of European local autonomies.[56] After that date, in his various positions as alderman or

---

[51] Transl. "AICCE political and juridical structure has proved to be the only one able to move around formal problems pertaining to the Italian regulations on local authorities. Local instituions therefore are steadily linked to European federalism, in the common goal to overtake central state bureaucratic monopoly, whose onlyinterest lies in the total preservation of national sovereignty".

[52] Transl. "the new Central Committee and all federalists, especially those residing in local institutions, to act without reservation in favour of the adhesion to AICCE of city, provincial and regional councils which haven't yet done so."

[53] "Membri italiani dell'Esecutivo del CCE".

[54] "Consiglio direttivo dell'AICCE".

[55] Among other initiatives, Lamberto Jori was one of the founders of the *Istituto storico della Resistenza* in Lombardy, which, created in June 1948, was initially hosted at Milan's *Castello Sforzesco*. The Lombard institute's executive committee was formed by its president Ferruccio Parri, Mario Bendiscioli, a professor at Pavia University, as the director of its archives, and Municipal Councillor Lamberto Jori as treasurer and secretary (Pavone (ed.), *Storia d'Italia nel secolo ventesimo. Strumenti e fonti*).

[56] See data bank at the AICCRE Archives in Rome.

municipal councillor, Lamberto Jori continued to play an active role in representing the city of Milan in the AICCE and in the CEM's international associations, establishing relations between the municipality of Milan and other European local institutions.[57]

The political and cultural activities of the reformist wing of Milanese and Lombard socialism concerning federalist and Europeanist issues was therefore totally clear; and they represented a role that in other Italian local institutions was almost exclusively the privilege of the DC. This process, which led to a clear political choice in favour of European integration,[58] was also made clear in articles that appeared in *Critica sociale*. In the August 15th-16th, 1947 issue, Ugoberto Alfassio Grimaldi[59] pointed out how the objective of creating a European federation had now become not only an issue to be debated but one on which political action should be taken. Socialists should acknowledge the need to create a European federation, and Saragat's party, which,

---

57 Traces of these activities that continued over the next decades are documented in "Il Direttivo dell'AICCE. Dibattito capitolino su fini e mezzi"; "Il dibattito politico" – on the basis of the minutes of the work done by the AICCE national executive board, it appears that Jori, who was no longer an alderman, attended the meeting as Milan's municipal councillor; "Ora drammatica" – at the AICCE's National council, Jori presented together with Mario Zagari and Carlo Zoli, among others, a unanimously approved document on the need to proceed on the path to a federal union of Europe that was, however, to take into account the role played by local institutions; "Assemblea dei delegati del CCE a Torino"; *Comuni d'Europa*, 11 (November 1964).

58 On the pro-western choice made by Italian reformists see Zagari, "Il socialismo italiano e l'europeismo. Testimonianza"; De Felice, "La socialdemocrazia e la scelta occidentale dell'Italia (1946-1947)"; Colarizi, *Storia dei partiti nell'Italia repubblicana*, pp. 151-154; De Felice, "Il PSLI e la scelta occidentale (1948-1949)".

59 Ugoberto Alfassio Grimaldi, from Voghera, was a representative of the Lombard school of reformists linked to *Critica sociale*, of which he became the editor-in-chief from 1974 to 1981, as well as a diehard Europeanist and federalist. Born in Asti on November 5th, 1915, he graduated in Law from Pavia University and then joined the fascist movement. In 1944 he was dismissed from his position as a teacher at the Voghera high school because he was considered an 'undesirable element.' This marked the beginning of his anti-fascist militancy, which resulted in his being responsible for the distribution of propaganda material against the regime in Salò. After the war, in 1946 he joined the socialist party, becoming a member of its central committee. A friend and advisor to Saragat, he followed him after the Palazzo Barberini scission in May 1947. A number of letters addressed to him, three from Mario Albertini, dated November 9th, December 13th and December 16th, 1954, and one from Gino (Luigi Vittorio) Majocchi reveal his close relations with federalists, among whom, in particular, Mario Albertini himself, the movement's leader and theoretician from the 1970s on. Albertini would send Alfassio Grimaldi texts of articles to be published in *Critica sociale*. Copies of these letters, of which the family has the originals, are now at Pavia University's *Centro interdipartimentale di ricerca e documentazione sulla storia del Novecento.*

after rifts and reunifications within the world of autonomist socialism, was in 1952 to take the name of the Italian Socialist Democratic Party (PSDI),[60] should commit "on the subject of Europe, immediately establishing contact with socialist parties in other countries" in order to draft a common programme for the creation of a United States of Europe.

While Ugoberto Alfassio Grimaldi along with Ivan Matteo Lombardo[61] can be considered a significant example of the attention of and the decisive choices made by Lombard and Milanese Social Democratic militants immediately after the war in favour of the struggle for European unity, different paths were followed by socialists who, while temporarily constrained in an alliance with no future with Italian Communists,[62] only with difficulty finally recognised Europe as a strategic objective to be conquered. As far as reformists who joined the PSI were concerned, one must bear in mind that, being loyal to the old internationalist tradition, they started to perceive the need for a European federation only in the late 1950s. In those years a number of Milanese militants embarked upon a Long March that, specifically on issues linked to foreign policy, such as the Hungarian uprising and the Khrushchev report, was to lead them to perceive Europe as a dynamic political entity extraneous to a rigid application of the Cold War rules. It was within this framework that there was a first attempt to create a centre-left municipal government in Milan in 1956. It was during those difficult years that the prestige and political ability of Milan's socialist administrators emerged, as they paid attention to both a dialogue with their citizens and to the evolution of national and European politics.[63]

---

60 Among the various books on this subject, see Righetti, *Contributo ad una storia della socialdemocrazia italiana* and Averardi, *I socialisti democratici*.

61 On the Europeanist activities of Ivan Matteo Lombardi see the essay by Caraffini, "Ivan Matteo Lombardo e l'unità europea"; as well as Preda, Daniela, *Storia di una speranza*.

62 Maggiorani and Ferrari (eds.), *L'Europa da Togliatti a Berlinguer*. On relations between federalists and the European left, see Pasquinucci, *Europeismo e democrazia*.

63 The prestige and political ability of Milan's socialist administrators was, however, obvious and, starting with Greppi – who until the beginning of 1949 managed to lead a municipal government in which there were two socialist parties, the Christian Democrats and the Communists, and, when that alliance was no longer possible, imposed an administration based on cooperation between the DC and his own party, the PSLI, which he continued to lead until the 1951 elections – adopted policies attentive to the city's needs as well as a European vision. Greppi's legacy to his successor and fellow party member Virgilio Ferrari was the formula involving centrism, which differed greatly from the Roman one and which in many ways prefigured the centre-left that, it is no coincidence, imposed itself in Milan before anywhere else both at a programmatic and at a political level. Formulas aside, what

In 1957 the Maximalist current of federalists led by Altiero Spinelli promoted the initiative of the Congress of European People in the six countries that had signed the Treaties of Rome and in Switzerland, in order to raise the awareness of democratic legitimacy denied to Europeans because of the absence of primary elections. In this manner, citizens in favour of summoning a constituent assembly for a United States of Europe would be called upon to choose delegates at a single European assembly or congress that would be capable of exercising public pressure to the extent of imposing the constituent will of the European people on governments.[64] The powerfully innovative and anti-government aspects of this operation encouraged the CEM to adopt a very cautious official attitude at an international level in order to avoid rifts between the various national sectors and with governments.[65] The

---

mattered most was the importance that socialism, albeit divided, continued to have in Milan. Starting with the 1948 general election and local elections held in 1951, social-democracy had in fact won far more votes in Milan than the national average, proving its grounding among Milanese citizens, which also depended on the stubbornness with which its representatives had supported within the city's administration the reasons of a reformative socialism, attentive to the needs of the people and the need to reconstruct the city, confirming its role as the primary driving force for the country's industrial and civil development. In alliance and also in competition with the Social-Democrats was also the Socialist Party, which was more persuasive than elsewhere when addressing autonomy and attempting to achieve socialist unity, as proved by the attempt in 1956 to create a centre-left municipal government. The events that followed are well-known. Milan continued over the next decades to have socialist mayors, with Ferrari succeeded by another Social-Democrat, Gino Cassinis, representing the first centre-left municipal government, then Piero Bucalossi, Aldo Aniasi, with whom power passed from the PSDI to the PSI, and then Carlo Tognoli and Paolo Pillitteri.

64 On the Congress of the European People see Spinelli, "Nuovo corso" and *idem*, "Il manifesto dei federalisti europei" in Spinelli, *Una strategia per gli Stati Uniti d'Europa*; *Actes et documents du Premier Congrès du Peuple Européen, Turin, 6-8 décembre 1957*; Publius [Albertini], "Esame tecnico della lotta per l'Europa"; Bolis e Marc, "Combat". For in-depth analysis see Guderzo, "Analisi sociale della votazione per il Congresso del Popolo Europeo nel comune di Pavia"; Levi and Pistone (eds.), *Trent'anni di vita del Movimento federalista europeo*, pp. 185-190; Preda, "All'avanguardia dell'Europa"; Rognoni Vercelli, "Il Congresso del popolo europeo".

65 On this subject there was an editorial, unsigned but attributable to the European secretary general Jean Bareth, that appeared in *Communes d'Europe*, in which, without mention of the Congress of the European People, it was stated that "s'il est difficile d'organiser dans les conditions actuelles un vaste référendum populaire rien n'interdit une telle action dans le cadre des communes. Le CCE pourrait ainsi se donner pour tache d'organiser de telle consultations dans les pays où elles seraient possibles et où les municipalités seraient d'accord pour les organiser" ("A Rome le Congrès interparlementaire du Mouvement Européen a demandé la création d'une Assemblée des communes et régions"; "Partecipations aux reunions internationales. II session Congrès du peuple européen, Lyon janvier 1959").

Italian section of the movement of European local autonomies sided instead very solidly with the federalist initiative and supported it, asking member municipalities to provide logistical support such as cabins, ballot boxes, panels, tables, as well as political backing. An analysis of accounts clearly indicates the importance of the support offered by Italian municipalities for these primary elections. In particular, the most important electoral results were achieved in Turin, where the mayor, Amedeo Peyron, was one of the initiative's strongest supporters, and in Milan, where the local political class governing the municipality provided public areas for electoral meetings and rallies as well as providing political support.[66] At an international level, the congress's organisers acknowledged that local administrators also played a particular political role as the "activators" for mobilising Europeans. They therefore managed to add to the Congress of the European People "cahiers de doléances" – words borrowed from the French Revolution indicating documents of political demands drafted by the various levels of European society – the theses at the basis of the creation of the CEM, thereby achieving for the first time a real unity of intentions between local powers and the struggle for a European federation.[67]

Within the dynamics of Milan's socialist world and its relations with the AICCE and the subject of European unity, one must also add the figure of Aldo Aniasi who, elected to Milan's Municipal council in 1951, considered himself the heir to the political and reformist tradition of Alessandro Schiavi, who in 1952 had been one of the co-founders of the AICCE. Aniasi is central to the subject of European twinnings since he was the first mayor to determinedly launch the municipality of Milan's international relations within the framework of the European integration process. On this subject, his political cooperation with the aforementioned Lamberto Jori – with whom he shared political ideas

66 The first elections, held all over Europe on November 24th, 1957, with the exception of Antwerp, where they were held on November 30th, saw a turnout of 16,959 voters in Turin and 8,386 in Milan. In the rest of Europe elections were held in Antwerp, Maastricht, Düsseldorf, Strasbourg, Lyon and Geneva. Starting in 1958 the congress saw a constant rise in the number of municipalities and thus in the number of voters involved. At the second Congress held in Lyon in 1958, there were 225,000 voters; at the third one held in Darmstadt in 1959, 400,000; at the fourth in Oostende in 1960, 500,000; then financial and organisational problems, and above all a sense of political impotence, calmed the initial enthusiasms and ended up by putting an end to a process that remains a unique example in European history. See Cabella, "C.P.E. (Congresso del Popolo Europeo)".

67 *Il Congresso del Popolo Europeo. Documenti*, pp. 18-24; Europa Nuova, *Tesi per la rivoluzione federalista*, pp. 9-10.

first within the PSLI, then in the PSDI, and later in the PSI[68] – was of great importance.

Jori's work in favour of relations between the municipality of Milan and the AICCE was fulfilled not only with the municipality formally joining the association of European local municipalities, but also with the organisation at Palazzo Marino, from February 9th to the 11th, 1959, of a session of an assembly of CEM international delegates on the subject of the representation of local autonomies in European institutions,[69] and the approval by Milan's Municipal Council on July 28th, 1961, of a proposal to participate in the European Institute of Studies and Intermunicipal Relations (from now on EISIR), with headquarters in Lugano.[70] This institute had been greatly desired and was created by Renato Brügner[71] (who worked closed with the AICCE's

---

68 Fiorini, *Il potere a Milano*. Aniasi and Jori's move from the PSDI to the PSI was prepared at length through the creation of the Movimento Unitario di Iniziativa Socialista. The new movement had been created to overcome the conditioning experienced by Saragat's party, which, according to the movement's founders, had lost its progressive force.

69 "I delegati del CCE riuniti a Milano".

70 Archivio civico del Comune di Milano (from here on AC, Milan), verbali del Consiglio comunale del 28 luglio 1961.

71 Renato Brügner (1894-1980) was born in Rome and joined the socialist party in the years leading up to World War I. He fought in the war as an officer. Although supervised by the military police since he was considered "subversive", he managed to meet and get to know Lenin during his brief periods of leave spent in Switzerland, where his mother lived at the time. After the war he continued his socialist militancy, taking part in the struggle against the rising fascist movement. When Mussolini came to power, together with other anti-fascists (such as Gullo, Mancini, and Merlin) he was sentenced to internal exile in Nuoro. After returning to Rome he graduated in engineering from the capital's university; however, unable to find a job he was obliged to open a photographic studio. He joined the Resistance and by pure chance after being questioned he was not taken to the Ardeatine Caves and shot. In 1944 he was appointed commissioner for sanctions against fascism, and in July 1945 he became the president of the Finance Ministry's Technical Committee for the Recall of all the Regime's assets; in October 1946 he was appointed a member of the Commission for the Publication of the O.V.R.A. lists. He took part in the founding of Adriano Olivetti's Italian Workers Socialist Party while also joining the MFE and the *Movimento Comunità*. As a local administrator and a federalist he took part in the founding of the Council of European Municipalities. In the CEM, Brügner, with his extensive knowledge of their respective juridical and political-administrative institutions, became a real bridge between the Italian and German institutions. He cooperated in the preliminary inquiry for the drafting of the ECLP, assisting with spreading knowledge of certain particular experiences, such as assistance provided to rural communities in Federal Germany. He was also the Italian delegate at the European Conference of Local Powers at the Council of Europe from 1957 to 1974, but above all in 1959 he founded and directed until 1973 the Lugano-based EISIR. Through the activities of this Institute, Brügner organised international meetings, conferences, study workshops on supranational and infra-national federalism, as well

secretary general Umberto Serafini), becoming the study-analysis centre for the association of European local autonomies. Brügner had also participated in the founding of the PSLI, becoming the secretary for the Lazio federation, and as a member was elected a provincial councillor for Rome from 1946 to 1952; he was later appointed a member of the provincial administrative government. From 1956 to 1958 he was a municipal councillor for Terracina, where he had been elected as a representative of Adriano Olivetti's *Movimento Comunità*. In the mid-1940s Brügner had also joined the MFE together with Serafini. As a local administrator and federalist he participated in the founding of the CEM and was one of the co-founders of the Italian section of the movement of European local autonomies, together with fellow party member Jori.[72]

In the CEM Brügner, together with Schiavi and Serafini, became an authentic bridge between the European administrative experiences and the reformist world, cooperating in the preliminary inquiry for the drafting of the European Charter of Local Freedoms, also becoming the Italian delegate at the European Conference of Local Powers (ECLP) at the Council of Europe[73] from 1957 to 1974. His most important contribution was, however, the founding in 1959 of the EISIR, which he directed until 1973, organising international meetings and study conferences on supranational and infra-national federalism and on international relations between municipalities. Its agreement with Jori's political choices and the shared attendance of the CEM's national and international institutions undoubtedly favoured the Municipality of Milan's decision to join and financially contribute to EISIR.[74]

After Milan joined the EISIR, as proposed by Mayor Gino Cassinis, its municipal council approved the first twinning between the Lombard capital and the city of Sao Paulo in Brazil.[75] This proposal was the result of an awareness that it would be possible to establish direct international relations between cities through twinnings. The objective was to develop economic-cultural exchanges, and it came about through relations between their respective Chambers of Commerce that started in 1960. This first twinning certainly had its institutional origins in the idea

as publications. On Brügner see [Serafini], "Renato Brügner" and Archivio Storico dell'Università degli Studi di Pavia (from here on ASUPv), Fondi aggregati, Fondo Brügner.

72 Zucca, *Autonomie locali e federazione sovranazionale*, pp. 205-212.

73 On the European Conference of Local Powers, the first example of European local autonomies participating in a European institutional assembly, see Zucca, "L'Europe des communes et des régions à travers l'action de deux de ses acteurs principaux".

74 AC, Milan, verbali del Consiglio comunale del 28 luglio 1961.

75 *Ibidem*.

of international relations between municipalities promoted by the CEM in the early 1950s and also spread by the EISIR. However, as instead happened for the next two twinnings with Chicago (1962) and Leningrad (1967), stipulated before Aldo Aniasi became mayor,[76] it did not have the European integration process as a reference framework, but rather the economic and international political relations that Milan and its political and economic classes had developed. The minutes of the debate in the municipal council also indicated that in all three cases the proposal of a twinning had come from the other three cities wishing to institutionalise the already consolidated economic, cultural and political relations.[77] The Milanese municipal councillors' concern was to ensure that the mayor and the municipal government would not allow international relations between municipalities to be reduced, as perceived in other cases, "simply to pleasure trips, but that these contacts must have consistency and practical results".[78] After being reassured that this would be achieved, all three twinnings were unanimously approved by the municipal council without the political conflict seen in other cities, as emphasised in previous chapters.

When in 1959 Aniasi[79] stood down as alderman of the municipality of Milan to join the PSI[80] together with Lamberto Jori and their

---

76 AC, Milan, verbali del Consiglio comunale del 25 giugno 1962 e del 2 ottobre 1967. Aniasi succeeded Pietro Bucalossi as mayor on November 16th, 1967.

77 The minutes of the debate in the June 25th, 1962, municipal council are of particular interest on this subject, with Mayor Cassinis revisiting the history of the twinning with Sao Paulo, the motivations that led to the idea of a twinning with Chicago, and the request for a twinning that came from Leningrad, now St Petersburg, presented by his predecessor Virginio Ferrari.

78 AC, Milan, verbali del Consiglio comunale del 25 giugno 1962.

79 For the moment there is no exhaustive biography of Aldo Aniasi. To partially reconstruct his work, among the various existing books see Morrone and Scirocco (eds.) *Grazie, Iso. Dall'Ossola a Palazzo Marino a Montecitorio*. In addition to essays with detailed historical reports, the book also contains many accounts by members of the Resistance, as well as by national and local politicians. In order to understand his political and administrative work, among others see Aniasi, *Vivere a Milano*; *idem*, *I socialisti per gli enti locali*; *idem*, "Introduzione", in Italia, Ministero per gli Affari regionali, *Rapporto 1982 sullo stato delle autonomie del Ministro per gli Affari regionali Aldo Aniasi*; *idem*, "Introduzione", in Craxi *et al.*, *La Conferenza programmatica del PSI*. On subjects linked to the partisans' struggle, among other works see Aniasi, *Parri. L'avventura umana, militare e politica di Maurizio*; Aniasi (ed.), *Ne valeva la pena. Dalla "Repubblica" dell'Ossola alla Costituzione repubblicana*. Aniasi is also mentioned in many books on the Resistance, on the history of the socialist and social-democratic parties, as well as in books on Milan's political-administrative history, but it is necessary to report the total lack of any overall study that sets a complex figure such as Aniasi within the context of Italian history in the second half of the 20th century. The hope is that the indexing of his personal archives and the accessibility of mayoral ones now preserved at Palazzo Marino may at last open research paths for scholars.

Movimento Unitario di Iniziativa Socialista (MUIS), he brought to the new political party his municipalist and Europeanist sensitivity, which was open to the role played by local autonomies at a national and international level.[81]

Pietro Bucalossi, on the eve of his rift with the Milanese PSDI that led to his joining the Italian Republican Party (PRI) and to the end of his experience as mayor, proposed to the municipal government and thus to the municipal council on September 26th, 1967, a twinning with the city of Lyon, to coincide with the twinning with Leningrad.[82] The two twinnings were approved unanimously, and this coinciding of both motions seems to perhaps have been political compensation between the various parties represented in the municipal council, thus becoming a means to achieve unanimous consensus. In the case of the twinning with Lyon there is no reference whatsoever to European unity or to municipal freedoms, while there were the usual economic and cultural motivations that did, however, confirm pre-existing direct relations between the twinned cities.

After a complex political crisis, Aldo Aniasi succeeded Bucalossi as mayor. While the Lombard capital's international activity certainly continued with Aniasi, compared to the previous period it was equally evident that there was an increased readiness to cooperate with federalist forces, and in particular with the AICCE, following both the PSI's now decidedly Europeanist political choice and sensitivities regarding the European integration process that former Social Democrats had brought to the Milan socialist party.

In May 1968, the repression of freedom in Czechoslovakia inspired Milanese federalists to promote initiatives in favour of the creation of a United States of Europe. The determining element for accelerating the process was identified as being the democratisation of municipalities and therefore the election by direct universal suffrage of a European parliament that would become the process's driving force. During an assembly of federalist militants, held on June 23rd, 1968, at the

80 See "Atmosfera pesante nel PSDI milanese".

81 The Aldo Aniasi Archives at the *Circolo De Amicis* in Milan (from here on Aldo Aniasi Archives); see the document "Le lunghe stagioni della Milano a democrazia partecipata", copy at the ASUPv, Fondi aggregati, c. Aldo Aniasi. Aniasi's personal library, now preserved at the *Circolo de Amicis* in Milan, includes a significant collection of books on federalist and Europeanist subjects. Among these an interesting read is the book published in 1948 by La Nuova Italia in Florence, entitled *Federazione europea;* this book also contains papers by Spinelli, Einaudi and the socialist Barbara Wootton, with a preface by Tristano Codignola.

82 AC, Milan, verbali del Consiglio comunale del 26 settembre 1967.

movement's headquarters in Milan,[83] it was proposed and then decided that the municipality should support the collection of signatures needed to present a people's draft bill for the election of Italians to the European parliament, to take place by direct universal suffrage. On the 25th anniversary of the founding of the MFE on August 27th-28th, 1943, the collection began for the fifty thousand signatures required for presenting the draft bill, as established by Article 71 of the constitution. In sponsoring this effort, the MFE was assisted by the AICCE, which mobilised member municipalities and mayors, finding great political and organisational support in the municipality of Milan, led by Aniasi.[84] At Milan's *Castello Sforzesco* on February 15th, 1969, an event was held to publicly announce that the target of fifty thousand signatures had been achieved and had been followed by the presentation of the draft bill to the Senate.[85] On that occasion, Aniasi reiterated the municipality's support and its role in the struggle for the democratisation of Europe.[86]

During a meeting of the MFE's central committee in Milan on October 4th, 1969, in the presence of Prime Minister Mariano Rumor, Mayor Aldo Aniasi made a speech in which he emphasised Milan's role as a European and federalist city. Aniasi totally supported the struggle for a new democratic and united Europe, emphasising that it was indispensable to involve citizens in the European creation process and thus to encourage "la piena partecipazione di Milano democratica alla lotta per un'Europa unita, nell'interesse di tutti i lavoratori, dei giovani e di ogni uomo libero".[87]

On the subject of the need to involve the "masses" in the struggle for a United States of Europe, Aniasi also spoke at a meeting of the European Movement at which, coherent with his reformist ideals, he emphasized how the idea of Europe was no longer the legacy of elites and avant-gardes but, thanks to the shared work undertaken by movements and municipalities, was increasingly becoming part of the

---

83 Majocchi and Rossolillo, *Il Parlamento europeo. Significato storico di un'elezione*, pp. 159-161.

84 "Un traguardo immediato per il CCE. Le elezioni europee", in particular p. 2 where there is the municipal government's motion authorising federalists to use the instruments needed to collect signatures.

85 Majocchi, "L'azione per il riconoscimento del diritto di voto europeo".

86 Aldo Aniasi Archives, AM 1969-2, Discorsi alla città (cultura europea), speech made at the Conference on the People's Participation in Europe's Political Unification, Milan, Castello Sforzesco 15/2/1969.

87 Aldo Aniasi Archives, 1969-10 AM cultura - Europa, Discorso del Sindaco Aldo Aniasi alla riunione del Comitato centrale del Movimento federalista europeo, 4 ottobre 1969.

"people's conscience".[88] Only the involvement of the masses could fulfil the process for the creation of a United States of Europe, which would have facilitated the fall of the Fascist regimes still present on the Old Continent and overcome the nationalistic idea of the state.

Aniasi's European activism and that of the municipality of Milan was also confirmed by the city's international relations, as Milan reacted positively to requests from Birmingham and Frankfurt, both twinned with Lyon, "for a multiple twinning" between the four European cities.[89] These twinnings were carried out within the framework of activities promoted directly by the AICCE and the CEM, assuming a political meaning for the first time in overcoming the barriers of the national states and in favour of European unity. Accompanied by a large Milanese delegation, Aniasi travelled to Lyon, where, on June 11th, 1969, he signed the twinning pact. In the speech he made on that occasion, in addition to speaking of the cultural and economic links between the two cities, he once again emphasised the role played by municipalities in the creation of "a new European spirit".[90] The next day Aniasi made another speech at the Rhone Prefecture in which he spoke for the first time of the need to organise in Milan a meeting of large cities to analyse the problems of industrial societies and large urban areas.[91]

The twinning with the city of Frankfurt was ratified by the municipal government on October 21st, 1969, and signed by the cities' mayors, but it was never presented for the approval of the municipal council,[92] while the twinning with Birmingham was only approved on June 5th, 1974.[93] These bureaucratic delays obviously took nothing away from the political importance of agreeing to twinnings sponsored by the CEM to encourage the international cooperation of European cities and the Europeanist spirit. In fact, the mayor of Milan travelled to Frankfurt on October 20th, 1970, to sign the twinning pact. Aniasi was aware that the "twinning pact" represented "the continuity and strengthening of the municipality of Milan's policy addressed at continually creating new

88 Aldo Aniasi Archives, AM 1969-2, Discorsi alla città (cultura europea), Intervento al Movimento europeo, s.d.

89 AC, Milan, verbali della seduta straordinaria del Consiglio comunale del giorno 5 giugno 1974. Attached to the minutes is a document on the motion with which Aniasi proposed, at a meeting held on June 22nd, 1969, that the city should proceed with a multiple twinning with the three European cities.

90 Aniasi, "Ogni lionese è cittadino di Milano".

91 Aniasi, "Non solo atto di generica simpatia".

92 AC, Milan, Atti del comune di Milano, seduta di Giunta municipale del giorno 21 ottobre 1969.

93 AC, Milan, verbali della seduta del Consiglio comunale del giorno 5 giugno 1974.

and valid ways of bringing together citizens from different nations." Aniasi took note of problems shared by the metropolitan areas of Milan, Birmingham, Frankfurt and Lyon, while speaking of the political role played by municipalities in contributing to "the creation of a Europe in which every citizen" would feel European.[94]

The multiple twinnings with Lyon, Frankfurt and Birmingham, the idea of Milan's international political role, the need to understand and address the dramatic problems in large metropolitan areas such as public transport, pollution and the reckless use of land, influenced a number of initiatives taken later by Aniasi. Starting in April 1972, meetings with the mayors of other large cities all over the world during the Milan Trade Fair had, unlike those organised by La Pira in Florence, both a political meaning, in terms of establishing direct international relations between large cities, and a practical one, as a moment for exchanging ideas and experiences.[95]

With this initiative, relations with twinned cities received a new breath of life. For example, at the 49th Trade Fair, the municipality of Milan organised working meetings for the delegates of the cities twinned with Milan,[96] while in an article published in the *Avanti*, Aniasi proposed the creation of a world conference of large cities. The idea was to create a global force to oppose the centralised state so that municipalities could regain their political and financial autonomy.[97] In 1972 Aniasi reiterated that cities had the right and the duty to develop a "diplomacy of cities", in the spirit of the first international organisations of municipalities, to address and resolve the problems of citizens.[98] Coherent with this spirit of international relations between cities, on April 23rd, 1974, Aniasi proposed a twinning with Dakar that was approved by the municipal council on June 3rd that same year.[99]

---

94 Aldo Aniasi Archives, Fondo Amministrazione Milano, c. 11, f. F1 gemellaggi e visite, speech by Aniasi for the signing of the twinning pact between Milan, Frankfurt, Birmingham and Lyon on 20/10/1970.

95 *Incontri dei sindaci delle grandi città del mondo: la qualità della vita* in http://www.fondazionealdoaniasi.it/aldo-aniasi/esperienza-amministrativa/aniasi-sindaco-di-milano/incontri-dei-sindaci-delle-grandi-citta-del-mondo-la-qualita-della-vita/.

96 Aldo Aniasi Archives, AM 1971-4, Relazioni internazionali, gemellaggi e visite, 14/4/1971. Meetings attended by delegates from the cities of Frankfurt, Leningrad, Lyon, and Sao Paolo of Brazil.

97 Aldo Aniasi Archives, f. 2, Grandi città del mondo. Articolo "Proposta del sindaco di Milano. Conferenza mondiale delle grandi città del mondo", in *Avanti*, August 26th, 1971.

98 Aldo Aniasi Archives, AM Relazioni internazionali grandi città del mondo, 16-17/4/1972.

99 AC, Milan, Gemellaggi.

Over time, further twinnings were added with Shanghai (1979), Osaka (1981), Tel Aviv (1997), Bethlehem (2000), Toronto (2003), Cracow (2003), Melbourne (2004) and Guadalajara (2008), but both the political meaning of these initiatives and potential concrete actions did not follow the path traced by Aldo Aniasi and, as far as the European spirit was concerned, as well as cooperation with the AICCE, were continued by Carlo Tognoli.[100] It was only after the election of Mayor Giuliano Pisapia that relations with the other European cities appeared to improve, and on this subject the opinion expressed by the mayor of Lyon, Gérard Colomb, was exemplary when, referring to a series of meetings with representatives of the new city government and with Pisapia himself, he said, "Lors du précédent mandat, le maire de Milan n'était pas très présent sur les réseaux européens. Les réseaux des maires en particulier".[101] Milan's absence from the context of international relations between European municipalities was thus perceived by the mayor of a twinned city as anomalous within the framework of a re-appropriation of rights that European cities had regained with such difficulty between the early decades of the 20th century and the new millennium.

[100] Zucca, "Il riformismo socialista lombardo e la questione dell'unità europea", pp. 570-577.

[101] See "Quand Milan s'intéresse au Grand Lyon" at http://www.Lyonmag.com/article/28587/quand-milan-s-interesse-au-grand-lyon.

CHAPTER 6

The Long March

The Representation of Local Institutions within European Institutions

The European Union is unquestionably a relatively new institution but, like national states created in the past, it is subject to a number of rules. It is not in fact possible to understand any national or international political-administrative system without placing it within the historical context through which it came into being. It is necessary to consider historically the nature and dynamics of the political, economic and social forces that continuously, but progressively, have changed the balance in play and also interact dynamically. In other words, the European Union must be observed within the context of the forces that created it, which interact with its current organisation or those still shaping it. As mentioned in the introduction, we can include among these players local European authorities that, over time, have increasingly become players in the integration process and that today are one of the Union's institutional bodies.

To the previous analysis of international relations activated through twinning one must therefore dynamically add that of the representation of territorial institutions within the European institutions.

Cultural diversity, which is Europe's great asset, has produced specific adaptations in relations between state and regional authorities[1] and has led to the creation of a broad range of regions,[2] which can be summarised in five categories, of which some at the federal level at times overlap within the same state:

1. Administrative districts (Portugal and the United Kingdom have both administrative districts and administrative regions, and, in the case of the United Kingdom, also autonomous or political regions).

---

1 On the state and territorial organisation of the various European states and current processes see Ferlaino and Molinari, *Neofederalismo, neoregionalismo e intercomunalità*, pp. 33-256. For a comparison between the various autonomist models see Schiera, *Le autonomie e l'Europa*.

2 Bolgherini, *Come le regioni diventano europee*.

2. Regions as second level territorial bodies in the form of groups of local institutions (Germany and the Netherlands).
3. Administrative regions (France, Portugal and the United Kingdom).
4. Autonomous or political regions (Belgium, Italy, the Netherlands, Portugal, the United Kingdom, Spain).
5. Federate regions (Austria, Belgium, Germany).

These differences reflect the variety of players and national or supranational processes and, in general, the profound reorganisation of the state and administrative framework currently taking place in European countries. These are, however, phenomena that have marked a strong discontinuity with the past and ones that must encourage the abandonment of traditional comparative modes for new conceptual models, in particular in order to understand the European Union's current institutional organisation in relation to local bodies and, in particular, the role played by the Committee of the Regions (CoR) regarding Parliament, the Commission and the Council.

One must also emphasise how these complex interrelations are in line with that of those who support Multi-level Governance (MLG)[3] as an alternative policy at a European level for the Integrated Governance Model (IGM) that initially characterised relations with the Community and later with the Union. In the IGM the main decision-making players are the states of the Union, while in MLG it is necessary to shift responsibility to both a higher level, that of European institutions, and to a lower one, that of territorial authorities.[4]

The local authorities' 'Long March' in relations with European institutions began the day after the creation in January 1951 of the Council of European Municipalities (CEM), which, as a federalist and Europeanist movement, immediately addressed the problem of its own representation to the European bodies founded at the time, unlike the International Union of Local Authorities (IULA).

This issue was particularly felt within the French federalist movement, *La Fédération*, which together with the Italian and Luxembourg

3 See *La Governance europea. Un libro bianco* at http://eur-lex.europa.eu/LexUriServ/site/it/com/2001/com2001_0428it02.pdf; see *Libro bianco del Comitato delle Regioni sulla governance multilivello* at http://cor.europa.eu/en/activities/governance/Documents/CoR's%20White%20Paper%20on%20Multilevel%20Governance/IT.pdf.

4 For a quick overview of the work done by the Italian regions in favour of their integration in European policies see Consiglio regionale della Lombardia, *Comunità europee e ruolo delle Regioni*; Caraffini, *Il Piemonte per l'Europa.* At a European level see Bitsch (ed.), *Le fait régional et la construction européenne.*

sections of the CEM, played a driving role. Ever since the CEM's constituent assembly, Jacques Chaban-Delmas, at the time mayor of Bordeaux, had provided precise indications concerning the need for local institutions to be in some way represented within the "différents Conseils qui dès à présent travaillent", later insisting on the creation of an assembly representing all municipalities, "a sort of European senate" as a democratic element within future European institutions. After a lengthy debate, the CEM's assembly passed two documents approving the observations presented by Chaban-Delmas. The CEM's objective, as stated in Paragraph IV of its Charter, was to "assurer la partecipation et la représentation des communes et collectivetés locales dans les organismes européens et internationaux" and, in Paragraph V, to "intégrer aux futures institutions européennes l'Assemblée représentative des communes et collectivités locales". The local institutions participated in the debate on European organisation, posing the problem of the representation of local communities.[5]

It was, however, the secretary of *La Fédération*, André Voisin, who obtained for the CEM the first political acknowledgement from European institutions. In April 1951, during a meeting of the executive committee of the European Movement (EM), Voisin contacted Paul-Henri Spaak, at the time president of the Council of Europe's Parliamentary Assembly and of the EM, informing him that the CEM had been founded. Spaak was favourably impressed and promised, "tout son appui" for the development of the municipal organisation.[6] To promote this new association, he agreed to receive a delegation from the CEM during the Council of Europe session scheduled for May. The official meeting, held in Strasbourg on May 7th, 1951, and the crowded press conference that followed were undoubtedly a political and public relations success for the CEM, to which Spaak publicly acknowledged the role of representing local European authorities and the potential for providing a "apport (...) au mouvement pour l'Europe (...) surtout au moment où se fait particulièrement sentir le besoin d'un grand effort de propagande pour l'unité du continent".[7] The Speaker of the Assembly

5 Archives d'État de la République et Canton de Genève (from now on AEG), Papiers Edgard Milhaud, c. *DOC. EM. Procès-verbaux des six séances de la conférence constitutive du Conseil des communes d'Europe. Genève 28-30 Janvier 1951.*

6 Archives Conseil des Communes et Régions d'Europe, Paris (from now on ACCRE, Paris), c. *Archives 1955-56*, f. *Cottier*, Letter from Jean Bareth to Fernand Cottier, dated April 24th, 1951, in which the CEM's secretary informs the president about action taken by Voisin.

7 Archives Association villes et communes luxembourgeoises, Luxembourg (from here on AVCL Archives, Luxembourg), c. *Conseil des communes d'Europe 1951. Réception, le lundi 7 mai 1951, de la délégation du Conseil d'Europe par M. P.H.*

committed to encouraging "la reconnaissance du Conseil des Communes d'Europe comme organisme qualifié pour apporter au Conseil de l'Europe ses avis et suggestions sur les incidences des problèmes européens dans les collectivités locales".[8]

The organisation of local European authorities hoped, however, to achieve further results, which were outlined by Voisin, while cultural aspects were entrusted to Alexandre Marc[9] who, under the aegis of the *Université Internationale* and in cooperation with the CEM's German section, summoned a "session d'études municipale" in Bad Dürkheim

---

Spaak, Président de l'Assemblée Consultative du Conseil de l'Europe et Président du Mouvement européen and Déclaration de M. Paul-Henri Spaak.

8 AVCL Archives, Luxembourg, c. *Conseil des communes d'Europe 1951*, Letter from Jean Bareth to Hubert Clément dated May 18th, 1951.

9 Alexandre Marc (whose real name was Aleksandre Markovitch Lipiansky, 1904-2000). His family, which was of Jewish origin, was obliged to leave Russia in 1918. He completed his education between Paris, Jena and Freiburg, and graduated in Paris in 1927 from the *École libre des sciences politiques.* His role in the infra-national and supranational federalist battle has yet to be defined, but he was certainly a leading player during the season of the federalist and Europeanist congresses, which between 1946 and 1949 resulted in the creation of the *Union européenne des fédéralistes*, of which he became the secretary general in 1946, and the founding of the first European Institutions such as the Council of Europe. From the mid-1950s onwards, Alexandre Marc worked for a federal European state, cooperating with Altiero Spinelli in promoting the Congress of the European People, the only really revolutionary attempt to create a supranational Europe by mobilising the European people. Simultaneously he cooperated in the founding of the *Centre international de formation européenne* (CIFE) and the *Institut européen des hautes études internationales* (IEHEI) in Nice, directing both. Between 1960 and 1970 Marc became committed to drafting the federalist school of thought as the global answer to contemporary society's needs. In 1960 he founded the magazine *Europe en formation*, the real educational workshop for integral federalist ideals. During the 1970s and 1980s Marc continued his work on the consolidation of the federalist idea and on promoting a federal society in Europe. After the fall of the Berlin Wall the work of the patriarch of integral federalism and of the many study centres inspired by its ideas also spread to Eastern European countries, providing possible solutions for the troubled and not yet completed events linked to post-communism (Rieben *et al.*, *Le fédéralisme et Alexandre Marc*; Gouzy, "Alexandre Marc soixante-quinze ans de combat fédéraliste"; *idem*, "Alexandre Marc"; Lega, "I novanta di Marc"; Marc, *Europa e federalismo globale*). According to information provided to me by Marc himself before he died, Christian Roy and Isabelle Lemoulec-Deschamps are preparing an analytical biographical reconstruction as well as a detailed study of his intellectual production. The two historians have had free access to Marc's personal archives, mostly "perdus, soit mangés par les rats (cachés dans une grange de la banlieue parisienne) soit brûlés par mégarde (par un personnage devenue célèbre, à savoir l'Abbé Pierre) – Archivio Storico dell'Università degli Studi di Pavia (from now on ASUPv), Fondo CCRE c. *Alexandre Marc*, Letter from Alexandre Marc to Fabio Zucca dated June 16th, 1994.

from March 14th to March 16th, 1952.[10] During the debate, Marc stated that European unity would only make sense if it were federal. It was therefore necessary to solemnly express the need to achieve municipal and regional freedom within a European framework by summoning the "États-Généraux des Communes d'Europe (...) germe d'une nouvelle institution européenne (...) la Chambre des Communes Européenne".[11] Thus, for the first time Marc demanded greater municipal autonomy not only at a national but also at a European level, as well as a role for local authorities within what was then perceived as the imminent unity of Western Europe.

Between January 12th and 14th, 1957, in Strasbourg, the Council of Europe summoned the first European Congress of Local Authorities (ECLA).[12] Officially this meeting was planned to allow representatives of local institutions to take part in the Parliamentary Assembly's activities when the assembly addressed issues concerning municipal or regional responsibilities.[13] Thus, for the first time the principle was established that international institutions were not authorised to adopt provisions concerning decentralised administrations without the municipalities or their representatives being previously consulted. In this sense the ECLA was a clear success achieved by the CEM, which, as previously mentioned, had listed among the association's objectives that of guaranteeing the participation and representation of local authorities within European institutions. For the federalists in the CEM, and in particular for Umberto Serafini, obtaining a summons for a congress at

---

10 The meeting was also useful in promoting the creation of the CEM's German section and was attended by about thirty local administrators and Austrian, French, Italian, Luxembourg and German federalists. Archives of the Conseil des communes et régions d'Europe, Roissy (from now on ACCRE, Roissy), c. *15*, f. *documents div. 1956-'57. Université internationale, Session d'études municipale (Bad Dürkheim, 13 au 16 mars 52). Ordre du jour*, Letter from Arthur Ladebeck to Alexandre Marc dated February 26th, 1952, and Letter from Ch. Laederich to Alexandre Marc dated March 12th, 1952. The ACCRE, Roissy, found in storage at Paris' Charles de Gaulle airport, was given to the Historical Archives of the European Union in Florence, thereby creating the aforementioned CCRE collection, but the new shelf marks match the previous ones, with those inventory numbers being used in this book.

11 ACCRE, Roissy, c. *15*, f. *documents div. 1956-'57*, Report on speeches made in Bad-Dürkheim entitled *Sous l'egide du C.C.E.*, p. 3.

12 Archives centrales du Conseil de l'Europe, Strasbourg (from here on ACCE, Strasbourg), *Dossier 0901, v. 4, 1954-1956-1957. Assemblée Consultative. Conférence européenne des pouvoirs locaux. Annuaire Janvier 1957*. On the ECLA see *La Conférence des pouvoirs locaux et règionaux de l'Europe*; Clotet y Mirò, *La cooperacion internacional*, pp. 97-185. Clotet y Mirò's work is restricted to the organisational aspects of the ECLA.

13 ACCE, Strasbourg, *Assemblée consultative, dossier 406, projet de résolution, 10 octobre 1955*, p. 2.

the Parliamentary Assembly was the premise for the creation of a similar institution at the European Coal and Steel Community (ECSC) and future European institutions.

The ECLA, however, was a consultative body, created to express opinions to a Parliamentary Assembly with no real power at all. Thus, it was nothing but a faded copy of the *Assemblée répresentative des communes et collectivités locales*, which CEM promoters would have liked to have partnered with a freely elected European parliament, partly following the model of the Federal Republic of Germany.

Action taken to promote a representation of local powers at the Strasbourg Assembly had been initiated by Jacques Chaban-Delmas.[14] In November 1951, a few months after the founding of the movement of European local autonomies, the mayor of Bordeaux asked the consultative assembly to add to the day's agenda a proposal promoting the creation of a Special Commission for Municipal and Regional Affairs. The grounds for this motion included an explicit reference to the founding of the Movement of European Municipalities and to the resolutions adopted during the constituent assembly. In his opinion, the fact that municipalities had set up an organisation at a European level proved that local authorities wished to actively participate in the integration process and emphasised the possibility of involving other forces in the battle for the continent's unity. His motion was supported by the presidency of the Assembly, which resulted in the approval, on September 20th, 1952, of resolution n° 20, which resulted in the creation of the Special Commission for Municipal and Regional Affairs. Its official task was to study the impact decisions made at a European level had on local affairs, and it was therefore authorised to establish contacts with government and municipal bodies.[15]

This first victory achieved by the CEM's French section, in particular by the mayor of Bordeaux (who in the meantime had been elected president of the commission), was received with a degree of disappointment by at least part of the CEM, in particular by Italian and Luxembourg federalists. During the constituent assembly it had, in fact, been decided to take action so that European local authorities would obtain representation in European institutions. As the chairman of the movement's European Action Committee, Jacques Chaban-Delmas had instead acted only in relation to the Council of Europe, where he played

---

[14] On the role played by Chaban-Delmas and Umberto Serafini in encouraging the representation of local authorities in European institutions see Zucca, *L'Europe des communes et des regions.*

[15] ACCE, Strasbourg, *Assemblée consultative. Texte adopté pendant la 4e Session Ordinaire (Deuxième partie). Résolution 20 tendant à la création d'une commission spéciale des Affaires communales et régionales.*

a direct political role. Divergences did of course emerge, also in the absence of Chaban-Delmas, during the second session of the movement's executive committee held in Palermo from January 30th to February 1st, 1953.[16] After a bitter debate, the various positions found common ground in a single document that included a number of observations made by constitutionalist federalists. Chaban-Delmas was then invited to also take action within the Ad hoc Assembly appointed at the time to draft the project for a Charter of European political authority. Once again he chose to operate within the framework of the Council of Europe, thereby extending the time frame for intervention. It was in fact only after he obtained a formal mandate from the Special Commission for Municipal and Regional Affairs that, on June 22nd, 1953, the mayor of Bordeaux wrote a letter to the president of the Ad hoc Assembly's Constitutional Commission inviting him to consider the possibility of studying ways of ensuring the representation "des collectivités locales dans les futures institutions européennes et notamment dans celles de la Communauté européenne".[17] While the modalities of his intervention were impeccable, it should be observed that it took place with serious delay compared to the requests in the Palermo mandate and the events linked to the Ad hoc Assembly. As was well known, the Charter of the EPC had been approved on March 10th, 1953, and the text had been the object of a debate during later intergovernmental conferences.

Continuing his work aimed at linking the CEM to the Council of Europe, the mayor of Bordeaux also organised the participation of one of the Special Commission's work groups at the October 1953 States-General of Versailles and later summoned a meeting of this commission during the holding of the second States-General of European Municipalities in October 1954 in Venice. Thanks to these initiatives, the reports and resolutions of the States-General[18] were officially sent to

---

16 ACCRE, Paris, *armoire D*, c. *Reunions statutaires, procès verbaux, 1951 à 1971. IIe session du comité exécutif, Palerme 30 janvier-1er février 1953. Procès-verbal*, p. 2. On that occasion four resolutions were presented addressing relations between the CEM, the Special Commission for Municipal and Regional Affairs and the Strasbourg Assembly. The first, presented by the French delegation, basically accepted the conduct of the mayor of Bordeaux; the others, drafted by the Italian delegation led by Umberto Serafini, secretary of the CEM's Italian section, disapproved of the decisions based on the charters and on programme documentation.

17 ACCE, Strasbourg, *Conseil de l'Europe, Assemblée consultative, dossier 0902-364. Commission spéciale des affaires communales et régionales, Strasburg, le 27 juin 1953.* Copy of the letter sent by Jacques Chaban-Delmas to Heinrich von Brentano on June 22nd, 1953.

18 ACCE, Strasbourg, *Assemblée consultative, dossier 0902-366, Commission spéciale des affaires communales et régionales. Compte rendu des États généraux des communes d'Europe réunis à Versailles les 16, 17 et 18 octobre 1953, auxquels participait un Groupe de travail délégué par la Commission spéciale des Affaires*

the Council of Europe. Among them, particular political importance was attributed to the resolution with which the Venice States-General asked the Council of Europe's Committee of Ministers to transform the Special Commission into a "Commission de plein exercice" and to constitute "un Groupe de travail permanent où les délégués des organisations communales et internationales pourraient collaborer étroitement".[19]

Once again as proposed by Chaban-Delmas,[20] the Parliamentary Assembly took the initiative. Making use of its right to consult experts, on October 14th, 1955, it deliberated to proceed with the summoning of "une conférence des représentants de toutes les associations nationales qualifiées de pouvoirs locaux des pays membres".

The CEM used its international organisation and its national sections to support the creation of an assembly of local European authorities as the precursor of a possible senate of local European bodies.[21] Between January and March 1956 pressure was applied on Spaak, Bech, Martino,[22] as well as on the German and French governments.[23] Thanks to such action, as the chairman of the CEM's European Action Committee, Jacques Chaban-Delmas was received by the Committee of Ministers in Strasbourg on March 1st. There he obtained a radical change in the attitude adopted by the committee, which, although postponing

---

communales et régionales. Strasbourg, le 15 mars 1953 (the correct date was March 15th, 1954).

19 ACCE, Strasbourg, *Assemblée consultative, dossier n. 0901, années 1956-1957-1958. Commissions des pouvoirs locaux. Conférence européenne des pouvoirs locaux, Strasbourg, le 17 octobre 1957*, p. 1 and following for other quotes.

20 ACCE, Strasbourg, *Comité des ministres, dossier 0902-368, Assemblée consultative, dossier 0902-368.* On the basis of previous deliberations and recommendations, the mayor of Bordeaux ensured that the Special Commission unanimously adopted a draft resolution envisaging a yearly summons of a conference of representatives of national associations of local authorities.

21 The decision was taken during the meeting of the *bureau international* held in Metz on January 21st and 22nd, 1956; see "L'action du C.C.E. en faveur de la Conférence européenne des pouvoirs locaux".

22 ACCRE, Roissy, c. *Bureau international, f. bureau international 1956.* Copy of the letter sent by Émile Hamilius to Gaetano Martino, dated April 9th, 1956. The president of the CEM requested an official meeting with the Italian Foreign Minister in order to discuss relations between the CEM, the Special Commission for Municipal and Regional Affairs, and the Council of Europe.

23 Joseph-Jean Merlot intervened with Paul Henri Spaak, Henry Cravatte met with Joseph Bech, Umberto Serafini spoke to Gaetano Martino, Heinz Hoose, secretary of the *Rat der Gemeinden Europas*, intervened with the German government, and Gaston Defferre, at the time president of the *Association française du Conseil des communes d'Europe* (AFCCE), addressed both the French government and the institutional bodies of the Council of Europe.

once again a decision to allocate funds needed to summon the conference, abandoned its prejudicially negative attitude. There is no doubt that the international political atmosphere, once again favourable to agreements between states within a European framework (the Rome Treaties were signed on March 25th 1957), facilitated the lobbying work undertaken by the CEM with governments, whose representatives approved the principle of summoning a "conférence de représentants des associations nationales de pouvoirs locaux des pays membres, proposée par la Résolution 76 (1955) de l'Assemblée Consultative".[24] In this case as well, the expected opposition was voiced, but it was in part overcome thanks to support from Fernand Dehousse, at the time president of the Strasbourg Assembly.[25] Residual unfavourable attitudes resulted in the conference not having a permanent status and the agenda for the day was restricted to a debate on subjects linked to "les intérêts régionaux et locaux dans le cadre de la construction européenne".[26]

The conference held its first session from January 12th to the 14th, 1957, and, as proposed by the CEM, Jacques Chaban-Delmas, whose role in these events escaped no one, was elected its first president. The ECLA's political importance was greater than that originally assigned to it by the permanent working group.[27] The Conference consisted of 135 members,[28] the same number as the Parliamentary Assembly appointed by the national and international associations of local authorities and by the Strasbourg Assembly.

The Strasbourg Assembly should have provided real answers to the demands presented by the ECLA, quite a difficult achievement considering the consultative assembly's lack of power. According to

24 ACCE, Strasbourg, doc. 527, *Assemblée consultative, huitième session ordinaire, 18 juillet 1956*, pp. 1-3.

25 Together with Bareth, Dehousse intervened to persuade the IULA to change its attitude to the summoning of a Conference of Local Authorities. The Assembly's president thereby started to work closely with the CEM and with Chaban-Delmas, who thanked him officially at the ECLA's first session (ACCE, Strasbourg, *dossier 0901, année 1956-1957-1958*, ECLA, *Strasbourg, le 17 janvier 1957, compte rendu des débats de la ECLA, 1re séance*, p. 12).

26 ACCE, Strasbourg, doc. 527, *Assemblée consultative, huitième session ordinaire, 18 juillet 1956*, p. 2.

27 For the CEM, the ECLA was the "première institution communale européenne: see "Conférence européenne des pouvoirs locaux".

28 ACCE, Strasbourg, *dossier 0901*. The CEM tried to guarantee adequate representation for its national sections. Its attempts clashed with those of the IULA, which in turn tried to influence the formation of delegations.

accounts by the Congress's secretary Alois Larcher,[29] even the ECLA's promoters were aware that it would be impossible over the short term to transform the Congress into a European senate equipped with power, but they had decided to pursue their work to create an institutional precedent.

It was left to the Italian federalist Natale Santero, a member of the Parliamentary Assembly's Commission of Local Authorities,[30] to propose and obtain,[31] in agreement with Umberto Serafini and the CEM's[32] international secretariat, the institutionalisation of the ECLA, which, equipped with its own charter on September 13th, 1961,[33] has continued until now with its meetings, playing a cultural role and providing a possible political-institutional example.

---

29 Alois Larcher, one of the ECLA's representatives at the Council of Europe, worked for Jacques Chaban-Delmas (as reported to me in Strasbourg on March 17th, 1995. A report is preserved at the ASUPv, c. Alois Larcher).

30 As requested by the CEM, in 1957 the Special Commission for Municipal and Regional Affairs was transformed into a permanent commission and its name changed to the Commission of Local Authorities (ACCRE, Roissy, c. 16. *Projet de procès verbal du Conseil de présidence, Luxembourg les 4 et 5 mai 1957*, p. 3). According to Larcher, the fact that there was no longer any reference to the regions in the new name did not hide any political choice but was the result of a bureaucratic oversight no one wished to correct (Alois Larcher, March 17th, 1995 see footnote 29). As always, in this first phase of the history of relations between local authorities and institutions in Strasbourg most of the credit for the positive results should be attributed to Chaban-Delmas. He applied pressure on his "cher ami" Fernand Dehousse so that the Parliamentary Assembly would approve the transformation of the commission as desired by the CEM (ACCE, Strasbourg, *dossier 02514, année 1952-1957*, Letter from Jacques Chaban-Delmas to Fernand Dehousse dated April 27th, 1957).

31 In April 1957 Natale Santero, representing the Commission of Local Powers, presented to the Parliamentary Assembly a project of recommendations that included a request that the ECLA should be summoned in 1958. After the second session of the conference was held, Santero once again requested that the ECLA be summoned in 1959 (ACCE, Strasbourg, *doc. 637, Assemblée consultative, rapport sur la représentation des pouvoirs locaux au sein des institutions européennes, 11 avril 1957*).

32 After initially experiencing perplexities, the entire CEM supported the experience of the ECLA, which in the movement's projects became a possible model for the representation of local authorities at future European institutions. Thus, after the summoning of the first Conference, the association of municipalities began to work on obtaining the summoning of the second session (ACCRE, Roissy, *c. 16. Projet de procès verbal du Conseil de presidénce, Luxembourg les 4 et 5 mai 1957*, p. 4).

33 Ministers' delegates "rendant hommage aux résultats obtenus par les conférences européennes ad hoc des pouvoirs locaux qui se sont réunis jusqu'à ce jour" adopted the *Charte de la Conférence européenne des pouvoirs locaux* on September 13th, 1961. The document envisaged the creation of the ECLA "sur une base biennale" (ACCE, Strasbourg, *dossier 0901 1956-1962, comité des ministres, résolution (61) 20 adoptée par les délégués des ministres le 13 septembre 1961*).

The Council of Europe's Parliamentary Assembly also later adopted the Congress's resolutions. However, in view of this assembly's aforementioned lack of political power, the proposals never had any real follow-up.[34]

In 1967, the CEM managed within the ECLA to promote and then create the consultative committee of the local authorities of the six countries of the EEC, which was to be acknowledged as the Community's interlocutor only in the 1970s.

Umberto Serafini, in a document dated 1960 entitled *Le regioni e l'Europa*, had equally stated that the ECLA would have to become one of the Council of Europe's permanent bodies and thus also one for the European Common Market (ECM). The objective was to lead local authorities, in particular the regional autonomies, to play the role of political interlocutors for the government of the community institutions[35] as set out during the third national congress of the AICCE held in Frascati in 1958.[36]

In October 1962 the EEC's Commission published a "Memorandum on the Community action programme during the second stage" which set out a number of general guidelines for long-term regional economic policies, with no mention, however, of a possible role for local authorities.[37] This document should not be considered surprising if one considers that the 1951 Treaty of Paris on the ECSC, the 1957 Treaty of Rome that gave life to the EEC, and the treaty on nuclear energy (EURATOM)[38] made no reference to local authorities if not in marginal notes of no political importance whatsoever. The preamble of the Treaty on the EEC only envisaged harmonious economic development between the various European regions with the objective of reducing differences

---

34 "L'Istituto europeo di credito comunale".

35 ASUPv, Fondi aggregati, Archivio Umberto Serafini, c. 4, f. 2. Document *s.d.* but dated 1960 entitled *Le regioni e l'Europa* later published in *La sentinella del canavese*, February 19th, 1960, p. 1.

36 "La rappresentanza dei poteri locali nel quadro della CEE".

37 Grosso, "Necessità di una strutturazione democratica", p. 3. The article written by Grosso, at the time mayor of Turin, is a summary of his report at the *Colloquio sulla politica regionale europea* sponsored by the CEM and by the European Community, held at *Europa-Haus* in Otzenhausen in Saar on February 6th to the 8th, 1967. This text is a precious document for reconstructing the events that resulted in local European bodies establishing a first link with the European Communities.

38 Among the many contributions available on the Treaties of Rome, see the following classics: Ferrari Agradi, *Europa: tappe e prospettive di unificazione*; Albonetti, *Euratom e sviluppo nucleare*; *idem*, *Preistoria degli Stati Uniti d'Europa*; Mellaerts, *La genèse du marché commun*; Hallestein, *L'Europe inachevée*; Gerbert, *La construction de l'Europe*; Cartou, *Communautés Européennes*; Serra (ed.), *Il rilancio dell'Europa e i Trattati di Rome*.

between the various European regions perceived more as a geographical reference than a political-territorial one.[39]

The first sign of a possible political cultural change in the EEC Commission's attitude to local authorities appeared in June 1963, when the CEM managed to directly involve the Commission in the organisation in Brussels of the Conference on Territorial Planning and Regional Policies. The conclusions drawn at this conference indicated how territorial institutions should be acknowledged as having competence regarding territorial planning and regional policies. It was also following these conclusions that, in 1964, the Commission formally invited the CEM to produce the first "Memorandum concerning regional policies in the Common Market", delivered in the first few months of 1965, which was the basis for the report made by MEP Giovanni Bersani in January 1966 to the European Parliament as Speaker of the Economic and Financial Commission on the Common Market's regional policies. The report, agreed on with the CEM, clearly acknowledged for the first time the need to adopt regional policies that also involved local institutions as the representatives both of particular and overall interests. After a wide-ranging debate, the document was unanimously approved by the European Parliament on May 8th, 1966. Following this first success, the CEM's objective was to continue the battle for Europe based on concrete directives that would lead to increasing integration, emphasising the power of the European Parliament, while waiting for it to be directly elected along with a decisive and broader role and participation of democratically organised authorities at regional and local levels.[40]

In the multi-decade long work of the Council of European Municipalities and Regions (CEMR) – the movement changed its name in 1984 – the issue of how local authorities would be represented in European institutions remained on the agenda and merged with that of the democratic political forces and of the economic, social and cultural personalities involved in the battle for European unity and its democratisation, with the election of the European parliament through direct and universal suffrage. It was in such a perspective that during the conference on *Il ruolo delle regioni in un'Europa federale*, held in Naples in July 1970 and organised by the *Consiglio Italiano del Movimento Europeo* (CIME), the AICCE director Gianfranco Martini[41]

---

39 Caciagli, *Regioni d'Europa*. On the CEM's role as a 'prompter' for ministers involved in drafting the treaties establishing the Communities, see Zucca's *Conseil des communes d'Europe e il rilancio europeo di Messina*.

40 Grosso, *Necessità di una strutturazione democratica*, p. 4.

41 Gianfranco Martini was born in Lucca on June 23rd, 1925. In 1943, to avoid forced recruitment by the army of the republic of Salò, he took refuge in Lendinara, in the

spoke of how the relationship between European regionalisation and integration was complementary, since both were the symptoms and effects of an overall crisis affecting the organisations and functioning of the centralised national state. There was therefore a need to transfer the power and sovereignty of states both downwards to the regions and upwards to a European federation. According to Martini, regionalisation, with the consequent acknowledgement of the role played by intermediate bodies at a European level, would have an explosive function going well beyond the problem of decentralisation, since it implied a profound change in the existing institutional system at a national and supranational level.[42] In closing the conference, Umberto Serafini, at the time the AICCE's secretary general and an authoritative member of the CEM's supranational bodies, explained how the direct election of the European Parliament would be the turning point for a renewed importance of the entire organisation of the Community and therefore also of the regions.[43]

The position adopted by the CEM in April 1975 during the States-General held in Vienna was of particular importance on the eve of the decision that led to the process destined to result in the first direct election of the European parliament, with the movement representing local autonomies committed to the battle addressed at supporting the direct election of the first European parliament and the representation of local and regional powers in the European institutions.[44] One should not forget that in the 1960's a close political link was established with the European Parliament, which was not yet elected by direct universal suffrage. The CEM had managed to set up a formal and informal series of meetings and debates with the European Parliament, Commissions

---

Polesine, where in 1951 he was elected mayor, a position he held for a decade; he later was elected councillor of the province of Rovigo. After ensuring his municipality joined the newly created Italian section of the CEM, he attended the first States-General of the Municipalities of Europe held in Versailles in 1953, and from then on became increasingly involved in the dual federalist battle for European unity and for municipal autonomy. In 1964, invited by Umberto Serafini, he moved to Rome, becoming one of the AICCE's (and thus also the CEMR's) highest-ranking managers. In this dual role he was appointed a member of the CLRA. He presided over the association of Local Democracy Agencies and was the European head of CEMR twinning. On Gianfranco Martini see Di Giovan Paolo and Gianfranco Martini, *Piccoli Padri.*

42 ASUPv, Fondi aggregati, Archivio Umberto Serafini, c. 4, f. 2, *Convegno di studi su: Il ruolo delle regioni in un'Europa federale, Napoli 4-5 luglio 1970*, paper presented by Gianfranco Martini, *p.* 3.

43 ASUPv, Fondi aggregati, Archivio Umberto Serafini, c. 4, f. 2, *Convegno di studi su: Il ruolo delle regioni in un'Europa federale, Napoli 4-5 luglio 1970*, paper presented by Umberto Serafini, p. 18.

44 Serafini, *Breve storia del Consiglio dei comuni e delle regioni d'Europa*, pp. 102-108.

and individual MEPs directly interested in regional and local affairs. This work led to the creation of the European Parliament's Group for local and regional problems, whose work ended only when parliament created the Commission for Regional Policies, since with its specific competence it seemed to be an essential, albeit not exclusive, reference point for regional and local authorities. In particular the Commission played an important role in promoting the European Community's Conference of Regions. It was the final document of the first Conference held in January 1984, which insisted on the need for the European Parliament to ensure the continuing and regular participation of regional and local authorities in its activities. Furthermore, this document also stated that other institutions must implement the repeated statements made in support of this aforementioned participation, officialising their relations with the suitably adapted, enlarged and reformed consultative council to offer all possible representation to the Community's regions, and recommended that the EC Commission should establish a direct dialogue with the regions for all matters concerning European territorial institutions, while respecting the competences of member states.[45] This tendency gradually increased and was further implemented when, elected by direct universal suffrage on June 7th-10th, 1979, the European Parliament held the first Conference of the Regions in Strasbourg on January 25th-27th, 1984.[46]

Between the 1970's and the 1980's, the Regions and the European territorial institutions began to play a role, both because a number of centralised member states reorganised themselves with increasingly emphasised administrative decentralisation – first Italy and France and then Spain – and because others, such as Belgium, implemented progressive federal reforms of their country's organisation.[47]

In 1975 the European Regional Development Fund was created, marking the beginning of a first embryonic European regional policy. Its implementation also took place due to the impulse provided by the entrance of new countries, such as Great Britain, which at least formally acknowledged the important role played by local government[48] as well as being the 'exchange currency' used to ensure Great Britain and Ireland would accept the mechanisms of European agricultural policy.

---

45 "La dichiarazione finale".

46 "Conferenza delle Regioni della Comunità europea e dei paesi candidati Spagna e Portogallo".

47 Ferlaino and Molinari, *Neofederalismo, neoregionalismo e intercomunalità. pp.* 33-256.

48 On the role played by local institutions in the evolution of democracy in Great Britain see Gasser, *Geschichte der Volksfreiheit und der Demokratie; idem, Gemeindefreiheit als Rettung Europas.*

In the mid 1970s, in cooperation with the IULA, the CEM fostered the Consultative Committee of Local and Regional Authorities with the objective of creating a forum for meetings and dialogue between European local authorities and the institutions, with Parliament and the Communities' Commission reacting in a positive manner by starting a constructive dialogue.[49]

Consistent with the policy of establishing a continuous relationship with the European institutions, in December 1982 the CEM had delivered to the European Parliament's Institutional Commission a broad ranging document in which, in addition to supporting the need for a reform of the Treaties in a federal sense, it documented and expressed the need, once again together with the IULA, for the institutionalisation of the *Comité Consultatif des Institutions Locales et Régionales des États membres de la Communauté*, a body identical to the economic and social committee already envisaged by the Treaties. The objective was to democratise the institutions, bringing local administrators to take part in establishing European policies. The CEM thereby proposed to amend the Treaties by including in the preamble the acknowledgement "que les Collectivités locales régionales constituent un des principaux fondements démocratiques de la construction de l'Europe à laquelle elles participent à leur niveau de compétence".

It was also proposed that a new article should be added, envisaging the institutionalisation of an "organe consultatif des collectivités locales et régionales, qui viendraient prendre sa place au sein des Institutions Communautaires".[50]

Simultaneously, thanks to the stubborn and strategically important work done by Umberto Serafini and Gabriele Panizzi,[51] the Draft Treaty Establishing the European Union, sponsored and drafted by Altiero Spinelli, voted in a plenary session by the European Parliament on September 14th, 1983, and approved by absolute majority on February

49 [Pellegrini],"Il Comitato delle regioni e degli enti locali".

50 ASUPv, Fondi aggregati, Archivio Umberto Serafini, c. 11, f. 27, *Contribution du C.C.E. aux travaux de la Commission institutionnelle du Parlement européen* on December 23rd, 1982.

51 Gabriele Panizzi was born in Latina on March 11th, 1938. He was a member of AICCRE and president of the Rome section of the *Movimento federalista europeo*, vice-president of the Altiero Spinelli Institute of Federalist Studies, municipal councillor for the Municipality of Terracina from 1960 to 2001, councillor for the Lazio Region from 1975 to 1990 and president of this region from 1984 to 1985, and a MEP representing the Italian Socialist Party in 1994. During the 1950s he met Umberto Serafini, who involved him in the battle for a United States of Europe, a battle he is coherently still fighting today. Interview with Gabriele Panizzi recorded in Rome on October 22nd, 2009, and preserved at the ASUPv, Fondo CCRE.

14th, 1984, officially acknowledged the need for local and regional authorities to participate in the creation of the European Union.[52] The preamble for the project for the new Treaty also stated: "The High Contracting Parties [are] Convinced of the need to enable local and regional authorities to participate by appropriate methods in the unification of Europe".

On April 13th, 1984, the European Parliament approved a resolution that basically indicated the need to involve local authorities in the European integration process,[53] while later constitutional projects drafted by the European Parliament clearly indicated the need to create a Committee of the Regions.[54]

The first appearance made by local authorities within the Community's institutions only took place in 1988, when, as proposed by parliament, the Commission at last created the Consultative Council of regional and local authorities with the decision no. 88/487/EEC dated June 1988.[55] The Council, installed on December 20th that same year, was organised as a subsidiary body composed of forty-two members appointed by the Commission following joint nominations by the Assembly of European Regions, the IULA and the CEMR. The new institution was to be consulted on common policy provisions of interest to the regions[56] and functioned until 1993, when it was replaced with new institutions created by the Maastricht Treaty.

According to Umberto Serafini and the federalists in the movement of local European autonomies, the role of the Regions and local authorities should in all events have been a political one, and therefore also supersede institutional aspects, which were perceived as a means. According to the federalist leader:

> le Regioni europee oltre i loro normali compiti sono venute ad ereditare anche un compito essenziale di supplenza: rappresentare la maggioranza europeista delle popolazioni quanto meno dei Paesi della "piccola" Europa e della Spagna, per rilanciare il cammino verso l'Unione politica sovranazionale europea. Le Regioni dovranno non estraniarsi, con illusioni corporative, dai minori livelli delle autonomie territoriali, ma mettersi alla loro testa [perché] sarà l'Europa delle Regioni a farci avanzare verso un

52 Panizzi, "La battaglia per l'Europa e il Comitato delle Regioni".

53 [Pellegrini], "Il Comitato delle regioni e degli enti locali".

54 Serafini, *Breve storia del Consiglio dei comuni e delle regioni d'Europa*, p. 154.

55 [Pellegrini], "Il Comitato delle regioni e degli enti locali".

56 Mascia, *Il Comitato delle Regioni nel sistema dell'Unione europea.*

democratico assetto federale: altrimenti la storia dell'Europa libera è finita e noi decadremo definitivamente a un rango coloniale.[57]

Loyal to these principles, Umberto Serafini asked Gabriele Panizzi, at the time a councillor for the Lazio Region, to present the draft law 204 dated April 8th, 1986, to the Lazio Regional Council. This law, with reference to the Treaty establishing the European Union approved by the European Parliament, set up the "Permanent Committee of local and regional power and activities for the European Union". According to its proponent, the Committee was expected to play an "autonomous innovative role within an organisational framework of interdependency from a municipal to a regional level, both national and supranational" as well as to represent a clear example of what should be done at a European institutional level.[58]

Meeting in Paris on May 23rd, 1990, the CEMR's presidency unanimously approved a political resolution asking Parliament and the Commission "that, in addition to the two houses of parliament, it should become compulsory to consult the Consultative Council of regional and local communities at the European Community's Commission".[59] This resolution was once again referred to during the XIII States-General of the Municipalities of Europe held in Lisbon in October, 1990, which, acknowledging the decisions taken by the European Council held in Dublin on June 25th and 26th, which envisaged a summoning of two Intergovernmental Conferences, the first to debate Economic and Monetary Union and the second to address political union, requested a European currency, the coordination of common policies, the integration of an authentic social Europe, and the ratification of a treaty for political union taking into account the territorial bodies. The final resolution stated the need for the:

---

57 ASUPv, Fondi aggregati, Archivio Umberto Serafini, c. 9, f. 2, document prepared for Panizzi for the Lazio Region on April 9th, 1986 (transl. "besides their usual institutional tasks, European Regions inherited an essential "covering duty": they represent the pro-Europe majority of the people, at least of the populations of "small" Europe countries and of Spain, willing to resume the march toward the European supranational political union. Regions should not withdraw, driven by corporative illusions, from the lower levels of local authorities, they should rather lead them [since] only a Europe of Regions will be able to move us forward the foundation of a democratic federation. The history of free Europe is otherwise over and we will once and for all descend to the status of a colony").

58 ASUPv, Fondi aggregati, Archivio Umberto Serafini, c. 4, f. 3, Regione Lazio. Proposta di legge n. 204 di iniziativa dei consiglieri: Mechelli, Panizzi, Marroni, Massolo, Molinari e Splendori. Iniziative della Regione e degli enti locali per l'Unione europea.

59 Serafini, *Breve storia del Consiglio dei comuni e delle regioni d'Europa*, p. 154.

> creazione dell'Unione europea dotata di un autentico potere esecutivo responsabile (derivato dalla Commissione comunitaria) e i cui poteri legislativi e di controllo sarebbero esercitati da un sistema bicamerale costituito: da un'Assemblea dei Popoli (il Parlamento europeo), da una Camera Alta che rappresenti gli Stati e assicuri una rappresentanza dell'ordinamento regionale e locale.[60]

It was only the complete application of the Maastricht Treaty, signed on February 7th, 1992, that in 1994 finally implemented all that had been deliberated ten years earlier by the European Parliament through the creation of the Committee of Regions, the objective of which was to encourage cooperation between the regions of the Union's member states. The Committee, which took office on March 9th and 10th, 1994, therefore became one of the Union's representative bodies alongside the Council of Ministers and the Parliament. The importance the interested bodies attributed to the Committee when it was created is confirmed by the fact that its members were important politicians from regional governments and mayors of large cities. Members of the Committee also recognised the essential role that the CEMR had played in its creation, electing as its first president France's Jacques Blanc – President of the Languedoc Roussillon Region, mayor of Canourgue, and a member of the CEMR's French section – and as the first vice-president the Catalan Pasqual Maragall – mayor of Barcelona – president of the CEMR.

The main function of this Committee, consisting of 189 incumbent members and as many substitutes, was to express opinions addressed to the Council and the Commission, but not to Parliament. Local institutions therefore acquired a new institutional role, albeit partly losing their privileged political relationship with the European Parliament. The issues on which it was compulsory to consult the Committee were education, within the framework of social policies, culture, public health, trans-European transport, telecommunications and energy networks, economic and social cohesion. The Committee was therefore in a category of community organisations having consultative functions together with the European Economic and Social Committee (EESC) and the European Parliament itself. Further enlargements of the Community preceding the Union then strengthened the perception of the

60 [Pellegrini], "Il Comitato delle regioni e degli enti locali" (transl. "foundation of the European Union, endowed with an actual and accountable executive power derived form the Communities' Commission. The legislative and control powers shall be exercised according to the bicameral system: by an Assembly of the Peoples (the European Parliament) and by an upper house representing not only the member States, but also regional and local authorities").

positive role European territorial institutions could play as strategic players for the integration of candidate countries.[61]

After its installation, the Committee of the Regions was reconfirmed along with the functions attributed to it during the 1997 Conference of Amsterdam, a decision that was renewed in 1998 and reformed with the Treaty of Nice approved at the European Council held in the French city on December 11th, 2000, and signed on February 26th, 2001. After being ratified by the then fifteen member states of the European Union, the treaty came into force on February 1, 2003. The Treaty establishing a Constitution for Europe (Constitutional Treaty signed in Rome on October 29th, 2004) further establishes that the Committee of the Regions is also a consultative body of the European Parliament, thereby becoming one of the instruments for a possible multilevel governance of a new Europe.

Nowadays the Committee of the Regions has its headquarters in Brussels and consists of 344 members representing regional and local institutions (Art. 263 of the Treaty as modified by the Treaty of Nice). As proposed by the central governments, since 1994 members are appointed every four years. It is obvious that this system must be overcome to guarantee greater democracy within the Committee, even though now the representatives already form alliances and oppose one another on the basis of their belonging to the various political groups, on the basis of national and regional delegations, as well as based on geographical criteria (thus for example a Mediterranean Group[62] has been formed) and inclusion in urban/industrial or agricultural regions with deliberative or only administrative powers, among regions in the North, the South and the East, and among representatives of Regions or other local bodies. These various aggregations prove the vitality and potential of possible new convergences of political and territorial interests rather than a weakness of the Committee as some have maintained.[63]

In view of this brief historical reconstruction that emphasises the role local European bodies have played in creating European integration through coherent work implemented for over half a century, a statement by Frédéric Vallier, secretary general of the CEMR, made in Berlin when he was elected, still seems valid today. According to Vallier, the role played by local authorities, also regarding the crisis that has profoundly affected European countries, remains that of providing a first

---

61 Comitato delle Regioni, *Un'Europa di città e regioni*.

62 On the work of the Mediterranean Regions see Bolgherini, *Come le regioni diventano europee*.

63 Caciagli, *Regioni d'Europa*, p. 105.

response for citizens, because they are clearly aware of the reality of a situation and are capable of mobilising consciences more that a state policy can. Local policies are the real spokesperson of the demands of the people, whose participation in the government decision-making process should be strengthened.[64] The CEMR, the European section of the IULA, in tune with the Committee of the Regions, is therefore preparing to embark upon a new battle for relations between citizens and the European Union at a time when the European Union is experiencing a serious crisis; as has always happened in the past, this may lead to positive new scenarios if the new leading players in this history will be capable of continuing the Europeanist and federalist work of their fathers.

64 Salerno, "Questo è il bello della democrazia".

References

"1912-1990", *XXe siècle fédéraliste. Pouvoir européen*, 1 (1991), pp. 2-3.

IIe Congrès international des Villes, Amsterdam 30 juin et 1 juillet 1924, Union international des villes, Brussels, 1924.

IIIe Congrès international des villes, Paris 28 septembre-4 octobre 1925, Union international des villes, Paris, [1925?], 3 vols.

"Les IVe États Généraux des communes d'Europe", *Communes d'Europe*, 33-34 (September-October 1958), pp. 34-37.

XXe siècle fédéraliste. Pouvoir européen, 1 (1993), p. 4.

Actes et documents du Premier Congrès du Peuple Européen, Turin, 6-8 décembre 1957, Strasbourg, 1957.

"L'action du C.C.E. en faveur de la Conférence européenne des pouvoirs locaux", *Communes d'Europe*, 3 (March 1956), p. 12.

L'action fédéraliste européenne, 3 (November 1946).

Adenauer, Konrad, *Erinnerungen 1945-1953*, Deutsche Verlags-Anstalt, Stuttgart, 1965.

"Adesione socialista", *L'Unità Europea*, 7 (November-December 1944), p. 3.

Aga Rossi, Elena (ed.), *Il piano Marshall e l'Europa*, Istituto della Enciclopedia italiana, Rome, 1983.

Agnelli, Arduino, "Da Coudenhove-Kalergi al piano Briand", in Sergio Pistone (ed.), *L'idea dell'unificazione europea dalla prima alla seconda guerra mondiale. Relazioni tenute al convegno di studi svoltosi presso la Fondazione Luigi Einaudi (Torino, 25-26 ottobre 1974)*, Fondazione Luigi Einaudi, Turin, 1975, pp. 40-57.

AICCE, *Il ruolo dei gemellaggi per l'Unione europea*, Broglio Editore, Rome, 1978.

"L'AICCRE la cittadinanza europea e i gemellaggi", in AICCRE, *Documento informativo*, AICCRE, Rome, 2011, p. 3.

[Albertini, Mario], "Esame tecnico della lotta per l'Europa", *Il federalista*, 2 (September 1959), pp. 86-111 (published under the pseudonym of Publius).

Albertini, Mario, *Lo Stato nazionale*, Giuffré, Milan, 1960.

Albertini, Mario, "Far partecipare le basi dei partiti alla elaborazione dei programmi elettorali europei", *L'Unità Europea*, 42 (August 1977), pp. 1-4.

Albertini, Mario, *Il federalismo. Antologia e definizione*, Il Mulino, Bologna, 1979.

Albertini, Mario, *Il Risorgimento e l'Unità europea*, Guida, Naples, 1979.

Albertini, Mario, *Tutti gli scritti*, Il Mulino, Bologna, 2006-2010, 9 vols.

Albertini, Mario - Chiti-Batelli, Andrea - Petrilli, Giuseppe, *Storia del federalismo europeo*, ERI, Turin, 1973.

"Alberto Cabella segretario nazionale aggiunto del M.F.E.", *Europa federata*, 51 (September 1951), p. 4.

Albonetti, Achille, *Euratom e sviluppo nucleare*, Edizioni di Comunità, Milan, 1958.

Albonetti, Achille, *Preistoria degli Stati Uniti d'Europa*, Giuffrè, Milan, 1960.

Alfassio Grimaldi, Ugoberto, "Il federalismo della 'Critica' mondolfiana", *Critica sociale*, 1 (1972), pp. 16-17.

Amato, Pasquale, *Il PSI tra frontismo e autonomia*, Lerici, Cosenza, 1978.

Aniasi, Aldo, "Non solo atto di generica simpatia", *Comuni d'Europa*, 6 (June 1969), p. 2.

Aniasi, Aldo, "Ogni lionese è cittadino di Milano", *Comuni d'Europa*, 6 (June 1969), pp. 1-2.

Aniasi, Aldo, *Vivere a Milano*, SugarCo, Milan, 1975.

Aniasi, Aldo, *I socialisti per gli enti locali*, Edizioni delle autonomie, Rome, 1979.

Aniasi, Aldo, "Introduzione", in Bettino Craxi *et al.*, *La Conferenza programmatica del PSI. Rimini, aprile 1982: i problemi istituzionali*, Edizioni del Circolo di Via De Amicis 17, Milan, 1982, pp. 5-12.

Aniasi, Aldo, "Introduzione", in Italia, Ministero per gli Affari regionali, *Rapporto sullo stato delle autonomie del Ministro per gli Affari regionali Aldo Aniasi*, Istituto poligrafico e zecca dello Stato, Rome, 1982, pp. 7-19.

Aniasi, Aldo, *Parri. L'avventura umana, militare e politica di Maurizio*, ERI, Turin, 1991.

Aniasi, Aldo (ed.), *Ne valeva la pena. Dalla "Repubblica" dell'Ossola alla Costituzione repubblicana*, M&B, Milan, 1997.

"Antonio Segni interviene al direttivo dell'AICCE", *Comuni d'Europa*, 5 (May 1962), p. 1.

Ardy, Silvio, "I rapporti del C.C.E. con l'Union International des Villes", *Nuova Rassegna di legislazione, dottrina e giurisprudenza. Rivista amministrativa quindicinale per i comuni, le provincie e per gli altri enti locali*, second series, 12 (June 1954), pp. 914-915.

Ardy, Silvio, "Realtà nell'utopia", *Nuova Rassegna di legislazione, dottrina e giurisprudenza. Rivista amministrativa quindicinale per i comuni, le provincie e per gli altri enti locali*, second series, 12 (June 1954), p. 893.

Ardy, Silvio (ed.), *Il Consiglio dei comuni d'Europa. Resoconto dei primi stati generali e della prima assemblea (Versaglia, 16-17-18 ottobre 1953)*, Noccioli, Florence, 1954, monographic issue of *Nuova Rassegna di legislazione, dottrina e giurisprudenza*, 12 (June 16th 1954), p. 913.

Arfè, Gaetano, "Presentazione", in Marta Petricioli (ed.), *La sinistra europea nel secondo dopoguerra (1943-1949)*, Sansoni, Florence, 1981.

Arfè, Gaetano, *Intellettuali e società di massa: i socialisti dal 1945 a oggi*, ECIG, Genoa, 1984.

Aron, Raymond and Lerner, Daniel (eds.), *La querelle de la CED. Essais d'analyse sociologique. Recueil d'études*, Colin, Paris, 1956.

"Assemblea dei delegati del CCE a Torino", *Comuni d'Europa*, 4 (April 1963), pp. 5-10.

Association française du Conseil des Communes et Régions d'Europe, *L'art du jumelage. Pourquoi, avec qui et comment jumeler sa commune*, AFCCRE, [Orléans, 1995?], p. 3.

Associazione Italiana per il Consiglio dei Comuni d'Europa, *Statuto e documenti fondamentali*, Tip. Castaldi, Rome, 1962, p. 27.

Associazione Italiana per il Consiglio dei Comuni e delle Regioni d'Europa, I *gemellaggi per l'unione europea e per la pace: guida ai vincoli permanenti di fraternità tra Comuni, Province e Regioni d'Europa aperti alle relazioni Est-Ovest, Nord-Sud* (ed. Mattia Pacilli), Salemi, Rome, 1990.

"Atmosfera pesante nel PSDI milanese. Aniasi e Jori lasciano gli assessorati in contrasto col sindaco Virgilio Ferrari", *Avanti* (February 6th 1959), p. 4.

Auriol, Vincent, *Journal du septennat (1947-1954)*, Colin, Paris, 1970-1978, 7 vols.

"Autonomie e Stato", *Comuni d'Europa*, 2-3 (January 1953), pp. 3-4.

Averardi, Giuseppe, *I socialisti democratici. Da Palazzo Barberini alla scissione del 4 luglio 1969*, SugarCo, Milan, 1977.

Babel, A., "A la mémoire du professeur Edgard Milhaud", *Le Coopérateur Suisse*, 57 (1965), no. 39, pp. 506-509.

Ballini, Pier Luigi, *Alcide De Gasperi*. III. *Dalla costruzione della democrazia alla "nostra patria Europa" (1948-1954)*, Rubbettino, Soveria Mannelli, 2009.

Bareth, Jean, *Le fédéralisme par la commune*, La Fédération, Paris, 1946.

Bareth, Jean, "Le fédéralisme c'est d'abord la commune", *Circulaire intérieure de la Fédération* (July-August 1946).

Bareth, Jean, *Le fédéralisme: un principe, une action*, La Fédération, Paris, 1947.

Bareth, Jean, *La Commune et l'Europe. Jumelages et rencontres intercommunales*, Conseil des communes d'Europe Geneva, [1953].

Bareth, Jean, *The Municipality and Europe. Twinning and Intermunicipal Encounters*, Council of european municipalities, Geneva, 1953.

Bareth, Jean, *L'Europe des Communes*, Section luxembourgeoise du Conseil des Communes d'Europe, Luxembourg, 1956.

Bareth, Jean, "46 Comuni francesi sono affratellati con altre città europee", *Comuni d'Europa*, 2 (February 1956), p. 1.

Bareth, Jean, "J'étais à Seelisberg", *Communes d'Europe*, new series, 15 (March-April 1961), p. 11.

Bareth, Jean, "Uno dei più esemplari sindaci europei", *Comuni d'Europa*, 9 (September 1965), p. 4.

[Bareth, Jean], "Mort d'Amedeo Peyron", *Communes d'Europe*, new series, 49 (September-October 1965), p. 7.

Barié, Ottavio, "Presentazione", in Guido Formigoni, *La Democrazia Cristiana e l'alleanza occidentale (1943-1953)*, Il Mulino, Bologna, 1996, pp. 7-10.

Barral, Pierre, *Il y a trente ans. La guerre froide*, Colin, Paris, 1984.

Bauer, Hans, *Les 50 ans de l'Union européenne de Suisse 1934-1984*, [s.n.], Berne, 1984.

Bechelloni, Antonio (ed.), *Metamorfosi di un modello repubblicano: Francia 1944-1993*, Unicopli, Milan, 1995.

Becker, Jean-Jacques, *Histoire politique de la France depuis 1945*, Colin, Paris, 1992.

Benzoni, Alberto and Tedesco, Viva, *Il movimento socialista del dopoguerra*, Marsilio, Padova, 1968.

Benzoni, Alberto - Guitti, Roberto - Landolfi, Antonio (eds.), *La dimensione internazionale del socialismo italiano. 100 anni di politica estera del PSI*, Ed. associate, Rome, 1993.

Berstein, Serge and Rudelle, Odile (eds.), *Le modèle républicaine*, Presses universitaires de France, Paris, 1992.

Berta, Giuseppe, "Fra centrismo e centro sinistra: Olivetti e il Movimento Comunità", *Studi storici*, 3 (1978), pp. 545-587.

Beyer, Henry, *Robert Schuman. L'Europe par la réconciliation franco-allemande*, Fondation Jean Monnet pour l'Europe, Lausanne, 1986.

Bianchi, Gianfranco, *Neutralismo elvetico (1814-1944). Vicende, problemi, documenti, testi*, Università di Trieste, Trieste, 1974.

Bjøl, Erling, *La France devant l'Europe. La politique européenne de la IV République*, Munksgaard, Copenhagen, 1966.

Bitsch, Marie Thérèse, "Le rôle de la France dans la naissance du Conseil de l'Europe", in Raymond Poidevin (ed.), *Histoire des débuts de la construction européenne (mars 1948 - mai 1950). Actes du Colloque de Strasbourg, 28-30 novembre 1984*, Bruylant *et al.*, Brussels *et al.*, 1986, pp. 165-198.

Bitsch, Marie Thérèse (ed.), *Jalons pour une histoire du Conseil de l'Europe. Actes du Colloque de Strasbourg, 8-10 juin 1995*, Peter Lang, Bern, 1997.

Bitsch, Marie-Thérèse (ed.), *Le fait régional et la construction européenne*, Bruylant, Brussels, 2003.

Bitsch, Marie Thérèse - Loth, Wilfried - Poidevin, Raymond (eds.), *Institutions européennes et identités européennes*, Bruylant, Brussels, 1998.

Bloch-Lainé, François and Bouvier, Jean, *La France restaureé 1944-1954. Dialogue sur les choix d'une modernisation*, Fayard, Paris, 1986.

Blum, Léon, *L'œuvre de Léon Blum*. IX. *1947-1950*, Michel, Paris, 1963.

Bobbio, Norberto, *Il federalismo nel dibattito politico e culturale della Resistenza*, Fondazione Luigi Einaudi, Turin, 1975.

Bobbio, Norberto, "Un uomo del secolo: Umberto Campagnolo", *Nuova Antologia*, 580 (1998), pp. 35-44.

Boffa, Giuseppe, *Storia dell'Unione Sovietica*. II. *Dalla guerra patriottica al ruolo di seconda potenza mondiale. Stalin e Cruscëv 1941-1964*, Mondadori, Milan, 1976-1979.

Bolgherini, Silvia, *Come le regioni diventano europee. Stile di governo e sfide comunitarie nell'Europa mediterranea*, Il Mulino, Bologna, 2006.

Bolis, Luciano and Marc, Alexandre, "Combat", *Quaderni federalisti*, 26 (February 1993), pp. 3ff.

Bonin, Hubert, *Histoire économique de la Quatrième République*, Masson, Paris, 1988.

Bossuat, Gérard, "La France et les constructions européennes 1943-1957", *Historiens et Géographes*, 319 (July-August 1988), pp. 145-165.

Bossuat, Gérard, *D'Alger à Rome (1943-1957). Choix de documents*, Ciaco, Louvain-la-Neuve, 1989.

Bossuat, Gérard, *La France, l'aide américaine et la construction européenne 1944-1954*, Comité pour l'histoire économique et financière de la France, Paris, 1992, 2 vols.

Bossuat, Gérard, *L'Europe occidentale à l'heure américaine. Le plan Marshall et l'unité européenne 1945-1952*, Complexe, Brussels, 1992.

Bourgeois, Daniel, *Le troisième Reich et la Suisse, 1933-1941*, Ed. de la Baconnière, Neuchâtel, 1974.

Bouvier, Jean *et al.*, *Histoire économique et sociale de la France*. IV. *L'ère industrielle et la société d'aujourd'hui, siècle 1880-1980* (eds. Fernand Braudel and Ernest Labrousse), Presses universitaires de France, Paris, 1979-1982.

Braga, Antonella, "La collaborazione con Ernesto Rossi nel lavoro di organizzazione e propaganda del Movimento federalista europeo in Svizzera", in Daniela Preda and Cinzia Rognoni Vercelli (eds.), *Dalla Resistenza all'Europa. Il mondo di Luciano Bolis*, TCP, Pavia, 2001, pp. 93-135.

Braga, Antonella, "Nazionalismo, federalismo e autonomie nel pensiero politico di Ernesto Rossi", in Daniela Preda and Cinzia Rognoni Vercelli (eds.), *Storie e percorsi del federalismo. L'eredità di Carlo Cattaneo*, Il Mulino, Bologna, 2005, vol. II, pp. 809-859.

Braga, Antonella, *Un federalista giacobino. Ernesto Rossi pioniere degli Stati uniti d'Europa*, Il Mulino, Bologna, 2007.

Braga, Antonella and Michelotti, Simonetta (eds.), *Ernesto Rossi. Un democratico europeo*, Rubbettino, Soveria Mannelli, 2009.

Braudel, Fernand, *Civiltà e imperi del Mediterraneo nell'età di Filippo II*, Einaudi, Turin, 1976, vol. I, pp. 94-236.

Breccia, Alfredo, *L'Italia e la difesa dell'Europa. Alle origini del Piano Pleven*, Istituto di studi europei A. De Gasperi, Rome, 1984.

Brugmans, Hendrik, *L'idée européenne 1920-1970*, De Tempel, Bruges, 1970.

Bufardeci, Giuseppe, "Il significato politico dei gemellaggi e le elezioni dirette del parlamento europeo. Relazione introduttiva al convegno europeo delle città gemellate. Lucca, 19/20 maggio 1972", in AICCE, *Il ruolo dei gemellaggi per l'Unione europea*, Broglio Editore, Rome, 1978, pp. 59-65.

Burban, Jean-Louis, *Le Conseil de l'Europe*, Presses universitaires de France, Paris, 1993.

Cabella, Alberto, "C.P.E. (Congresso del Popolo Europeo)", *Comuni d'Europa*, 5 (May 1974), p. 11.

Caciagli, Mario, *Regioni d'Europa. Devoluzioni, regionalismi, integrazione europea*, Il Mulino, Bologna, 2003.

Cadeddu, Davide, *Il valore della politica in Adriano Olivetti*, Fondazione Adriano Olivetti, Rome, 2007.

Caizzi, Bruno, *Camillo e Adriano Olivetti*, UTET, Turin, 1962.

Calchi Novati, Gianpaolo, *Neutralismo e guerra fredda*, Edizioni di Comunità, Milan, 1963.

Canavero, Alfredo, "Pietro Nenni, i socialisti italiani e l'Internazionale socialista tra Est e Ovest dopo la seconda guerra mondiale", in *Les Internationales et le problème de la guerre au XXe siècle. Actes du colloque de Rome, 22-24 novembre 1984*, École française de Rome, Rome, 1987, pp. 241-264.

Canavero, Alfredo, *Alcide De Gasperi. Cristiano, democratico, europeo*, Rubbettino, Soveria Mannelli, 2003.

Canavero, Alfredo *et. al.*, *Alcide De Gasperi*. I. *Dal Trentino all'esilio in patria (1881-1943)*, Rubbettino, Soveria Mannelli, 2009.

Canavero, Alfredo and Durand, Jean-Dominique (eds.), *Il fattore religioso nell'integrazione europea. Programma di ricerca "Les identités européennes au XXe siècle" coordinato dall'Institut Pierre Renouvin (Université Paris 1 - Panthéon Sorbonne)*, Unicopli, Milan, 1999.

Caraffini, Paolo, *Il Piemonte per l'Europa: venticinque anni di attività della Consulta regionale europea 1976-2001*, Celid, Turin, 2002.

Caraffini, Paolo, "Ivan Matteo Lombardo e l'unità europea", in Fabio Zucca (ed.), *Europeismo e federalismo in Lombardia dal Risorgimento all'Unione europea*, Il Mulino, Bologna, 2007, pp. 333-373.

Caraffini, Paolo, *Costruire l'Europa dal basso. Il ruolo del Consiglio italiano del Movimento europeo (1948-1985)*, Il Mulino, Bologna, 2008.

"Carta europea delle libertà locali", *Comuni d'Europa*, 2-3 (January 1953), p 3.

Cartou, Louis, *Communautés Européennes*, Dalloz, Paris, 1986.

Carucci, Paola, "Lo scarto come elemento qualificante delle fonti per la storiografia", *Rassegna degli Archivi di Stato*, 35 (1975), pp. 250-264.

Catala, Michel (ed.), *Histoire de la construction européenne. Cinquante ans après la déclaration Schuman*, Ouest Editions, Nantes, 2001.

Catalano, Franco, *Europa e Stati Uniti negli anni della guerra fredda. Economia e politica 1944-1956*, Istituto Librario internazionale, Milan, 1972.

Cattaneo, Carlo, *Stati Uniti d'Italia* (ed. and with an Introduction by Norberto Bobbio), Chiantore, Turin, 1945.

Catti De Gasperi, Maria Romana, *La nostra patria Europa. Il pensiero europeistico di Alcide De Gasperi*, Mondadori, Milan, 1969.

Catti De Gasperi, Maria Romana, *De Gasperi e l'Europa*, Morcelliana, Brescia, 1979.

Cerchiai, Geri and Rota, Giovanni (eds.), *Eugenio Colorni e la cultura italiana fra le due guerre*, Lacaita, Manduria - Bari - Rome, 2011.

Chanoux, Émile, *Écrits* (ed. Paolo Momigliano Levi), Institut historique de la Résistance en Vallée d'Aoste, Aosta, 1994.

Chaunu, Pierre, *La conquista e l'esplorazione dei nuovi mondi (XVI secolo)*, Mursia, Milan, 1977.

Chaunu, Pierre, *L'espansione europea dal XIII al XV secolo*, Mursia, Milan, 1979.

Chenaux, Philippe, *Une Europe vaticane? Entre le Plan Marshall et les Traités de Rome*, Ciaco, Brussels, 1990.

Chiti-Batelli, Andrea, "Mazzini, précurseur de l'idée de la fédération européenne?", *Bulletin du Centre interdisciplinare de Recherches sur l'Italie de l'Université de Strasbourg*, 1 (1974), pp. 16-71.

Chiti-Batelli, Andrea, *La dimensione europea delle autonomie e l'Italia. Regione, ente intermedio, autonomie nella prospettiva federalista*, Franco Angeli, Milan, 1984.

Chiti-Batelli, Andrea, *Regionalismo, federalismo, razzismo*, published by author, Rome, 1994.

Chiti-Batelli, Andrea, "L'idea federalista nel pensiero di Adriano Olivetti", in Sergio Pistone and Corrado Malandrino (eds.), *Europeismo e federalismo in Piemonte tra le due guerre mondiali. La Resistenza e i Trattati di Roma (1957). Atti del Convegno tenuto presso la Fondazione Luigi Einaudi, Torino, 9 e 10 ottobre 1997*, Olschki, Florence, 1999, pp. 251-263.

Chiti-Batelli, Andrea, *Oltre il sistema rappresentativo? Per un superamento della democrazia partitica alla luce della proposta di Adriano Olivetti in un ambito federale europeo. Materiali per un dibattito*, Franco Angeli, Milan, 2006.

Cialdea, Basilio, "Presupposti di un'Unione Europea", *Politica Estera*, 4-5 (1945), pp. 78-83.

"Cittadinanza europea e gemellaggi", *Comuni d'Europa*, new series, 27 (March 2011).

Citterio, Ferdinando and Vaccaro, Luciano (eds.), *Quale federalismo per quale Europa. Il contributo della tradizione cristiana*, Morcelliana, Brescia, 1996.

Ciuffoletti, Zeffiro *et al.*, *Storia del P.S.I.*, Laterza, Rome-Bari, 1992-1993.

Clesse, Armand, *Le project de C.E.D. du Plan Pleven au "crime" du 30 août: histoire d'un malentendu européen*, Nomos, Baden-Baden, 1989.

Clotet y Mirò, Maria-Angels, *La cooperación internacional de los municipios en el marco del Consejo de Europa. La obra de la Conferencia permanente de poderes locales y regionales de Europa*, Civitas, Madrid, 1992.

Codiroli, Pierre, *L'ombra del Duce. Lineamenti di politica culturale del fascismo nel Canton Ticino (1921-1943)*, Franco Angeli, Milan, 1988.

Cofrancesco, Dino, "La battaglia federalista di U. G. Mondolfo", *Quaderni di scienze sociali*, 3 (1969), pp. 25-48.

Cofrancesco, Dino, "La 'Battaglia per il socialismo' di U.G. Mondolfo. Riflessioni sullo Stato nazionale e l'Europa", in Gaetano Arfè *et al.*, *Socialismo e socialisti dal Risorgimento al fascismo*, De Donato, Bari, 1974, pp. 309-357.

Cofrancesco, Dino, *Europeismo e cultura. Da Cattaneo a Calogero*, ECIG, Genova, 1981.

Cofrancesco, Dino, *Per una analisi critica della destra rivoluzionaria. Dal nazionalsocialismo al fascismo*, ECIG, Genova, 1984.

Colarizi, Simona, *Storia dei partiti nell'Italia repubblicana*, Laterza, Rome-Bari, 1996.

Collotti, Enzo, *Solidarietà europea e prospettive di un nuovo ordine internazionale nel pensiero della Resistenza italiana*, in *Annali della Facoltà di Lettere e Filosofia dell'Università di Trieste* (Trieste, 1965-1966), vol. II.

Collotti, Enzo, *Nazismo e società tedesca 1933-1945*, Loescher, Turin, 1982.

Colombo, Ornella, *Per una storia del federalismo italiano: il dibattito interno del Movimento Federalista Europeo dal 1945 al 1948*, Degree thesis debated at the Faculty of Humanities and Philosophy at Pavia University, academic year 1983-1984, Thesis Director Giulio Guderzo.

Colorni, Eugenio, *La malattia della metafisica. Scritti filosofici e autobiografici* (eds. Geri Cerchiai and Giovanni Rota), Einaudi, Turin, 2009.

Comitato delle Regioni, *Un'Europa di città e regioni. Strategie e prospettive per un'Unione europea allargata*, Ufficio delle pubblicazioni ufficiali delle Comunità europee, Luxembourg, 2002.

Comitato direttivo nazionale del MFE, "Verso il IV Congresso del MFE", *Europa federata*, supplement for no. 41 (1951), pp. I-III.

Comité pour la commémoration du 100e anniversaire de Robert Schuman, *Les racines et l'œuvre d'un grand Européen. Robert Schuman 1886-1986*, Ville de Luxembourg, Luxembourg, 1986.

"Comment organiser un jumelage!", *Communes d'Europe*, 23 (November 1957), p. 9.

Commissione delle Comunità europee, *I comuni e l'Europa. Guida pratica dei gemellaggi*, Ufficio delle pubblicazioni ufficiali delle Comunità europee, Brussels-Luxembourg, 1992.

Il comune di Firenze e l'Europa, in Ufficio Stampa del comune di Firenze (ed.), *Firenze. Rassegna del comune 1951-1960*, Florence, 1960, single edition, October 1960, p. 115.

Comuni d'Europa, 11 (November 1964).

Comuni d'Europa, 6 (June 1984).

Comuni d'Europa, new series, 10 (December 2005).

"Conférence européenne des pouvoirs locaux", *Communes d'Europe*, 13 (January 1957), p. 2.

La Conférence des pouvoirs locaux et régionaux de l'Europe. Pour une Europe plus démocratique et équilibrée. La participation des communes et régions à la construction de l'Europe, Conseil d'Europe, Strasbourg, 1980.

"Conferenza delle Regioni della Comunità europea e dei paesi candidati Spagna e Portogallo", *Comuni d'Europa*, 2 (February 1984), p. XIII.

Il Congresso del Popolo Europeo. Documenti, Tip. Angelucci, Rome, [s.d.].

"Il Consiglio dei Comuni d'Europa", *Europa Federata*, 40 (February 1951), p. 4.

"Consiglio direttivo dell'AICCE", *Comuni d'Europa*, 1 (February 1954), p. 2.

Consiglio regionale della Lombardia, *Comunità europee e ruolo delle Regioni. Atti del Convegno tenutosi a Milano il 26 e 27 ottobre 1979*, Giuffrè, Milan, 1981.

Conte, Pietro, *I papi e l'Europa. Documenti (PIO XII-Giovanni XXIII-Paolo VI)*, Elledici, Turin, 1978.

"Il convegno costitutivo dell'Associazione italiana per il Consiglio dei comuni d'Europa (Rome 26th-27th January 1952)", *Comuni d'Europa*, 1 (April 1952).

Coudenhove-Kalergi, Richard, *Crusade for Pan-Europe. Autobiography of a man and a movement*, G. P. Putnam's sons, New York, 1943.

Coudenhove-Kalergi, Richard, *Pan-Europe*, Presses universitaires de France, Paris, 1988.

"Cronaca del Movimento", *Rivista del movimento comunità*, 13 (January 1952), p. 2.

"Cronaca del movimento. Riunione della D.P.E. del Movimento Comunità", *Comunità*, 19 (June 1953), pp. I-II.

La cultura delle riforme in Italia fra Otto e Novecento. I Montemartini. Atti del seminario nazionale, Pavia, 15 dicembre 1984, Amministrazione provinciale, Pavia, 1986.

Curcio, Carlo, *Europa. Storia di un'idea*, ERI, Turin, 1978.

D'Agata, Raffaele, *Le origini del Movimento federalista europeo (1941-1946)*, Elengraf, Rome, 1976.

Damilano, Andrea (ed.), *Atti e documenti della Democrazia cristiana 1943-1967*, Cinque Lune, Rome, 1968, vol. I.

Debré, Michel, *Trois républiques pour une France. Mémoires*, Michel, Paris, 1984-1988, vols. 1-2.

Decleva, Enrico, "La politica estera: dal frontismo alla riscoperta dell'Europa", in Fondazione Brodolini (ed.), *Storia del Partito socialista*. III. *Dalla guerra fredda all'alternativa*, Marsilio, Venice, 1980, pp. 21-51.

Decleva, Enrico, "I socialisti fra unità europea e politica dei blocchi", in Arturo Colombo (ed.), *La Resistenza e l'Europa. Atti del convegno di studi storici. Como, 28-31 maggio 1983*, Le Monnier, Florence, 1984, pp. 136-181.

De Felice, Alessandro, "La socialdemocrazia e la scelta occidentale dell'Italia (1946-1947)", *Storia contemporanea*, 1 (1995), pp. 5-43.

De Felice, Alessandro, "Il PSLI e la scelta occidentale (1948-1949)", *Storia contemporanea*, 1 (February 1996), pp. 69-112.

De Felice, Renzo, *Mussolini il fascista*. I. *La conquista del potere 1921-1925*, Einaudi, Turin, 1966.

Defferre, Gaston, "Depuis Genève, le C.C.E. fut son œuvre", *Communes d'Europe*, new series, 68 (December 1969), p. 3.

De Gasperi, Alcide, *De Gasperi scrive. Corrispondenza con capi di stato, cardinali, uomini politici, giornalisti, diplomatici* (ed. Maria Romana Catti De Gasperi), Morcelliana, Brescia, 1974, 2 vols.

De Gaulle, Charles, *L'esprit de la Vème République. Mémoires d'espoir. Suivi d'un choix d'allocutions et messages sur la IVème et la Vème Républiques 1946-1969*, Plon, Paris, 1994.

Degl'Innocenti, Maurizio, "Introduzione a Eugenio Colorni", in Degl'Innocenti, Maurizio (ed.), *Eugenio Colorni dall'antifascismo all'europeismo socialista e federalista*, Lacaita, Manduria-Bari-Rome, 2010, pp. 5-108.

Degl'Innocenti, Maurizio (ed.), *Eugenio Colorni dall'antifascismo all'europeismo socialista e federalista*, Lacaita, Manduria-Bari-Rome, 2010.

Dehio, Ludwig, *Gleichgewicht oder Hegemonie. Betrachtungen uber ein Grundproblem der neuren Staaten-geschichte*, Scherpe, Krefeld, 1948.

Dehio, Ludwig, *Equilibrio o egemonia. Considerazioni sopra un problema fondamentale della storia politica moderna*, Morcelliana, Brescia, 1954.

Dehio, Ludwig, *Deutschland und die Weltpolitik im XX Jahrhundert*, Oldenbourg, Munich, 1955.

Dehio, Ludwig, *La Germania e la politica mondiale del XX secolo*, Edizioni di Comunità, Milan, 1962.

Dehousse, Fernand, *L'Europe et le Monde. Recueil d'études, de rapports et de discours 1945-1960*, Librairie générale de droit et de jurisprudence, Paris, 1960.

Deighton, Anne (ed.), *Western European Union 1954-1997. Defence, Security, Integration*, St. Antony's College, Oxford, 1997.

"I delegati del CCE riuniti a Milano", *Comuni d'Europa*, 3 (March 1959), p. 1 e pp. 12-13.

De Luna, Giovanni, *Storia del Partito d'Azione 1942-1947*, Feltrinelli, Milan, 1982.

Del Vecchio, Edoardo, "Dalla CED all'UEO", in Roman H. Rainero (ed.), *Storia dell'integrazione europea*. I. *L'integrazione europea dalle origini alla nascita della Cee*, Marzorati - Editalia, Settimo Milanese - Rome, 1997, pp. 155-204.

Denna, Frank Fleming, *Storia della guerra fredda (1917-1960)*, Feltrinelli, Milan, 1964.

De Rougemont, Denis, "Vers une fédération des Régions", in *Naissance de l'Europe des Régions*, Institut universitaire d'Etudes européennes, Geneva, 1968.

De Rougemont, Denis, *Œuvres complètes de Denis de Rougemont*. III. *Écrits sur l'Europe*, Éditions de la différence, Paris, 1994.

De Siervo, Ugo - Giovannoni, Gianni - Giovannoni, Giorgio (eds.), *Giorgio La Pira sindaco. Scritti, discorsi e lettere*, Cultura Nuova Editrice, Florence, 1988-1989, 3 vols.

De Tocqueville, Alexis, *Scritti politici*. II. *La democrazia in America* (ed. Nicola Matteucci), UTET, Turin, 1968.

De Tocqueville, Alexis, "L'antico regime e la rivoluzione", in Alexis de Tocqueville, *Scritti politici. I. La rivoluzione democratica in Francia* (ed. Nicola Matteucci), UTET, Turin, 1969.

Devani, Giulia, "Altiero Spinelli e il Conseil des Communes (et des Régions) d'Europe", in Daniela Preda (ed.), *Altiero Spinelli e i movimenti per l'unità europea*, CEDAM, Padova, 2010, pp. 231-242.

"La dichiarazione finale", *Comuni d'Europa*, 2 (February 1984), p. XXIII.

"Il dibattito politico", *Comuni d'Europa*, 7-8 (July August 1960), p. 15.

"Il dibattito politico generale: cosa possono attendersi le autorità locali e regionali dalle elezioni europee a suffragio universale diretto?", *Comuni d'Europa*, 7-8 (August 1979), pp. 3-6.

Di Giovan, Paolo Roberto and Martini, Gianfranco, *Piccoli padri. Una conversazione sulla nascita dell'Unione europea e il suo futuro*, Iacolbelli, Pavona di Albano Laziale, 2010.

Di Nolfo, Ennio, *Vaticano e Stati Uniti 1939-1952 (dalle carte di Myron C. Taylor)*, Franco Angeli, Milan, 1978.

Di Nolfo, Ennio, "La guerra fredda", in *La Storia. I grandi problemi dal Medioevo all'età contemporanea*. IX. *L'età contemporanea*. 4. *Dal primo al secondo dopoguerra*, UTET, Turin, 1986-1988, pp. 659-684.

Di Nolfo, Ennio, *Storia delle relazioni internazionali 1918-1992*, Laterza, Rome-Bari, 1994.

Di Nolfo, Ennio - Rainero, Romain H. - Vigezzi, Brunello (eds.), *L'Italia e la politica di potenza in Europa (1938-40)*, Marzorati, Settimo Milanese, 1988.

"Il direttivo A.I.C.C.E. del 3 gennaio. Nuovi incarichi nel comitato esecutivo dell'AICCE", *Comuni d'Europa*, 1 (January 1957), p. 6.

"Il Direttivo dell'AICCE. Dibattito capitolino su fini e mezzi", *Comuni d'Europa*, 2 (February 1959), p. 9.

"Le Discours de M. Robert Schuman", *Le Bulletin fédéraliste*, 62 (April 1952), p. 3.

Dogliani, Patrizia, "La sinistra europea alle origini del movimento comunale internazionale", in Patrizia Dogliani and Oscar Gaspari (eds.), *L'Europa dei comuni, Origini e sviluppo del movimento comunale dalla fine dell'Ottocento al secondo dopoguerra*, Donzelli, Rome, 2003, pp. 167-200.

Dogliani Patrizia and Gaspari, Oscar, "Origini e sviluppo del movimento comunale europeo nel Novecento" in Patrizia Dogliani and Oscar Gaspari (eds.), *L'Europa dei comuni, Origini e sviluppo del movimento comunale dalla fine dell'Ottocento al secondo dopoguerra*, Donzelli, Rome, 2003, pp. 7-28.

Dogliani, Patrizia (ed.), *Europeismo e municipalismo. Alessandro Schiavi nel secondo dopoguerra*, Il ponte vecchio, Cesena, 1996.

Dogliani, Patrizia and Gaspari, Oscar (eds.), *L'Europa dei comuni. Origini e sviluppo del movimento comunale dalla fine dell'Ottocento al secondo dopoguerra*, Donzelli, Rome, 2003.

Duclos, Pierre, *La réforme du Conseil de l'Europe*, Librairie générale de droit et de jurisprudence, Paris, 1958.

Duclos, Pierre, *Le Conseil de l'Europe*, Presses universitaires de France, Paris, 1964.

Dumoulin, André and Remacle, Eric, *L'Union de l'Europe occidental. Phénix de la défense européenne*, Bruylant, Brussels, 1998.

Dumoulin, Michel (ed.), *Plans des temps de guerre pour l'après-guerre 1940-1947. Actes du colloque de Bruxelles, 12-14 mai 1993*, Bruylant *et al.*, Brussels *et al.*, 1995.

Dumoulin, Michel (ed.), *L'échec de la CED (1954). Leçons pour demain?*, Peter Lang, Bern, 1999.

Dumoulin, Michel - Girauld, René - Trausch, Gilbert (eds.), *L'Europe du patronat. De la guerre froide aux années soixante. Actes du colloque de Louvain-la-Neuve des 10 et 11 mai 1990*, Peter Lang, Bern, 1993.

Duroselle, Jean-Baptiste, *L'idea d'Europa nella storia*, Edizioni Milano Nuova, Milan, 1964.

Duroselle, Jean-Baptiste, "Les 'invariants' de la politique étrangère de la France", *Politique étrangère*, 51 (1986), 1, pp. 13-23.

Duroselle, Jean-Baptiste, *Storia diplomatica dal 1919 ai nostri giorni*, LED, Milan, 1998.

Duverger, Maurice, *La repubblica tradita*, Edizioni di Comunità, Milan, 1960.

Einaudi, Luigi, *La guerra e l'unità europea*, Il Mulino, Bologna, 1986.

Elgey, Georgette, *Histoire de la Quatrième République*, Fayard, Paris, 1965-1968, 2 vols.

Ellwood, David William, *L'Europa ricostruita. Politica ed economia tra Stati Uniti ed Europa occidentale 1945-1955*, Il Mulino, Bologna, 1994.

"Émile Hamilius président d'honneur du C.C.E., ancien bourgmestre de Luxembourg", *Communes d'Europe*, new series, 73 (March 1971), p. 29.

Esterbauer, Fried - Héraud, Guy - Pernthalter, Peter (eds.), *Föderalismus als Mittel permanenter Konfliktregelung*, Braumüller, Vienna, 1977.

Esterbauer, Fried *et al.* (eds.), *Von der freien Gemeinde zum föderalistischen Europa. Festschrift für Adolf Gasser zum 80. Geburtstag*, Duncker & Humblot, Berlino, 1983.

Europa Nuova, *Tesi per la rivoluzione federalista. Sette argomenti proposti da Europa Nuova per l'azione verso il Congresso del Popolo Europeo*, Europa Nuova, Turin, 1957.

Faure, Edgar, *Mémoires*, Plon, Paris, 1982-1985, 2 vols.

Fauvet, Jacques, *La Quatrième République*, Fayard, Paris, 1959.

La Fédération, mouvement fédéraliste français, La Fédération, Paris, 1994, pp. 1-3.

Felisini, Daniela, *1943-1957. Il Partito socialista italiano e l'integrazione europea*, extracted from: *Annali dell'Istituto Ugo La Malfa*, 3 (1987), pp. 213-350.

Ferlaino, Fiorenzo and Molinari, Paolo, *Neofederalismo, neoregionalismo e intercomunalità. Geografia amministrativa dell'Italia e dell'Europa*, Il Mulino, Bologna, 2009.

Ferrari Agradi, Mario, *Europa: tappe e prospettive di unificazione*, Cinque Lune, Rome, 1958.

Fiori, Giuseppe, *Una storia italiana: vita di Ernesto Rossi*, Einaudi, Turin, 1997.

Fiorini, Sergio, *Il potere a Milano. Prove generali di centrosinistra (1959-1961)*, Bruno Mondadori, Milan, 2006.

Fleury, Antoine, "La Suisse et la préparation à l'après guerre", in Michel Dumoulin (ed.), *Plans des temps de guerre pour l'après-guerre 1940-1947. Actes du colloque de Bruxelles, 12-14 mai 1993*, Bruylant *et al.*, Brussels *et al.*, 1995, pp. 175-195.

Fondation archives européennes, *Le Plan Briand d'union fédérale européenne. Documents*, Fondation archives européennes, Geneva, 1991.

Fondation Spaak, *Les pères de l'Europe. 50 ans après. Perspectives sur l'engagement européen*, Bruylant, Brussels, 2001.

Fontaine, Andrè, *Histoire de la guerre froide*, II, *De la guerre de Corée à la crise des alliances 1950-1967*, Fayard, Paris, 1967.

"Forlì e Firenze nell'AICCE", *Comuni d'Europa*, 2-3 (January 1953), p. 5.

Franzinelli, Mimmo and Braga, Antonella (eds.), *Ernesto Rossi. Una vita per la libertà (1897-1967). Bio-bibliografia*, Istituto storico della Resistenza e della società contemporanea nel Novarese e nel Verbano Cusio-Ossola "Piero Fornara", [Novara], 2007.

"Fratellanze intercomunali", *Comuni d'Europa*, 1 (February 1954), p. 3.

Frosio Roncalli, Moris, "La segreteria nazionale del MFE a Milano: la gestione Umberto Campagnolo", in Fabio Zucca (ed.), *Europeismo e federalismo in Lombardia dal Risorgimento all'Unione europea*, Il Mulino, Bologna, 2007, pp. 273-295.

Fursdon, Edward, *The European Defence Community. A History*, MacMillan, London, 1980.

Gagliano, Ernesto, "Amedeo Peyron", in Ferruccio Borio (ed.), *I sindaci della libertà. Torino dal 1945 ad oggi*, EDA, Turin, 1980.

Gagliano, Stefano (ed.), *La personalità poliedrica di Mario Alberto Rollier. Ricordo di un milanese protestante, antifascista, federalista e uomo di scienza. Atti della giornata di studi promossa in Milano dalla Associazione Piero Guicciardini, 14 novembre 2009*, Biblion, Milan, 2010.

Galante, Severino, *Il Partito comunista italiano e l'integrazione europea. Il decennio del rifiuto: 1947-1957*, Liviana, Padova, 1988.

Galante, Severino, *L'autonomia possibile. Il Pci del dopoguerra tra politica estera e politica interna*, Ponte alle Grazie, Florence, 1991.

Galli, Giorgio, *Storia del socialismo italiano*, Laterza, Rome-Bari, 1980.

Galli, Giorgio, *Storia del PCI. Livorno 1921, Rimini 1991*, Kaos, Milan, 1993.

Gallino, Luciano, *L'impresa responsabile. Un'intervista su Adriano Olivetti* (ed. Paolo Ceri), Edizioni di Comunità, Turin, 2001.

Gaspari, Oscar, "Alle origini del movimento comunale europeo: dall'Union Internationale des Villes al Consiglio dei comuni d'Europa (1913-1953)",

Memoria e Ricerca. Rivista di storia contemporanea, first series, 10 (1997), pp. 147-163.

Gaspari, Oscar, *L'Italia dei municipi. Il movimento comunale in età liberale (1879-1908)*, Donzelli, Rome, 1998, pp. 78-81.

Gasser, Adolf, *Geschichte der Volksfreiheit und der Demokratie*, Verlag Sauerländer, Aarau, 1939.

Gasser, Adolf, *Storia della libertà popolare e della democrazia*, La Fiaccola, Milan, post 1939 (clandestine edition).

Gasser, Adolf, *Grundlinien einer ethischen Geschichtauffassung*, Verlag Bucherfreunde, Basel, 1943.

Gasser, Adolf, *Gemeindefreiheit als Rettung Europas. Grundlinien einer ethischen Geschichtsauffassung*, Verlag Bucherfreunde, Basel, 1943.

Gasser, Adolf, *L'autonomia comunale e la ricostruzione dell'Europa*, La Fiaccola, Milan, 1946.

Gasser, Adolf, *L'autonomie communale et la reconstruction de l'Europe. Principes d'une interprétation éthique de l'histoire*, Éditions de la Baconnière, Neuchâtel, 1946.

Gasser, Adolf, *Ausgewählte historische Schriften, 1933-1983*, Helbing & Lichtenhahn, Basel, 1983.

Gasser, Adolf, "Three kinds of new Europe", in Walter Lipgens (ed.), *Documents on the History of European Integration*. I. *Continental Plans for European Union 1939-1945*, Walter de Gruyter, Berlin-New York, 1985.

Gentile, Emilio, *Storia del partito fascista 1919-1922. Movimento e milizia*, Laterza, Rome-Bari, 1989.

Gerbet, Pierre, *La construction de l'Europe*, Imprimerie Nazionale, Paris, 1983.

Gerbert, Pierre, *Le relèvement 1944-1949*, Imprimerie Nazionale, Paris, 1991.

Girault, René, "The French Decision-makers and their Perception of French Power in 1948", in Josef Becker and Franz Knipping (eds.), *Power in Europe? Great-Britain, France, Italy and Germany in a post-war World 1945-1950*, Walter de Gruyter, Berlin-New York, 1986, pp. 47-64.

Girault, René, "La France entre l'Europe et l'Afrique", in Enrico Serra (ed.), *Il rilancio dell'Europa e i Trattati di Roma. Actes du Colloque de Rome, 25-28 mars 1987*, Bruylant *et al.*, Brussels *et al.*, 1989, pp. 351-378.

Girault, René and Frank, Robert (eds.), *La puissance française en question 1945-1949*, Paris, 1988.

Giscard d'Estaing, Valéry, "Prefazione. Il CCRE: cinquant'anni al servizio degli enti locali e regionali europei", in Fabio Zucca, *Autonomie locali e federazione sovranazionale. La battaglia del Conseil des Communes et Régions d'Europe per l'unità europea*, Il Mulino, Bologna, 2001, p. 13.

Gouzy, Jean-Pierre, "I movimenti per l'unità europea in Francia", in Sergio Pistone (ed.), *I movimenti per l'unità europea dal 1945 al 1954. Atti del convegno internazionale, Pavia 19-20-21 ottobre 1989*, Jaca Book, Milan, 1992, pp. 61-89.

Gouzy, Jean-Pierre, "Alexandre Marc soixante-quinze ans de combat fédéraliste", *L'Europe en formation*, 291 (Winter 1993-1994), pp. 7-14.

Gouzy, Jean-Pierre, "Alexandre Marc", in Denis de Rougemont (ed.), *Dictionnaire international du fédéralisme*, Bruylant, Brussels, 1994, pp. 219-227.

Graglia, Piero S., "L'Associazione Federalisti Europei di Firenze (A.F.E.) ed il I Congresso Federalista di Venezia (January 1945-October 1946)", *Storia contemporanea*, XXIV (August 1993), 4, p. 568.

Graglia, Piero S., *Unità europea e federalismo. Da "Giustizia e libertà" ad Altiero Spinelli*, Il Mulino, Bologna, 1996.

Graglia, Piero S., *Altiero Spinelli*, Il Mulino, Bologna, 2008.

Grange, Daniel, "La politique européenne de Pierre Mendès-France vue par les diplomates italiens", in *Pierre Mendès-France et le rôle de la France dans le monde. Colloque organisé par l'Institut Pierre Mendès-France à l'Assemblée nationale les 10 et 11 janvier 1991*, Presses universitaires de Grenoble, Grenoble, 1991, pp. 55-80.

Grazi, Laura, *La questione urbana nel processo di integrazione europea (1957-1999)*, Il Mulino, Bologna, 2006.

Greilsammer, Alain, *Les mouvements fédéralistes en France de 1945 à 1974*, Presses d'Europe, Nice, 1975.

Greppi, Antonio, *La coscienza in pace. Cinquant'anni di socialismo*, Edizioni Avanti!, Milan, 1963.

Greppi, Edoardo, "Il Consiglio d'Europa: l'istituzionalizzazione della cooperazione politica tra Stati sovrani", in Roman H. Rainero (ed.), *Storia dell'integrazione europea. I. L'integrazione europea dalle origini alla nascita della Cee*, Marzorati - Editalia, Settimo Milanese - Rome, 1997, pp. 87-116.

Grosser, Alfred, *Affaires extérieurs. La politique de la France, 1944-1984*, Flammarion, Paris, 1984.

Grosso, Giuseppe, *Commemorazione dell'avvocato Amedeo Peyron ex sindaco di Torino. Consiglio comunale, 26 luglio 1965*, Città di Torino, Turin, 1965.

Grosso, Giuseppe, "Necessità di una strutturazione democratica della politica regionale della Comunità", *Comuni d'Europa*, 3 (March 1967), pp. 3-4.

La Governance europea. Un Libro Bianco. Website. http://eur-lex.europa.eu/LexUriServ/LexUriServ.do?uri=COM:2001:0428:FIN:IT:PDF [access April 2012].

Gualtieri, Roberto, *Togliatti e la politica estera italiana: dalla Resistenza al trattato di pace, 1943-1947*, Editori Riuniti, Rome, 1995.

Guderzo, Giulio, "Analisi sociale della votazione per il Congresso del Popolo Europeo nel comune di Pavia", *Il Federalista*, 3 (November 1959), pp. 162-166.

Guercio, Maria, "La selezione dei documenti archivistici nel recente dibattito internazionale: evoluzione e continuità nella metodologia e nella prassi", *Archivi per la storia*, 11/1 (1998), pp. 43-64.

Guillen, Pierre, "L'Europe remède à l'impuissance française? Le gouvernement Guy Mollet et la négociation des Traités de Rome (1955-1957)", *Revue d'Histoire diplomatique*, 102 (1988), pp. 319-335.

Guillen, Pierre, "La France et la construction européenne dans les années cinquante", *Storia delle relazioni internazionali*, VIII (1992), 1-2, p. 23.

Hallstein, Walter, *L'Europe inachevée*, Laffont, Paris, 1970.

Hamilius, Émile, "Préface", in Jean Bareth, *La Commune et l'Europe. Jumelages et rencontres intercommunales*, Conseil des communes d'Europe, Genève, [1953], p. 5.

Héraud, Guy, *Peuples et Langues d'Europe*, Denoël, Paris, 1968.

Héraud, Guy, *L'Europe des ethnies*, Presses d'Europe, Paris-Nice, 1974.

Hick, Alan, "Il movimento europeo", in Sergio Pistone (ed.), *I movimenti per l'unità europea dal 1945 al 1954. Atti del convegno internazionale, Pavia 19-21 ottobre 1989*, Jaka Book, Milan, 1992, pp. 171-181.

Hirschmann, Ursula, *Noi senza patria*, Il Mulino, Bologna, 1993.

Hubert Clément. Un humaniste du travail, Éditions de l'Imprimerie coopérative luxembourgeoise, Esch-sur-Alzette, 1954, 2 vols.

Ignazi, Pietro (ed.), *Ernesto Rossi, una utopia concreta*, Edizioni di Comunità, Milan, 1991.

Incontri dei sindaci delle grandi città del mondo: la qualità della vita. Website. http://www.fondazionealdoaniasi.it/aldo-aniasi/esperienza-amministrativa/aniasi-sindaco-di-milano/incontri-dei-sindaci-delle-grandi-citta-del-mondo-la-qualita-della-vita/ [access May 2012].

"Incontro delle città europee a Magonza", *Comuni d'Europa*, 10 (October 1978), pp. 4-13.

Innamorati, Serena, *Mario Fabiani. Il sindaco della ricostruzione. Appunti per una storia*, Comune di Firenze, Florence, 1984.

"L'Istituto europeo di credito comunale", *Bollettino Associazione nazionale dei comuni italiani*, 4 (April 1958), p. 3.

Jílek, Lubor, *L'esprit européen en Suisse de 1860 à 1940*, Cahiers d'Histoire Contemporaine, Geneva, 1990.

Jílek, Lubor, "Un choix d'Europe en 1938: fédéralisme suisse entre le Vorbild et le Sonderfall", *Revue d'Allemagne et des pays de langue allemande*, 23 (1991), 3, pp. 340-354.

Jílek, Lubor, "L'idée d'Europe devant la guerre: les exilés et le fédéralisme européen en Suisse, 1938-1945", in Andrea Bosco (ed.), *The federal idea*. II. *The history of federalism since 1945*, Lothian Foundation Press, London-New York, 1992.

Jílek, Lubor, "L'Union européenne a Bâle entre 1938 et 1946: pôle helvétique et versant mondial dans les projets d'une association européaniste", in Michel Dumoulin (ed.), *Plans des temps de guerre pour l'après-guerre 1940-1947. Actes du colloque de Bruxelles, 12-14 mai 1993*, Bruylant *et al.*, Brussels *et al.*, 1995.

Jost, Hans-Ulrich, "Minaccia e ripiegamento (1914-1945)", in *Nuova storia della Svizzera e degli Svizzeri*, Casagrande, Lugano-Bellinzona, 1982-1983, vol. III, pp. 98-184.

"Jumelages", *Communes d'Europe*, 2-3 (January 1953), p. 5.

"Jumelages et échanges intercommunaux", *Bulletin du Conseil des communes d'Europe*, 18 (November 1954), p. 2.

"Jumelages Troyes-Tournai, Montbéliard-Ludwisburg", *Le Bulletin fédéraliste*, 56 (January 1952), p. 4.

Kerr, Philip H. (Marquis of Lothian), "The Prevention of War", in Philipp H. Kerr Marquis of Lothian and Lionel Curtis (eds.), *The Prevention of War*, Yale University Press for the Institute of Politics of Williamstown, New Haven, 1923.

Kerr, Philip H. (Marquis of Lothian), *Pacifism is not enough, nor patriotism either. Being the Burge memorial lecture for the year 1935*, The Clarendon press, Oxford, 1935.

Landoni, Enrico, *Il laboratorio delle riforme. Milano dal centrismo al centro-sinistra (1956-1961)*, Lacaita, Manduria-Bari-Rome, 2007.

Landoni, Enrico, "L'attività dell'Amministrazione Comunale da Cassinis ad Aniasi", in Carlo G. Lacaita and Maurizio Punzo (eds.), *Milano. Anni Sessanta. Dagli esordi del centrosinistra alla contestazione*, Lacaita, Manduria-Bari-Rome, 2008, pp. 243-285.

Landuyt, Ariane, "Un tentativo di rinnovamento del socialismo italiano. Silone e il Centro estero di Zurigo", in Gaetano Arfè *et al.*, *L'emigrazione socialista nella lotta contro il fascismo, 1926-1939*, Sansoni, Florence, 1982, pp. 71-104.

Landuyt, Ariane and Preda, Daniela (eds.), *I movimenti per l'unità europea 1970-1986*, Il Mulino, Bologna, 2000, 2 vols.

La Pira, Giorgio, "Nuova Europa", *Comuni d'Europa*, 2 (October 1954), p. 5.

La Pira, Giorgio, "Il valore delle città. Discorso pronunciato a Ginevra il 12 aprile 1954 alla riunione del Comitato Internazionale della Croce Rossa", in Ufficio Stampa del comune di Firenze (ed.), *Convegno a Firenze dei Sindaci delle Capitali, 2-6 ottobre 1955*; Noccioli, Florence, 1956, p. 7.

La Pira, Giorgio, "Discorso per il gemellaggio di Firenze con Reims", in Ugo De Siervo, Gianni Giovannoni, Giorgio Giovannoni (eds.), *Giorgio La Pira sindaco. Scritti, discorsi e lettere*, Cultura Nuova Editrice, Florence, 1988-1989, vol. I, pp. 427-432.

Lathière, Valérie, *François Mitterrand et l'unification européenne 1945-1957*, Maîtrise, Paris-1, 1989, Thesis Director Réne Girault.

"I lavori del Comitato federale a Monaco", *L'Unità Europea*, 42 (August 1977), p. 1 e pp. 4-6.

"Il lavoro dell'AICCE. Un comitato regionale piemontese", *Nuova rassegna*, 12 (June 1954), pp. 979-980.

Lega, Achille, "I novanta di Marc", *Cuore e Critica*, second series, 17 (May 1994), pp. 46-47.

Lejeune, René, *Robert Schuman, une âme pour l'Europe*, Editions Saint-Paul, Paris-Fribourg, 1986.

Leone, Ugo, *Le origini diplomatiche del Consiglio d'Europa*, Giuffrè, Milan, 1966.

Levi, Lucio, "Internazionalismo marxista e federalismo", *Mondo Operaio*, 7-8 (July-August 1976), pp. 78-84.

Levi, Lucio, "Internazionalismo marxista e federalismo", *Mondo Operaio*, 10 (October 1976), pp. 76-81.

Levi, Lucio, *Federalismo e integrazione europea*, Palumbo, Palermo, 1978.

Levi, Lucio, *L'unificazione europea. Trent'anni di storia*, Società Editrice Internazionale, Turin, 1979.

Levi, Lucio, *Il federalismo*, Franco Angeli, Milan, 1987.

Levi, Lucio and Pistone, Sergio (eds.), *Trent'anni di vita del Movimento federalista europeo*, Franco Angeli, Milan, 1973.

Libro bianco del Comitato delle Regioni sulla governance multilivello. Website. http://www.europarl.europa.eu/meetdocs/2009_2014/documents/afco/dv/livre-blanc_/livre-blanc_it.pdf [access April 2012].

Linz, Juan J. - Farneti, Paolo - Lepsius, Mario Rainer, *La caduta dei regimi democratici*, Il Mulino, Bologna, 1981.

Lipgens, Walter, *Europa-Föderationspläne der Widerstandsbewegungen 1940-1945, eine Dokumentation Gesammelt und eingeleitet von Walter Lipgens*, R. Oldembourg, Munich, 1968.

Lipgens, Walter, *Die Anfänge der europäischen Einigungspolitik 1945-1950*, Ernst Klett, Stuttgart, 1977.

Lipgens, Walter, *Sources for the History of european Integration (1945-1955). A guide to Archives in the Countries of the Community*, Sijthoff *et al.*, Leyden *et al.*, 1980.

Lipgens, Walter, *A History of European Integration*. I. *The formation of the European Unity Movement 1945-1947*, Clarendon Press, Oxford, 1982.

Lipgens, Walter, "Swiss plans for the Postwar Order in Europe", in Walter Lipgens (ed.), *Documents on the History of European Integration*. I. *Continental Plans for European Union 1939-1945*, Walter de Gruyter, Berlin-New York, 1985.

Lipgens, Walter (ed.), *Documents on the History of European Integration*. II. *Plans for European Union in Great Britain and in exile 1939-1945*, Walter de Gruyter, Berlin-New York, 1986.

Lipgens, Walter and Loth, Wilfried (eds.), *Documents on the History of European Integration*, Walter de Gruyter, Berlin-New York, 1985-1991, 4 vols.

Lizzadri, Oreste, *Il socialismo italiano dal frontismo al centro sinistra*, Lerici, Rome, 1969.

Logiou, Laurent, *Mémoire sur le Conseil des communes et Régions d'Europe*, D.E.S.S. Administration internationale, année 1985-1986, Paris I.

Loth, Wilfried, "Il Movimento Socialista per gli Stati Uniti d'Europa", in Sergio Pistone (ed.), *I movimenti per l'unità europea dal 1945 al 1954. Atti del convegno internazionale. Pavia 19-20-21 ottobre 1989*, Jaca Book, Milan, 1992, pp. 253-264.

Loubet Del Bayle, Jean-Louis, *Les non-conformistes des années 30: une tentative de renouvellement de la pensée politique française*, Seuil, Paris, 1969.

Loubet Del Bayle, Jean-Louis, *I non conformisti degli anni Trenta*, Cinque Lune, Rome, 1972.

Louvain, Roberto *et al.*, *Émile Chanoux et le débat sur le fédéralisme* (ed. Paolo Momigliano Levi), Presses d'Europe, Nice, 1997.

Lyttelton, Adrian, *La conquista del potere. Il fascismo dal 1919 al 1929*, Laterza, Rome-Bari, 1974.

Maggia, Giovanni (ed.), *Bibliografia degli scritti di Adriano Olivetti*, Università degli Studi di Siena, Facoltà di Scienze economiche e bancarie, Siena, 1983, 2 vols.

Maggiorani, Mauro, *L'Europa degli altri. Comunisti italiani e integrazione europea (1957-1969)*, Carocci, Rome, 1998.

Maggiorani, Mauro and Ferrari, Paolo (eds.), *L'Europa da Togliatti a Berlinguer. Testimonianze e documenti 1945-1984*, Il Mulino, Bologna, 2005.

Magnani, Alberto, *Luigi Montemartini nella storia del riformismo italiano*, La Nuova Italia, Florence, 1990.

Majocchi, Luigi Vittorio, "Ludwig Dehio", *Il Federalista*, 30 (1988), no. 2, pp. 134-162.

Majocchi, Luigi Vittorio, *La difficile costruzione dell'unità europea*, Jaca Book, Milan, 1996.

Majocchi, Luigi Vittorio, "L'azione per il riconoscimento del diritto di voto europeo", in Sergio Pistone (ed.), *I movimenti per l'unità europea 1954-1969. Atti del Convegno internazionale, Genova, 5-6-7 novembre 1992*, PIME, Pavia, 1996, pp. 438-441.

Majocchi, Luigi Vittorio, "Prefazione", in Antonella Braga, *Un federalista giacobino. Ernesto Rossi pioniere degli Stati uniti d'Europa*, Il Mulino, Bologna, 2007, pp. 11-17.

Majocchi, Luigi Vittorio and Rossolillo, Francesco, *Il Parlamento europeo. Significato storico di un'elezione*, Guida, Naples, 1979.

Majocchi, Luigi Vittorio (ed.), *Messina quarant'anni dopo. L'attualità del metodo in vista della conferenza intergovernativa del 1996*, Cacucci, Bari, 1996.

Majocchi, Luigi Vittorio and Vitale Marco (eds.), *Europa 1992. Dall'Atto Unico al governo europeo*, Il Sole 24 Ore Libri, Milan, 1990.

Malandrino, Corrado (ed.), *Alle origini dell'europeismo in Piemonte. La crisi del primo dopoguerra, la cultura politica piemontese e il problema dell'unità europea. Atti del convegno tenuto presso la Fondazione Luigi Einaudi (Torino, 28-29 novembre 1991)*, Fondazione Luigi Einaudi, Turin, 1993.

Malgeri, Francesco, *Alcide De Gasperi*. II. *Dal fascismo alla democrazia (1943-1947)*, Rubbettino, Soveria Mannelli, 2009.

Mammarella, Giuseppe, *Storia d'Europa dal 1945 a oggi*, Laterza, Rome-Bari, 1992, pp. 87-204.

Mammarella, Giuseppe, *Europa-Stati Uniti, un'alleanza difficile 1945-1985*, Laterza, Rome-Bari, 1996.

Mammarella, Giuseppe, and Cacace, Paolo, *Storia e politica dell'Unione europea (1926-2005)*, Laterza, Rome-Bari, 2005.

Mancuso, Francesco, "Il federalismo democratico di Umberto Campagnolo", *Federalismo e società*, 2 (1996), pp. 231-244.

"Manifestazioni in Toscana per il XXV dei Trattati di Roma", *Comuni d'Europa*, 4 (April 1982), p. 16.

Mantelli, Brunello and Artico, Davide (eds.), *Ideologia e geopolitica all'ombra della guerra fredda. Conflitti materiali e simbolici in Europa dal 1945 ai primi anni Cinquanta*, UTET, Turin, 2012.

Marc, Alexandre, *Du communalisme au fédéralisme intégral*, La Fédération, Paris, [1948].

Marc, Alexandre, "Avant le congrès de La Haye", *La Fédération*, 36 (January 1948), p. 5.

[Marc, Alexandre], "Un procès en paternité. La Haye 1948", *L'Europe en formation*, 292 (Spring 1994), pp. 46-50.

Marc, Alexandre, *Europa e federalismo globale*, Il ventilabro, Florence, 1996.

Martin, Jean-Maurice, "Défendons nos libertés locales", *Le Bulletin fédéraliste*, 10 (July-August 1949), p. 1.

Martin, Jean-Maurice, "Bilan de dix ans d'efforts 1944-1954", *La Fédération. Revue de l'ordre vivant*, supplement for no. 120 (November 1954), pp. 1-13.

Mascia, Marco, *Il Comitato delle Regioni nel sistema dell'Unione europea*, CEDAM, Padova, 1996.

Masini, Carlo, "Filippo Turati e gli Stati Uniti d'Europa", *Critica Sociale*, 1 (January 1972), pp. 14-15.

Mayeur, Jean-Marie, "Pie XII et l'Europe", *Relations internationales*, 28 (Winter 1981), pp. 413-425.

Melchionni, Maria Grazia, "Genèse de la proposition européenne avancée par Alcide De Gasperi en 1951", in *L'Union européenne à l'aube d'un nouveau siècle*, Euroius Editorial Juridica, Madrid, 1997, pp. 123-144.

Melandri, Pierre, *Les États-Unis face à l'unification de l'Europe 1945-1954*, Pedone, Paris, 1980.

Mellaerts, Gaetan, *La genèse du marché commun*, Centre de recherches européennes, Lausanne, 1968.

"Membri italiani dell'Esecutivo del CCE", *Comuni d'Europa*, 1 (February 1954), p. 2.

Milhaud, Edgard, "Au seuil de la 50e année des 'Annales'. Un regard en arrière. Quelques grandes heures des 'Annales' et du Ciriec", *Annales de l'Économie collettive*, 46 (1958), pp. 1-6.

Milward, Alan S., "The International Committee of the Movements for European Unity", in Walter Lipgens, *A History of European Integration*, Clarendon Press, Oxford, 1982, pp. 657-684.

Mitterrand, François, *Aux frontières de l'union française. Indochine, Tunisie*, Juillard, Paris, 1953.

Mitterrand, François, *Le coup d'État permanent*, Union Général, Paris, 1964.

Mitterrand, François, *Ma part de vérité. De la rupture à l'unité*, Fayard, Paris, 1969.

Mitterrand, François, *Ici et maintenant. Conversations avec Guy Claisse*, Fayard, Paris, 1980.

"La mobilitazione del CCE per le elezioni del Parlamento europeo", *Comuni d'Europa*, 1 (January 1979), p. 16.

Momigliano, Francesco, *Carlo Cattaneo e gli Stati Uniti d'Europa*, Treves, Milan, 1919.

Mondo europeo. Rivista di civiltà europea, 7 (July-August 1946).

Monnet, Jean, *Mémoires*, Fayard, Paris, 1976.

Monnet, Jean and Schuman, Robert, *Correspondance 1947-1953*, Fondation Jean Monnet pour l'Europe, Centre de recherches europeénnes, Lausanne, 1986.

Monteleone, Renato, "Le ragioni teoriche del rifiuto della parola d'ordine degli Stati Uniti d'Europa nel movimento comunista internazionale", in Sergio Pistone (ed.), *L'idea dell'unificazione europea dalla prima alla seconda guerra mondiale: relazioni tenute al convegno di studi svoltosi presso la Fondazione Luigi Einaudi (Torino, 25-26 ottobre 1974)*, Fondazione Luigi Einaudi, Turin, 1975, pp. 77-97.

Montemartini, Giovanni, *Municipalizzazione dei pubblici servigi*, Società Editrice Libraria, Milan, 1902.

Monti, Fabrizio and De Maria, Carlo, *Inventari delle carte e bibliografia degli scritti di Alessandro Schiavi negli archivi forlivesi*, Lacaita, Manduria, 2003.

Moreau-Defarges, Philippe, "La France et l'Europe: le rêve ambigu ou la mesure du rang", *Politique étrangère*, 51 (1986), 1, pp. 199-218.

Morelli, Umberto, "L'Unione europea dei federalisti e il Movimento federalista europeo sovranazionale", in Sergio Pistone (ed.), *I movimenti per l'unità europea 1954-1969. Atti del Convegno internazionale, Genova, 5-6-7 novembre 1992*, PIME, Pavia, 1996, pp. 179-227.

Morelli, Umberto, "Il Movimento federalista europeo sovranazionale e l'Unione europea dei federalisti", in Ariane Landuyt and Daniela Preda (eds.), *I movimenti per l'unità europea 1970-1986*, Il Mulino, Bologna, 2000, vol. II, pp. 665-741.

Morlino, Leonardo, *Dalla democrazia all'autoritarismo. Il caso spagnolo in prospettiva comparata*, Il Mulino, Bologna, 1981.

Mornese, Michele, *L'eresia politica di Adriano Olivetti*, Lampi di stampa, Milan, 2005.

Morrone, Gino and Scirocco, Giovanni (eds.), *Grazie, Iso. Dall'Ossola a Palazzo Marino a Montecitorio. Atti della giornata di studio su Aldo Aniasi: il partigiano, l'amministratore, il politico*, M&B, Milan, 2007.

Movimento Comunità, *Linee e mezzi d'azione. Punti programmatici e statuto (provvisorio)*, Tipografia Giglio Tos, Ivrea, 1949.

Movimento Comunità, *Tempi nuovi metodi nuovi*, Edizioni di Comunità, Milan, 1953.

Murgia, Ivo, "I cattolici e l'Europa", *Studium*, 2 (1955), pp. 84-88.

Napolitano, Daniela, *Il socialismo federalista di Ignazio Silone: Europa e socialismo nel pensiero siloniano dalle Tesi del Terzo fronte a Europa socialista*, Regione Abruzzo - Centro studi Ignazio Silone, L'Aquila - Pescina, 1996.

Negruzzo, Simona and Zucca, Fabio (eds.), *Gli archivi storici delle Università italiane e il caso pavese. Atti del convegno nazionale (Pavia, 28-29 novembre 2000)*, Tipografia popolare, Pavia, 2001, monographic issue of the *Annali di Storia Pavese*.

Neri Gualdesi, Marinella, "La battaglia dei federalisti italiani per costruire l'alternativa europea federale (1950-1956)", in Roman H. Rainero (ed.), *Storia dell'integrazione europea*. I. *L'integrazione europea dalle origini alla nascita della Cee*, Marzorati - Editalia, Settimo Milanese - Rome, 1997, pp. 331-370.

Nicolet, Claude, *L'idée républicaine en France 1789-1924. Essai d'histoire critique*, Gallimard, Paris, 1982.

Occhiena, Mario, "Amedeo Peyron, un sindaco europeista", *La voce del popolo*, 44 (November 1985), p. 2.

Ochetto, Valerio, *Adriano Olivetti*, Mondatori, Milan, 1985.

Olivetti, Adriano, *Società, Stato, Comunità. Per una economia e politica comunitaria*, Edizioni di Comunità, Milan, 1952.

Olivetti, Adriano, *Per una libera comunità del Canavese. Discorso pronunciato nei comuni del Canavese in occasione della campagna elettorale, giugno 1953*, Movimento Comunità, Ivrea, 1953.

Olivetti, Adriano, *Città dell'uomo*, Edizioni di Comunità, Milan, 1960.

Olivetti, Adriano, *L'ordine politico delle comunità. Le garanzie di libertà in uno Stato socialista*, Edizioni di Comunità, Milan, 1970.

Olivier, Anne-Laure, "Entre Europe et Afrique: Gaston Defferre et les débuts de la construction européenne", *Terrains et travaux*, 8 (2005), pp. 14-33.

"Ora drammatica", *Comuni d'Europa*, 11 (November 1962).

Orsina, Giovanni (ed.), *Partiti e sistemi di partito in Italia e in Europa nel secondo dopoguerra*, Rubbettino, Soveria Mannelli, 2011.

Palayret, Jean-Marie, "Le Mouvement européen 1954-1969. Histoire d'un groupe de pression", in René Girault and Gérard Bossuat (eds.), *Europe brisée, Europe retrovée. Nouvelle réflexion sur l'unité européenne au XXe siècle*, Publications de la Sorbonne, Paris, 1994, pp. 365-383.

Palayret, Jean-Marie, "Il movimento europeo", in Sergio Pistone (ed.), *I movimenti per l'unità europea 1954-1969. Atti del convegno internazionale, Genova 5-6-7 novembre 1992*, PIME, Pavia, 1996, pp. 337-347.

Palayret, Jean-Marie, "Il Movimento Europeo Internazionale e la battaglia per l'Unione Europea", in Ariane Landuyt and Daniela Preda (eds.), *I movimenti per l'unità europea 1970-1986*, Il Mulino, Bologna, 2000, vol. II, pp. 743-781.

Pampaloni, Geno, *Adriano Olivetti: un'idea di democrazia*, Edizioni di Comunità, Milan, 1980.

Panizzi, Gabriele, "La battaglia per l'Europa e il Comitato delle Regioni", *Comuni d'Europa*, new series, 15 (March 2007), p. 49.

Paolini, Edmondo, "Pensiero e azione dei federalisti europei. La campagna per l'elezione del Parlamento europeo", *Comuni d'Europa*, 10 (October 1978), pp. 16-19.

Paolini, Edmondo, *Altiero Spinelli. Appunti per una biografia*, Il Mulino, Bologna, 1988.

Paolini, Edmondo (ed.), *Altiero Spinelli e l'unificazione dell'Europa*, [s.l., s.n.], Rome, [1990 or 1991].

Paolini, Edmondo, "Il Consiglio dei Comuni d'Europa", in Sergio Pistone (ed.), *I movimenti per l'unità europea dal 1945 al 1954. Atti del convegno internazionale. Pavia 19-20-21 ottobre 1989*, Jaca Book, Milan, 1992, p. 210.

Paolini, Edmondo, *Altiero Spinelli. Dalla lotta antifascista alla battaglia per la federazione europea 1920-1948: documenti e testimonianze*, Il Mulino, Bologna, 1996.

"Partecipations aux réunions internationales. II session Congrès du peuple européen, Lyon janvier 1959", *Communes d'Europe*, 28-29, (February-March 1959), p. 22.

Pasquinucci, Daniele, *Europeismo e democrazia. Altiero Spinelli e la sinistra europea 1950-1986*, Il Mulino, Bologna, 2000.

Pastorelli, Pietro, "La politica europeistica di De Gasperi", Storia *e politica*, 23 (1984), pp. 330-392.

Pastorelli, Pietro, *La politica estera italiana del dopoguerra*, Il Mulino, Bologna, 1987.

Patriciello, Aldo, *European twinning. Speciale dossier "gemellaggi europei"* Website. http://eacea.ec.europa.eu/citizenship/programme/documents/2011/programme_guide_it.pdf [access May 2012].

Pavone, Claudio (ed.), *Storia d'Italia nel secolo ventesimo. Strumenti e fonti.* III. *Le fonti documentarie*, Ministero per i beni e le attività culturali, Dipartimento per i beni archivistici e librari, Direzione generale per gli archivi, Rome, 2006.

Payre, Renaud and Saunier, Pierre-Yves, "L'Union internationale des villes o l'Internazionale municipale (1913-1940)", *Amministrare. Rivista quadrimestrale dell'Istituto per la Scienza dell'Amministrazione pubblica*, 1-2 (January-August 2000), pp. 217-242.

[Pellegrini, Fabio], "Il Comitato delle regioni e degli enti locali", *Comuni d'Europa*, 3 (March 1994), p. 5.

Pennera, Christian, *Robert Schuman, la jeunesse et les débuts politiques d'un grand européen de 1886 a 1924*, Pierron, Sarreguemines, 1985.

Petrella, Enrico, "I due Peyron", *Gazzetta di San Donato e Parella*, 7 (July 1989), p. 3.

Petrilli, Giuseppe, *La politica estera ed europea di De Gasperi*, Cinque Lune, Rome, 1975.

Petrini, Francesco, "Gli industriali lombardi, la Confindustria e l'Europa negli anni Cinquanta. La costruzione del grande mercato", in Fabio Zucca (ed.), *Europeismo e federalismo in Lombardia dal Risorgimento all'Unione europea*, Il Mulino, Bologna, 2007, pp. 627-651.

Peyron, Amedeo, "Torino e l'Europa", *Comuni d'Europa*, 6 (June-July 1956), p. 1.

Peyron, Amedeo, "Il discorso del sindaco Peyron alla Paulskirche", *Comuni d'Europa*, 11 (December 1956), p. 2.

Philippovich, Thomas, "I nuovi compiti del CCE per le elezioni del Parlamento europeo", *Comuni d'Europa*, 7-8 (August 1979), pp. 6-7.

Pio XII, "Pio XII ammonisce a non far dei gemellaggi pure cerimonie esteriori", *Comuni d'Europa*, 3 (March-April 1956), p. 10.

Pistone, Sergio, *Ludwig Dehio*, Guida editori, Naples, 1977.

Pistone, Sergio, *L'Italia e l'unità europea. Dalle premesse storiche all'elezione del Parlamento europeo*, Loescher, Turin, 1982.

Pistone, Sergio, *Ragion di Stato, relazioni internazionali, imperialismo._Corso di storia del pensiero politico contemporaneo a.a. 1983-1984*, Celid, Turin, 1984.

Pistone, Sergio, "Ludwig Dehio e l'interpretazione federalista dell'epoca delle guerre mondiali e del fascismo", *PiemontEuropa* (December 1988), pp. 24-27.

Pistone, Sergio, "Introduzione", in Sergio Pistone (ed.), *I movimenti per l'unità europea dal 1945 al 1954. Atti del convegno internazionale, Pavia 19-20-21 ottobre 1989*, Jaca Book, Milan, 1992, p. 11.

Pistone, Sergio, "La lotta del Movimento Federalista Europeo dalla Resistenza alla caduta della Comunità Europea di Difesa nel 1954", in Sergio Pistone (ed.), *I movimenti per l'unità europea dal 1945 al 1954. Atti del convegno internazionale. Pavia 19-20-21 ottobre 1989*, Jaca Book, Milan, 1992, pp. 17-60.

Pistone, Sergio, *Un'Italia federale in un'Europa federale*, Cesfer, Pavia, 1993.

Pistone, Sergio, "I movimenti per l'unità europea in Italia", in Sergio Pistone (ed.), *I movimenti per l'unità europea 1954-1969. Atti del Convegno internazionale, Genova, 5-6-7 novembre 1992*, PIME, Pavia, 1996, pp. 17-53.

Pistone, Sergio, "Il contributo del movimento Federalista Europeo del Piemonte alla lotta per l'unità europea negli anni 1945-1957", in Sergio Pistone and Corrado Malandrino (eds.), *Europeismo e federalismo in Piemonte tra le due guerre mondiali. La Resistenza e i Trattati di Roma (1957). Atti del Convegno tenuto presso la Fondazione Luigi Einaudi, Torino, 9 e 10 ottobre 1997*, Olschki, Florence, 1999.

Pistone, Sergio, "I movimenti per l'Unità europea in Italia", in Ariane Landuyt and Daniela Preda (eds.), *I movimenti per l'unità europea 1970-1986*, Il Mulino, Bologna, 2000, vol. I, pp. 39-100.

Pistone, Sergio (ed.), *Politica di potenza e imperialismo. L'analisi dell'imperialismo alla luce della dottrina della ragion di Stato*, Franco Angeli, Milan, 1973.

Pistone, Sergio (ed.), *L'idea dell'unificazione europea dalla prima alla seconda guerra mondiale. Relazioni tenute al Convegno di studi svoltosi presso la Fondazione Luigi Einaudi (Torino, 25-26 ottobre 1974)*, Fondazione Luigi Einaudi, Turin, 1975.

Pistone, Sergio (ed.), *I movimenti per l'unità europea 1954-1969. Atti del convegno internazionale, Genova 5-6-7 novembre 1992*, PIME, Pavia, 1996.

Pistone, Sergio and Malandrino, Corrado (eds.), *Europeismo e federalismo in Piemonte tra le due guerre mondiali. La Resistenza e i Trattati di Roma (1957). Atti del Convegno tenuto presso la Fondazione Luigi Einaudi, Torino, 9 e 10 ottobre 1997*, Olschki, Florence, 1999.

Plana, Manuel, *La Spagna franchista*, Guaraldi, Rimini-Florence, 1977.

Poggiolini, Ilaria, "Europeismo degasperiano e politica estera dell'Italia: un'ipotesi interpretativa (1947-1949)", *Storia delle relazioni internazionali*, 1 (1985), pp. 67-94.

Poher, Alain, "L'Europe, cette commune patrie à laquelle Jean Bareth a tant rêvé", *Communes d'Europe*, new series, 68 (December 1969), pp. 6-7.

Poidevin, Robert, *Robert Schuman. Homme d'État, 1886-1963*, Imprimerie Nationale, Paris, 1986.

Pombeni, Paolo, *Demagogia e tirannide. Uno studio sulla forma partito del fascismo*, Il Mulino, Bologna, 1984.

Pozzoli, Francesca, *Il federalismo europeo organizzato in Svizzera 1943-1945*, Degree thesis debated at the Faculty of Humanities and Philosophy at Pavia University, academic year 1994-1995, Thesis Director Luigi Vittorio Majocchi.

Preda, Daniela, "All'avanguardia dell'Europa: i primi vent'anni del Movimento federalista a Pavia", *Bollettino della Società Pavese di Storia Patria*, 85 (1985), pp. 182ff.

Preda, Daniela, *Storia di una speranza. La battaglia per la CED e la Federazione europea nelle carte della delegazione italiana (1950-1952)*, Jaca Book, Milan, 1990.

Preda, Daniela, *Sulla soglia dell'Unione. La vicenda della Comunità politica europea (1952-1954)*, Jaca Book, Milano, 1994.

Preda, Daniela, "Declino e rilancio del MFE tra fine della guerra e Piano Marshal", in Michel Dumoulin (ed.), *Plans des temps de guerre pour l'après-guerre 1940-1947. Actes du colloque de Bruxelles, 12-14 mai 1993*, Bruylant *et al.*, Brussels *et al.*, 1995, pp. 489-525.

Preda, Daniela, "La commissione istituzionale del Movimento europeo e le proposte per la riforma istituzionale dell'Unione europea", in Ariane Landuyt and Daniela Preda (eds.), *I movimenti per l'unità europea 1970-1986*, Il Mulino, Bologna, 2000, vol. I, pp. 569-602.

Preda, Daniela, *Alcide De Gasperi federalista europeo*, Il Mulino, Bologna, 2004.

Preda, Daniela (ed.), *Altiero Spinelli e i movimenti per l'unità europea*, CEDAM, Padova, 2010.

Preda, Daniela and Rognoni Vercelli, Cinzia (eds.), *Dalla Resistenza all'Europa. Il Mondo di Luciano Bolis*, TCP, Pavia, 2001.

Preda, Daniela and Levi, Guido (eds.), *L'europeismo in Liguria. Dal Risorgimento alla nascita dell'Europa comunitaria*, Il Mulino, Bologna, 2002.

Preda, Daniela and Rognoni Vercelli, Cinzia (eds.), *Storia e percorsi del federalismo. L'eredità di Carlo Cattaneo*, Il Mulino, Bologna, 2005, 2 vols.

Preda, Daniela and Pasquinucci, Daniele (eds.), *The Road Europe Travelled Along. The Evolution of the EEC/EU Institutions and Policies*, PIE Peter Lang, Brussels, 2010.

"Prefazione", in Lisa Conti Riccioli (ed.), *Scritti di Menotti Riccioli*, Tipografia Giuntina, Florence, 1979.

Premier Congrès international et exposition comparée des Villes, organisé sous le Haut Patronage et avec le concours de la Ville de Gand, à l'occasion de l'Exposition Universelle, en cette ville, 1913, et sous les auspices de l'Union des villes et communes belges. II. *Organisation de la vie communale*, Union internationale des villes, Brussels, 1913.

Press release dated January 31st, 2011, from the CoR. Website. http://www.cor.europa.eu/pages/PressTemplate.aspx?view=detail&id=545cd53a-9dc3-427f-876b-0706e7bbefe3 [access April 2012].

Press release dated June 16th 2011 from the CoR. Website. http://www.cor.europa.eu/pages/PressTemplate.aspx?view=detail&id=5cd9a64f-8ce0-411a-a29a-8f130c3f6c85 [access April 2012].

"Primo progetto di una Carta delle libertà comunali e regionali", *Comuni d'Europa*, 1 (April 1952), p. 10.

"Un primo resoconto del Congresso di Forlì", *Comuni d'Europa*, 4 (April 1955), pp. 1-3.

"Programma del Partito democratico cristiano", *L'Unità Europea*, 8 (January-February 1945), p. 8.

Punzo, Maurizio, *Dalla Liberazione a Palazzo Barberini. Storia del Partito Socialista Italiano dalla ricostruzione alla scissione del 1947*, Celuc, Milan, 1973.

Punzo, Maurizio, "Gino Cassinis, sindaco di Milano", in Enrico Decleva (ed.), *Il Politecnico di Milano nella storia italiana (1914-1963)*, vol. 1, *Rivista milanese di economia*, supplement for no. 28 (October-December 1988), pp. 319-335.

"Quand Milan s'intéresse au Grand Lyon". Website. http://www.lyonmag.com/article/28587/quand-milan-s-interesse-au-grand-lyon [access April 2012].

Quazza, Guido (ed.), *Fascismo e società italiana*, Einaudi, Turin, 1973.

Ragusa, Andrea, *Il manifesto elettorale. Mezzo secolo di propaganda dai fondi Schiavi di Forlì*, Lacaita, Manduria-Bari-Rome, 2004.

Ragusa, Andrea, "Eugenio Colorni dall'antifascismo all'Europeismo socialista e federalista. Convegno di studi sotto l'Alto patronato del presidente della Repubblica", *Storia e Futuro. Rivista di storia e storiografia*, 20 (June 2009).

"La rappresentanza dei poteri locali nel quadro della CEE", *Comuni d'Europa*, 10 (October 1958), p. 11.

"Rapprochement entre deux villes du Benelux Esch-sur-Alzette et Amersfoort", in *Hubert Clément. Un humaniste du travail*, Édition de l'Imprimerie coopérative luxembourgeoise, Esch-sur-Alzette, 1954, vol. I, pp. 141-142.

"Ratificare la "Carta" e aderire al Consiglio dei Comuni d'Europa: questi sono i compiti immediati", *Comuni d'Europa*, 1 (February 1954), p. 1.

"Raymond Mondon", *Communes d'Europe*, new series, 73 (March 1971), p. 28.

Régions et communes d'Europe, 72 (April-May 2011).

"Regolari adesioni scritte e sottoscritte ricevute entro il 24-IV-1952", *Comuni d'Europa*, 1 (April 1952), p. 8.

"Relazione organizzativa del Segretario aggiunto per il VI Congresso nazionale del MFE, Genova 11-13 giugno 1954", *Europa federata*, supplement for no. 4 (1954).

"Relazione sull'opera di Antoine Élisée Cherbuliez intitolata 'La democrazia in Svizzera'", in Alexis de Tocqueville, *Scritti politici*. I. *La rivoluzione democratica in Francia*, UTET, Turin, 1969.

Renouvin, Pierre, *Histoire des relations internationales*. VII. *Les crises du XXe siècles. De 1914 à 1929*, Hachette, Paris, 1957.

Renouvin, Pierre, *Histoire des relations internationales*. VIII. *Les crises du XXe siècles. De 1929 à 1945*, Paris, Hachette, 1958.

Ricciardelli, Chiara, *Olivetti: una storia, un sogno ancora da scrivere. La sociologia del lavoro italiana nell'esperienza di Ivrea*, Franco Angeli, Milan, 2001.

Riccioli, Menotti, *Profilo programmatico del Partito Repubblicano Italiano*, Partito repubblicano italiano, Rome, 1944.

Riccioli, Menotti, *La federazione europea in marcia*, Stabilimento grafico commerciale, Florence, [1953].

Richard, Max, "Soixante années de connivence", *XXe siècle fédéraliste. Pouvoir européen*, 1 (1991), pp. 5-7.

Ridolfi, Maurizio (ed.), *Alessandro Schiavi. Indagine sociale, culture politiche e tradizione socialista nel primo '900*, Il ponte vecchio, Cesena, 1994.

Rieben, Henri *et al.*, *Le fédéralisme et Alexandre Marc*, Centre de recherches européennes, Lausanne, 1974.

Righetti, Umberto, *Contributo ad una storia della socialdemocrazia italiana*, Società editrice democratica, Rome, 1962.

Rings, Werner, *La Svizzera in guerra 1933-1945*, Mondadori, Milan, 1975.

Rioux, Jean-Pierre, *La France de la Quatrième République*, Seuil, Paris, 1980-1983, 2 vols.

"Le risoluzioni dell'incontro di Magonza del Consiglio dei comuni d'Europa", *Comuni d'Europa*, 10 (October 1978), pp. 13-14.

Robbins, Lionel, *Economic Planning and International Order*, MacMillan, London, 1937.

Robertson, Arthur Henry, *Le Conseil de l'Europe. Sa structure, ses fonctions et ses réalisations*, Sijthoff, Leyde, 1962.

Rognoni Vercelli, Cinzia, *Mario Alberto Rollier: un valdese federalista*, Jaca Book, Milan, 1991.

Rognoni Vercelli, Cinzia, "L'Unione europea dei federalisti", in Sergio Pistone (ed.), *I movimenti per l'Unità europea dal 1945 al 1954. Atti del convegno internazionale, Pavia 19-20-21 ottobre 1989*, Jaca Book, Milan, 1992, pp. 183-204.

Rognoni Vercelli, Cinzia, "Il Congresso del popolo europeo", in Sergio Pistone (ed.), *I movimenti per l'unità europea 1954-1969. Atti del Convegno internazionale, Genova, 5-6-7 novembre 1992*, PIME, Pavia, 1996, pp. 373-397.

Rognoni Vercelli, Cinzia, "Gli archivi dei movimenti per l'unità europea e il ruolo della Fondazione Bolis", in Maria Grazia Melchionni (ed.), *Fonti e luoghi della documentazione europea. Istruzioni per l'uso. Atti del Seminario organizzato dal Polo Universitario Europeo Jean-Monnet - Luigi Einaudi (Roma, 19-20 febbraio 1999)*, Università degli Studi di Roma "La Sapienza", Rome. 2000, pp. 69-83.

Rognoni Vercelli, Cinzia, "Gli archivi federalisti ed europeisti e il ruolo della Fondazione Bolis", in Simona Negruzzo and Fabio Zucca (eds.), *Gli archivi storici delle Università italiane e il caso pavese*, Tipografia popolare, Pavia, 2001, monographic issue of the *Annali di Storia Pavese*, pp. 181-191.

Rognoni Vercelli, Cinzia, Con Spinelli alla testa del MFE, in Daniela Preda and Cinzia Rognoni Vercelli (eds.), *Dalla Resistenza all'Europa. Il Mondo di Luciano Bolis*, TCP, Pavia, 2001, pp. 217-248.

Rognoni Vercelli, Cinzia, *Luciano Bolis dall'Italia all'Europa*, Il Mulino, Bologna, 2007.

"A Rome le Congrès interparlementaire du Mouvement Européen a demandé la création d'une Assemblée des communes et régions", *Communes d'Europe*, 18, (June-July 1957), p. 39.

Rosboch, Michele, "La figura di Amedeo Peyron dalla ricostruzione alle celebrazioni di Italia '61", in Michele Rosboch and Daniele Gigli (eds.), *Sintaksis. Raccolta di studi*, La locanda del Re Pescatore, Turin, 2010, vol. 3, pp. 97-116.

Rosboch Michele (ed.), *L'opera del sindaco Amedeo Peyron: la dimensione europea di Torino. Atti del Convegno promosso dal Centro Culturale Pier Giorgio Frassati nel centenario della nascita dell'avv. Amedeo Peyron (1903-2003), sindaco di Torino dal 1951 al 1962: Torino, 8 novembre 2003*, L'Artistica, Savigliano, 2005.

Rosboch Michele and Sabatino Alfonso (eds.), *Atti del seminario Torino città europea. Il ruolo del Sindaco di Torino Amedeo Peyron (1951-1962) presidente dell'Associazione Italiana per il Consiglio dei Comuni d'Europa (1957-1965)*, Torino, 4 luglio 2008, CESI, Turin, 2009.

Rossi, Ernesto, *Un democratico ribelle. Cospirazione antifascista, carcere, confino: scritti e testimonianze* (ed. Giuseppe Armani), Guanda, Parma, 1975.

Rossi, Ernesto, *Guerra e dopoguerra. Lettere 1915-1930* (ed. Giuseppe Armani), La Nuova Italia, Florence, 1978.

Rossi, Ernesto, *Miserie e splendori dal confino di polizia. Lettere da Ventotene 1939-1943* (ed. Manlio Magini), Feltrinelli, Milan, 1981.

Rossi, Ernesto, *Nove anni sono molti. Lettere dal carcere 1930-1939* (ed. Mimmo Franzinelli), Bollati Boringhieri, Turin, 2001.

Rotelli, Ettore, *L'avvento della Regione in Italia. Dalla caduta del regime fascista alla Costituzione repubblicana (1943-1947)*, Giuffré, Milan, 1967.

Roveri, Alessandro, *Le cause del fascismo. Origini storiche del regime reazionario di massa in Italia e Germania*, Il Mulino, Bologna, 1985.

Ruffieux, Roland, *La Suisse de l'entre-deux-guerres*, Payot, Lausanne, 1974.

Rugge, Fabio, *I regimi delle città. Il governo municipale in Europa tra '800 e '900*, Franco Angeli, Milan, 1992.

Saint-Gille, Anne-Marie, *La Paneurope. Un débat d'idées dans l'entre-deux-guerres*, Presses de l'Université de Paris-Sorbonne, Paris, 2003.

Salerno, Daniele, "Questo è il bello della democrazia. Intervista a Frédéric Vallier nuovo segretario generale del CCRE", *Comuni d'Europa*, new series, 25 (April 2010), pp. 9-11.

Salvatorelli, Luigi, "Mazzini e gli Stati Uniti d'Europa", *Rassegna storica del Risorgimento*, 37 (1950), pp. 453-458.

Salvi, Sergio, *Le nazioni proibite. Guida a dieci colonie "interne" dell'Europa occidentale*, Vallecchi, Florence, 1973.

Salvi, Sergio, *L'Italia non esiste*, Camunia, Florence, 1996.

Santarelli, Enzo, *Storia del movimento e del regime fascista*, Editori riuniti, Rome, 1967, 2 vols.

Sapelli, Giulio and Chiarini, Roberto, *Fini e fine della politica. La sfida di Adriano Olivetti*, Edizioni di Comunità, Milan, 1990.

Scalfaro, Oscar Luigi and Porcellana, Giovanni, "Amedeo Peyron un uomo, una città", *Vita sociale*, 129 (December 1985).

Schiavi, Alessandro, *Il comune ieri, oggi, domani*, Opere Nuove, Rome, 1956.

Schiavi, Alessandro, *Le piaghe d'Italia. Disoccupazione, analfabetismo, tuguri, miseria*, Opere Nuove, Rome, 1958.

Schiavi, Alessandro, *Carteggi*. I. *1892-1926* (ed. Carlo De Maria), Lacaita, Manduria-Bari-Rome, 2003.

Schiavi, Alessandro, *Diari e note sparse (1894-1964)* (eds. Carlo De Maria and Stefano Mengozzi), Lacaita, Manduria, 2003.

Schiavi, Alessandro, *Carteggi*. II. *1927-1965* (ed. Carlo De Maria), Lacaita, Manduria-Bari-Rome, 2004.

Schiavi, Alessandro, *Nel socialismo italiano ed europeo* (ed. Gianni Silei), Lacaita, Manduria, 2005.

Schiera, Pierangelo, *Le autonomie e l'Europa. Profili storici comparati*, Il Mulino, Bologna, 1993.

Schulze, Hagen, *La repubblica di Weimar: la Germania dal 1917 al 1933*, Il Mulino, Bologna, 1987.

Schuman, Robert, "Origines et élaboration du Plan Schuman. Bruges 22 et 23 octobre 1953", *Cahiers de Bruges* (December 1953).

Schuman, Robert, *Pour l'Europe*, Nagel, Paris, 1963.

Sebastiani, Pietro, *Laburisti inglesi e socialisti italiani. Dalla ricostruzione del PSI(UP) alla scissione di Palazzo Barberini, da Transport House a Downing Street, 1943-1947*, Elengraf, Rome, 1985.

Segretariato generale del Consiglio d'Europa, *Il Consiglio d'Europa*, Istituto poligrafico dello Stato, Rome, 1971.

[Serafini, Umberto], "Il MFE per i comuni d'Europa. Due risoluzioni del Congresso di Torino", *Comuni d'Europa*, 2-3 (January 1953), p. 7.

[Serafini, Umberto], "Le spese superflue di molti viaggi", *Comuni d'Europa*, 3, (March-April 1956), p. 10.

Serafini, Umberto, *Adriano Olivetti: ci ha lasciato uno dei più grandi maestri del federalismo integrale*, Castaldi, Rome, 1960.

Serafini, Umberto, *Adriano Olivetti e le dottrine politiche*, Fondazione Adriano Olivetti, Ivrea, 1962.

[Serafini, Umberto], "La morte di Alessandro Schiavi", *Comuni d'Europa*, 6 (June 1965), p. 3.

Serafini, Umberto, "Amedeo Peyron", *Comuni d'Europa*, 9 (September 1965), pp. 1-4.

Serafini, Umberto, "Jean Bareth", *Comuni d'Europa*, 12 (December 1969), p. 2 and pp. 7-10.

Serafini, Umberto, "Gli enti locali e le elezioni europee", *Il comune democratico*, 8-9 (August-September 1978), pp. 60-72.

[Serafini, Umberto], "Renato Brügner", *Comuni d'Europa*, 4 (April 1980), pp. 5-7.

Serafini, Umberto, "Gli europei adulti: le elezioni europee e i compiti politici dei poteri locali e regionali. Relazione generale politica all'incontro delle 1.000 città europee gemelle, Magonza (Germania federale) 28-29 September 1978", *Gli inserti di Comuni d'Europa* (June 1978-December 1981), p. VII.

Serafini, Umberto, *Adriano Olivetti e il Movimento Comunità: una anticipazione scomoda, un discorso aperto*, Officina, Rome, 1982.

Serafini, Umberto, "Convertito ai gemellaggi", in Associazione Italiana per il Consiglio dei Comuni e delle Regioni d'Europa, I *gemellaggi per l'unione europea e per la pace: guida ai vincoli permanenti di fraternità tra Comuni, Province e Regioni d'Europa aperti alle relazioni Est-Ovest, Nord-Sud*, Salemi, Rome, 1990, pp. 18-24.

Serafini, Umberto, *I libri e il prossimo. Un esercizio di memoria, un esame di coscienza*, Passigli, Florence, 1991.

Serafini, Umberto, "Quarant'anni di storia, X Congresso nazionale AICCRE, Roma 7-9 Marzo 1991", *Comuni d'Europa*, 3 (March 1991), p. 2.

Serafini, Umberto, "La comunità di Adriano Olivetti e il federalismo", *Comuni d'Europa*, 3 (March 1993), pp. 1-8.

Serafini, Umberto, *Breve storia del Consiglio dei comuni e delle regioni d'Europa nel quadro di due secoli di lotta federalista*, Salemi, Rome, 1995.

Serafini, Umberto, *La mia guerra contro la guerra*, Europea editrice, Rome, 2002.

Sereni, Emilio, *Argomenti per l'Europa: contro la CED e il riarmo tedesco*, Comitato dei Partigiani della pace, [s.l.], 1954.

Sereni, Emilio, *L'europeismo, l'Italia e la CED. Conferenza tenuta al teatro municipale di Reggio Emilia il 17 gennaio 1954 dal Sen. Emilio Sereni*, Comitato dei Partigiani della pace, Reggio Emilia, 1954.

Sergent, Lucien, "Nous poursuivrons sa tâche", *Communes d'Europe*, new series, 68 (December 1969), p. 9.

Serra, Enrico (ed.), *Il rilancio dell'Europa e i Trattati di Roma. Actes du Colloque de Rome, 25-28 mars 1987*, Bruylant *et al.*, Brussels *et al.*, 1989.

Settia, Aldo Angelo, *Rapine, assedi, battaglie. La guerra del medioevo*, Laterza, Rome-Bari, 2002.

Signori, Elisa, *Ignazio Silone nell'esilio svizzero*, Le Monnier, Florence, 1979.

Signori, Elisa, *La Svizzera e i fuorusciti: aspetti e problemi dell'emigrazione politica, 1943-1945*, Franco Angeli, Milan, 1983.

"Sindaci di capoluogo firmatari dell'impegno per la Costituente", *Comuni d'Europa*, 1 (January 1953), p. 5.

"Il sindaco Peyron riceve a Strasburgo il "Premio Europa" per la nostra città", *La Nuova stampa* (October 20th 1957), p. 2.

Smith, Joseph, *La guerra fredda 1945-1991*, Il Mulino, Bologna, 2000.

Soavi, Giorgio, *Adriano Olivetti. Una sorpresa italiana*, Rizzoli, Milan, 2001.

I socialisti e l'Europa. Annali della Fondazione G. Brodolini e della Fondazione di studi storici Filippo Turati, Franco Angeli, Milan, 1989.

Solari, Leo, *I giovani di "Rivoluzione socialista"*, IEPI, Rome, 1964.

Solari, Leo, "Colorni e il federalismo socialista", *Mondoperaio*, 3 (March 1979), pp. 123-129.

Spinelli, Altiero, *L'Europa non cade dal cielo*, Il Mulino, Bologna, 1960.

Spinelli, Altiero, *Come ho tentato di diventare saggio*. I. *Io Ulisse*, Il Mulino, Bologna, 1984.

Spinelli, Altiero, *Il progetto europeo*, Il Mulino, Bologna, 1985.

Spinelli, Altiero, *Come ho tentato di diventare saggio*. II. *La goccia e la roccia*, Il Mulino, Bologna, 1987.

Spinelli, Altiero, *Discorsi al Parlamento europeo 1976-1986* (ed. Pier Virgilio Dastoli), Il Mulino, Bologna, 1987.

Spinelli, Altiero, "Il manifesto dei federalisti europei", in Altiero Spinelli, *Una strategia per gli Stati Uniti d'Europa*, Il Mulino, Bologna, 1989.

Spinelli, Altiero, "Nuovo corso", in Altiero Spinelli, *Una strategia per gli Stati Uniti d'Europa*, Il Mulino, Bologna, 1989.

Spinelli, Altiero, *Una strategia per gli Stati Uniti d'Europa* (ed. Sergio Pistone), Il Mulino, Bologna, 1989.

Spinelli, Altiero, *Diario europeo* (ed. Edmondo Paolini), Il Mulino, Bologna, 1989-1992, 3 vols.

Spinelli, Altiero, L'Europa tra Ovest e Est (ed. Cesare Merlini), Il Mulino, Bologna, 1990.

Spinelli, Altiero, *La crisi degli Stati nazionali* (ed. Lucio Levi), Il Mulino, Bologna, 1991.

Spinelli, Altiero, *Il Manifesto di Ventotene*, Il Mulino, Bologna, 1991.

Spinelli, Altiero and Rossi, Ernesto, *Problemi della federazione europea*, preface by Eugenio Colorni, Edizioni del Movimento italiano per la Federazione europea, Rome, 1944.

S.S. Pie XII parle de l'Europe (1948-1957), Office catholique d'information sur les problèmes européens, Strasbourg, 1958.

Staatsarchiv Basel, *Sammlung biographischer Zeitungsausschnitte, Adolf Gasser (1903-1985)* (ed. Marcus Mattmüller), Basel, 1985.

"Storia della democrazia", *La vetrina libraria*, 2 (February 1946), p. 3.

Suffert, Georges, *De Defferre à Mitterrand, la campagne présidentielle*, Seuil, Paris, 1966.

Taddei, Francesca, *Il socialismo italiano del dopoguerra: correnti ideologiche e scelte politiche (1943-1947)*, Franco Angeli, Milan, 1984.

Tamames, Ramon, *La República. La era de Franco*, Alianza editorial, Madrid, 1973.

Tasca, Angelo, *Nascita e avvento del fascismo*, Laterza, Bari, 1971.

Témoignages, *Guy Mollet, 1905-1975*, Fondation Guy Mollet, Paris, 1977.

"Tesi politiche federaliste", *L'Unità europea*, 3 (September 1943), pp. 2-3.

Terracini, Umberto, *Al bando dal Partito. Carteggio clandestino dall'isola e dall'esilio 1938-1945* (ed. Alessandro Coletti), La Pietra, Milan, 1976.

Terracini, Umberto, *Intervista sul comunismo difficile* (ed. Arturo Gismondi), Laterza, Rome-Bari, 1978.

"Terza seduta plenaria al Palazzo municipale di Versaglia", *Nuova Rassegna*, second series, 12 (June 1954), pp. 956-958.

Thamer, Hans-Ulrich, *Il Terzo Reich. La Germania dal 1933 al 1945*, Il Mulino, Bologna, 1993.

Togliatti, Palmiro, "Il Piano Marshall", *Rinascita*, 6 (June 1947), p. 139.

La Toscana per la pace. I gemellaggi in Toscana, Pagnini e Martinelli, Florence, 1999.

"Un traguardo immediato per il CCE. Le elezioni europee", *Comuni d'Europa*, 1 (January 1969), pp. 1-5.

Tramarollo, Giuseppe, *L'Europa di Mazzini*, Domus Mazziniana, Pisa, 1962.

Tranfaglia, Nicola, "La prima guerra mondiale e il fascismo", in *Storia d'Italia*, UTET, Turin, 1995, pp. 131ff.

Turati, Filippo, *Trent'anni di Critica sociale*, Zanichelli, Bologna, 1921.

Ufficio Stampa del comune di Firenze (ed.), *Convegno a Firenze dei Sindaci delle Capitali, 2-6 ottobre 1955*, Noccioli, Florence, 1956.

Ufficio Stampa del comune di Firenze (ed.), Firenze. *Rassegna del comune 1951-1960*, Florence, 1960, single edition, October 1960.

Ulam, Adam Bruno, *Stalin. The Man and his Era*, Allen Lane, London, 1974.

Unger, Gérard, *Gaston Defferre*, Fayard, Paris, 2011.

L'Unità europea, 10 (May 6th 1945).

L'Unità europea, 17 (September 1948).

Valeri, Antonio, "L'idea federalista e l'Internazionale nella 'Critica' turatiana", *Critica sociale*, 1 (1972), pp. 12-14.

Varsori, Antonio, "De Gasperi, Nenni, Sforza e il loro ruolo nella politica estera italiana del secondo dopoguerra", in Ennio Di Nolfo - Romain H. Rainero - Brunello Vigezzi (eds.), *L'Italia e la politica di potenza in Europa (1945-1950)*, Marzorati, Settimo Milanese, 1988, pp. 59-91.

Varsori, Antonio, "L'Italia fra Alleanza Atlantica e CED (1949-1954)", *Storia delle relazioni internazionali*, IV (1988), 1, pp. 125-165.

Varsori, Antonio, "Il Congresso dell'Europa dell'Aja 7-10 maggio 1948", in Sergio Pistone (ed.), *I movimenti per l'unità europea dal 1945 al 1954. Atti del convegno internazionale, Pavia 19-21 ottobre 1989*, Jaca Book, Milan, 1992, pp. 311-341.

Veneruso, Danilo, *L'Italia fascista (1922-1945)*, Il Mulino, Bologna, 1981.

"Il ventennale di un gemellaggio", *Comuni d'Europa*, 10 (October 1982), p. 5.

Vial, Philippe, "Jean Monnet, un père pour la CED?", in René Girault and Gérard Bossuat (eds.), *Europe brisée, Europe retrovée. Nouvelle réflexion sur l'unité européenne au XXe siècle*, Publications de la Sorbonne, Paris, 1994, pp. 197-262.

Vigezzi, Brunello, "De Gasperi, Sforza, la diplomazia italiana e la percezione della politica di potenza dal trattato di pace al Patto Atlantico (1947-1950)", *Storia contemporanea*, 16 (1985), 4, pp. 661-685.

Vincent, Gilbert and Willaime, Jean Paul (eds.), *Réligions et transformations de l'Europe*, Presses universitaires de Strasbourg, Strasbourg, 1993.

Vion, Antoine, *La constitution des enjeux internationaux dans le gouvernement des villes françaises (1947-1995)*, Doctoral thesis in Political Science, University of Rennes 1, 2001.

Vion, Antoine, "Europe from the Bottom Up: Town Twinning in France during the Cold War", *Contemporary european history*, XI (November 2002), p. 623.

Vion, Antoine, "Superare i conflitti: il gemellaggio tra città europee dopo la seconda guerra mondiale", in Patrizia Dogliani and Oscar Gaspari (eds.), *L'Europa dei comuni. Origini e sviluppo del movimento comunale europeo dalla fine dell'Ottocento al secondo dopoguerra*, Donzelli, Rome, 2003, pp. 249-272.

Visconti, Dante, *La concezione unitaria dell'Europa nel Risorgimento italiano e nei suoi precedenti storici*, Vallardi, Milan, 1948.

Vivarelli, Roberto, *Le origini del fascismo. L'Italia dalla grande guerra alla marcia su Roma*, Il Mulino, Bologna, 1991, 2 vols.

Voyenne, Bernard, *Histoire de l'idée fédéraliste*, Presses d'Europe, Nice, 1973-1981, 3 vols.

Waltz, Kenneth N., *Teoria della politica internazionale*, Il Mulino, Bologna, 1987.

Werth, Alexander, *France 1940-1955*, Hale, London, 1957.

Yergin, Daniel, *Shattered peace. The origins of the Cold War and the national Security State*, Houghton Mifflin, Boston, 1977.

Zagari, Mario, "Il socialismo italiano e l'europeismo. Testimonianza", in *I socialisti e l'Europa. Annali della Fondazione G. Brodolini e della Fondazione di studi storici Filippo Turati*, Franco Angeli, Milan, 1989, pp. 245-261.

Zanni Rosiello, Isabella, "Spurghi e distruzioni di carte d'archivio", *Quaderni storici*, 18 (1983), pp. 985-1017.

Zanzi, Luigi, *Le Alpi nella storia d'Europa. Ambienti, popoli, istituzioni e forme di civiltà del mondo alpino dal passato al futuro*, CDA & Vivalda, Turin, 2004.

Zoli, Giancarlo, "Testimonianza", in *Il clero toscano nella Resistenza. Atti del Convegno, Lucca, 4-5-6 aprile 1975*, La Nuova Europa, Florence, 1975, pp. 109-110.

Zoli, Giancarlo, "Il nostro messaggio", *Comuni d'Europa*, 12 (December 1982), p. 12.

Zoli, Giancarlo, "Non poteva esistere la sola libertà del villaggio: la sconfitta del nazismo era un traguardo europeo", *Comuni d'Europa*, 4 (April 1987), p. 11 and p. 16.

Zucca, Fabio, *La contribution du Conseil des communes d'Europe à la première élection du Parlement européen*, Groupe de liaison des historiens auprès des Communautés, Louvain-la-Neuve, 1996.

Zucca, Fabio, "Il Conseil des communes d'Europe e il rilancio europeo di Messina", in Luigi Vittorio Majocchi, (ed.), *Messina quarant'anni dopo. L'attualità del metodo in vista della conferenza intergovernativa del 1996*, Cacucci, Bari, 1996, pp. 243-260.

Zucca, Fabio, "Émile Chanoux e Adolf Gasser: ipotesi di organizzazione statale dagli anni Trenta alla Carta europea delle libertà locali", in Paolo Momigliano Levi (ed.), *Émile Chanoux et le débat sur le fédéralisme*, Presses d'Europe, Nice, 1997, pp. 87-102.

Zucca, Fabio, "Amedeo Peyron. Un sindaco federalista", in Sergio Pistone and Corrado Malandrino (eds.), *Europeismo e federalismo in Piemonte tra le due guerre mondiali. La resistenza e i Trattati di Roma (1957). Atti del Convegno tenuto presso la Fondazione Luigi Einaudi, Torino, 9 e 10 ottobre 1997*, Olschki, Florence, 1999.

Zucca, Fabio, *Autonomie locali e federazione sovranazionale. La battaglia del Conseil des Communes et Régions d'Europe per l'unità europea*, Il Mulino, Bologna, 2001.

Zucca, Fabio, "L'azione di Luciano Bolis per la costituzione dell'Associazione italiana per il Consiglio dei Comuni d'Europa", in Daniela Preda and Cinzia Rognoni Vercelli (eds.), *Dalla Resistenza all'Europa. Il Mondo di Luciano Bolis*, TCP, Pavia, 2001, pp. 249-270.

Zucca, Fabio, "Il riformismo socialista lombardo e la questione dell'unità europea", in Fabio Zucca (ed.), *Europeismo e federalismo in Lombardia dal Risorgimento all'Unione europea*, Il Mulino, Bologna, 2007, pp. 533-577.

Zucca, Fabio (ed.), *Europeismo e federalismo in Lombardia dal Risorgimento all'Unione europea*, Il Mulino, Bologna, 2007.

Zucca, Fabio, "Umberto Serafini e Altiero Spinelli fra federalismo infranazionale e sovranazionale", *Comuni d'Europa*, new series, 20 (June 2008), pp. 20-36.

Zucca, Fabio, "I gemellaggi della città di Torino e l'azione di Amedeo Peyron", in Michele Rosboch and Alfonso Sabatino (eds.), *Atti del seminario Torino città europea. Il ruolo del sindaco di Torino Amedeo Peyron (1951-1962) presidente dell'Associazione Italiana per il Consiglio dei Comuni d'Europa (1957-1965)*, Torino, 4 luglio 2008, CESI, Turin, 2009, pp. 19-67.

Zucca, Fabio, "Eugenio Colorni, Guglielmo Usellini e l'Unità europea", in Maurizio Degl'Innocenti (ed.), *Eugenio Colorni dall'antifascismo all'europeismo socialista e federalista*, Lacaita, Manduria-Bari-Rome, 2010, pp. 251-273.

Zucca, Fabio, "L'Europe des communes et des régions à travers l'action de deux de ses acteurs principaux: Jacques Chaban-Delmas et Umberto Serafini", in Sylvain Schirmann (ed.), *Quelles architectures pour quelle Europe? Des projects d'une Europe unie à l'Union européenne (1945-1992). Actes des deuxièmes journées d'étude de la Maison de Robert Schuman. Metz, 9, 10 et 11 mai 2010*, PIE Peter Lang, Brussels, 2011, pp. 91-111.

Zucca, Fabio, "L'organisation du consensus parmi les administrateurs locaux européens", in Daniela Preda and Daniele Pasquinucci (eds.), *International Conference. The Evolution of the Consensus to European Integration 1950-2005*, Genova, May 5th-6th 2010 (currently being published).

Zucca, Fabio (ed.), *Eugenio Colorni federalista*, Lacaita, Manduria-Bari-Rome, 2011.

EUROCLIO – Published Books

N° 72 – *The International Relations of Local Authorities. From Institutional Twinning to the Committee of the Regions: Fifty Years of European Integration History.* Fabio ZUCCA, 2012.

N° 71 – *Histoire du Conseil de l'Europe (1949-2009).* Birte WASSENBERG, 2012.

N° 70 – *The EU, Security and Transatlantic Relations.* Finn LAURSEN (ed.), 2012.

N° 69 – *Européanisation au XXᵉ siècle. Un regard historique / Europeanisation in the 20ᵗʰ Century. The Historical Lens.* Matthieu OSMONT, Émilia ROBIN-HIVERT, Katja SEIDEL, Mark SPOERER & Christian WENKEL (dir./eds.), 2012.

N° 68 – *Consensus and European Integration. An Historical Perspective / Consensus et intégration européenne. Une perspective historique.* Daniela PREDA & Daniele PASQUINUCCI (eds./dir.), 2012.

N° 67 – *Générations de fédéralistes européens depuis le XIXᵉ siècle. Individus, groupes, espaces et réseaux.* Geneviève DUCHENNE et Michel DUMOULIN (dir.), 2012.

N° 66 – *Raymond Aron, penseur de l'Europe et de la nation.* Giulio DE LIGIO (dir.), 2012.

N° 65 – *Europe Twenty Years after the End of the Cold War. The New Europe, New Europes? / L'Europe vingt ans après la fin de la guerre froide. Nouvelle Europe, nouvelles Europes?* Bruno ARCIDIACONO, Katrin MILZOW, Axel MARION & Pierre-Étienne BOURNEUF (eds./dir.), 2012.

N° 64 – *Aux origines de la diplomatie européenne. Les Neuf et la Coopération politique européenne de 1973 à 1980.* Maria Gainar, 2012.

N° 63 – *Europe and the Middle East. The hour of the East?* Birte WASSENBERG & Giovanni FALEG (eds.), 2012.

N° 62 – *Quelle architecture pour un code européen de droit international privé ?* Marc FALLON, Paul LAGARDE, Sylvaine POILLOT-PERUZZETTO (dir.), 2011.

N° 61 – *La construction d'un espace euro-méditerranéen. Genèses, mythes et perspectives.* Houda BEN HAMOUDA et Mathieu BOUCHARD (dir.), 2012.

N° 60 – *Innovations et transferts de technologie en Europe du Nord-Ouest aux XIXᵉ et XXᵉ siècles.* Jean-François ECK et Pierre TILLY (dir.), 2011.

N° 59 – *Novel Outlooks on the Marshall Plan. American Aid and European Re-Industrialization.* Fransceca FAURI & Paolo TEDESCHI (eds.), 2011.

N° 58 – *Europe in the International Arena during the 1970s. Entering a Different World / L'Europe sur la scène internationale dans les années 1970. À la découverte d'un nouveau monde.* Antonio VARSORI & Guia MIGANI (eds./dir.), 2011.

N° 57 – *Cultures nationales et identité communautaire. Un défi pour l'Europe ? / National Cultures and Common Identity. A Challenge for Europe?* Marloes BEERS & Jenny RAFLIK (dir./eds.), 2010.

N° 56 – *Les trajectoires de l'innovation technologique et la construction européenne. Des voies de structuration durable ? / Trends in Technological Innovation and the European Construction. The Emerging of Enduring Dynamics?* Christophe BOUNEAU, David BURIGANA & Antonio VARSORI (dir./eds.), 2010.

N° 55 – *L'OTAN et l'Europe. Quels liens pour la sécurité et la défense européenne ?* Birte WASSENBERG, Giovanni FALEG et Martin W. MLODECKI (dir.), 2010.

N° 54 – *The Road Europe Travelled Along.* Daniele PASQUINUCCI and Daniela PREDA (eds.), 2010.

N° 53 – *Vivre et construire l'Europe à l'échelle territoriale de 1945 à nos jours.* Yves DENÉCHÈRE et Marie-Bénédicte VINCENT (dir.), 2010.

N° 52 – *De l'esprit de la Résistance jusqu'à l'idée de l'Europe. Projets européens et américains pour l'Europe de l'après-guerre (1940-1950).* Veronika HEYDE, 2010.

N° 51 – *Le dernier carré. Les charbonniers belges, libres entrepreneurs face à la CECA (1950-1959).* Roch HANNECART, 2010.

N° 49 – *Le « Congrès de l'Europe » à La Haye (1948-2008).* Jean-Michel GUIEU et Christophe LE DRÉAU (dir.), 2009.

N° 48 – *The Road to a United Europe. Interpretations of the Process of European Integration.* Morten RASMUSSEN & Ann-Christina L. KNUDSEN (eds.), 2009.

N° 47 – *L'Europe au cœur. Études pour Marie-Thérèse Bitsch.* Martial LIBERA et Birte WASSENBERG (dir.), 2009.

N° 46 – *Les deux Europes. Actes du IIIe colloque international RICHIE/ The Two Europes. Proceedings of the 3rd international RICHIE conference.* Michele AFFINITO, Guia MIGANI & Christian WENKEL (dir./eds.), 2009.

N° 45 – *Pardon du passé, Europe unie et défense de l'Occident. Adenauer et Schuman docteurs* honoris causa *de l'Université catholique de Louvain en 1958.* Geneviève DUCHENNE et Gaëlle COURTOIS (dir.), 2009.

N° 44 – *From* Détente *in Europe to European* Détente. *How the West Shaped the Helsinki CSCE.* Angela ROMANO, 2009.

N° 43 – *L'Espagne et l'Europe. De la dictature de Franco à l'Union européenne.* Matthieu TROUVÉ, 2008.

Euroclio European Network

together with the SEGEI Network

Coordination : Chaire Jean Monnet d'histoire de l'Europe contemporaine (Cehec)
Collège Erasme, 1, place Blaise-Pascal, B-1348 Louvain-la-Neuve

Germany
Jürgen Elvert
Wilfried Loth

Belgium
Julie Cailleau
Jocelyne Collonval
Yves Conrad
Gaëlle Courtois
Pascal Deloge
Geneviève Duchenne
Vincent Dujardin
Michel Dumoulin
Roch Hannecart
Pierre-Yves Plasman
Béatrice Roeh
Corine Schröder
Caroline Suzor
Pierre Tilly
Arthe Van Laer
Jérôme Wilson
Natacha Wittorski

Spain
Enrique Moradiellos
Mercedes Samaniego Boneu

France
Françoise Berger
Marie-Thérèse Bitsch
Gérard Bossuat
Éric Bussière
Jean-François Eck
Catherine Horel
Philippe Mioche
Marine Moguen-Toursel
Sylvain Schirmann
Matthieu Trouvé
Laurent Warlouzet
Emilie Willaert

Hungary
Gergely Fejérdy

Italy
David Burigana
Elena Calandri
Eleonora Guasconi
Luciano Segreto
Antonio Varsori

Luxemburg
Charles Barthel
Etienne Deschamps
Jean-Marie Kreins
René Leboutte
Robert Philippart
Corine Schröder
Gilbert Trausch

The Netherlands
Anjo Harryvan
Jan W. Brouwer
Jan van der Herst

Poland
Józef Laptos
Zdzisiaw Mach

Switzerland
Antoine Fleury
Lubor Jilek

FSC
www.fsc.org
MIX
Papier | Fördert
gute Waldnutzung
FSC® C083411

Kolibri 360 GmbH
Ferdinand-Jühlke-Straße 7
99095 Erfurt, Deutschland
produktsicherheit@kolibri360.de